Syntax of Scope

Linguistic Inquiry Monographs
Samuel Jay Keyser, general editor

1. *Word Formation in Generative Grammar*
   Mark Aronoff
2. *$\bar{X}$ Syntax: A Study of Phrase Structure*
   Ray Jackendoff
3. *Recent Transformational Studies in European Languages*
   Samuel Jay Keyser, editor
4. *Studies in Abstract Phonology*
   Edmund Gussmann
5. *An Encyclopedia of AUX: A Study in Cross-Linguistic Equivalence*
   Susan Steele
6. *Some Concepts and Consequences of the Theory of Government and Binding*
   Noam Chomsky
7. *The Syntax of Words*
   Elisabeth Selkirk
8. *Syllable Structure and Stress in Spanish: A Nonlinear Analysis*
   James W. Harris
9. *CV Phonology: A Generative Theory of the Syllable*
   George n. Clements and Samuel Jay Keyser
10. *On the Nature of Grammatical Relations*
    Alec Marantz
11. *A Grammar of Anaphora*
    Joseph Aoun
12. *Logical Form: Its Structure and Derivation*
    Robert May
13. *Barriers*
    Noam Chomsky
14. *On the Definition of Word*
    Anna-Maria Di Sciullo and Edwin Williams
15. *Japanese Tone Structure*
    Janet Pierrehumbert and Mary Beckman
16. *Relativized Minimality*
    Luigi Rizzi
17. *Types of $\bar{A}$-Dependencies*
    Guglielmo Cinque
18. *Argument Structure*
    Jane Grimshaw
19. *Locality: A Theory and Some of Its Empirical Consequences*
    Maria Rita Manzini
20. *Indefinites*
    Molly Diesing
21. *Syntax of Scope*
    Joseph Aoun and Yen-hui Audrey Li

Syntax of Scope

Joseph Aoun and
Yen-hui Audrey Li

The MIT Press
Cambridge, Massachusetts
London, England

© 1993 Massachusetts Institute of Technology

All rights reserved. No part of this book may be reproduced in any form or by any electronic or mechanical means (including photocopying recording, or information storage and retrieval) without permission in writing from the publisher.

This book was set in Times Roman by Asco Trade Typesetting Ltd., Hong Kong, and was printed and bound in the United States of America.

Library of Congress Cataloging-in-Publication Data

Aoun, Joseph.
  Syntax of scope / Joseph Aoun and Yen-hui Audrey Li.
    p. cm—(Linguistic inquiry monographs; 21)
  Includes bibliographical references and index.
  ISBN 0-262-01133-6 (hc).—ISBN 0-262-51068-5 (pbk.)
  1. Grammar, Comparative and general—Syntax. 2. Generative grammar.
I. Li, Yen-hui Audrey, 1954– II. Title. III. Series.
P291.A57 1993
415—dc20   92-30929
                                                                  CIP

To the memory of our friend and
colleague Osvaldo Jaeggli

Contents

Series Foreword   xi

Acknowledgments   xiii

Introduction   1

Chapter 1
Interpretive Invariance: QP/QP Interaction   11

1.1 Problems   13

1.2 Proper Binding of Variables   19

1.3 Chains   21

1.4 Constituency Difference between English and Chinese   22

1.5 The Analysis   25

1.6 Conclusion   38

Chapter 2
Comparative Dimension: QP/*Wh* Interaction   39

2.1 QP/*Wh* Interaction   40

2.2 A Unified Account for QP/*Wh* Interaction   56

2.3 Conclusion   71

Chapter 3
Syntax of Scope 73

3.1
NP-Traces and Quantifier-Raising 74

3.2
Chains and Scope Interaction 83

3.3
Conclusion 88

Chapter 4
Nominal Structures and Scope 91

4.1
Exocentric Behavior of Operators 92

4.2
Endocentric Behavior of Operators 100

4.3
Summary 121

Chapter 5
Construal, Indices, Domain, and Scope 123

5.1
Indices by Interpretive Rules 125

5.2
English Complex NPs 127

5.3
Chinese Complex NPs 128

5.4
QP/*Wh* Interaction in Chinese Complex NPs 142

5.5
Summary 147

Chapter 6
QP/*Wh*-Adjunct Interaction 151

6.1
A Typology of Adjuncts 152

6.2
Referential Adjuncts and QPs 155

6.3
Nonreferential Adjunct/QP Interaction in English 157

Contents

	6.4 Nonreferential Adjunct/QP Interaction in Chinese 164
	6.5 Summary 186
Chapter 7 **A Case Study: Japanese** 189	7.1 QP/QP Interaction 189
	7.2 QP/*Wh* Interaction 194
	7.3 Conclusion 198

Notes 199

References 213

Index 221

Series Foreword

We are pleased to present this monograph as the twenty-first in the series *Linguistic Inquiry Monographs*. These monographs will present new and original research beyond the scope of the article, and we hope they will benefit our field by bringing to it perspectives that will stimulate further research and insight.

Originally published in limited edition, the *Linguistic Inquiry Monograph* series is now available on a much wider scale. This change is due to the great interest engendered by the series and the needs of a growing readership. The editors wish to thank the readers for their support and welcome suggestions about future directions the series might take.

Samuel Jay Keyser
for the Editorial Board

Acknowledgments

For their help, we wish to thank many friends and colleagues: Sylvia Chen, Yu-chin Chien, Noam Chomsky, Larry Cohen, Mürvet Enç, Tom Ernst, Robert Freidin, Ken Hale, James Higginbotham, Hajime Hoji, Norbert Hornstein, James Huang, Wesley Hudson, S. Jay Keyser, Hilda Koopman, S. Yuki Kuroda, Richard Larson, Howard Lasnik, Thomas Lee, Horng-yi Lee, Anne Mark, Barry Schein, Patricia Schneider-Zioga, Tim Shi, Dominique Sportiche, Tim Stowell, Hiraoki Tada, Jean-Roger Vergnaud, Cathy Wei, Edwin Williams, Sheng-tai Zhang, Maria Luisa Zubizarreta.

Chapter 1 of this book is based on Aoun and Li 1989, and chapter 2 on Aoun and Li 1991.

Introduction

The treatment of quantifier scope in generative grammar has been directly inspired by the standard logic treatment of these elements. The Extended Standard Theory elaborated in Chomsky 1977 and Chomsky and Lasnik 1977 postulates the existence of a discrete interpretive level, the Logical Form (LF) component, and the existence of LF representations as representations of sentences determined by general rules and principles of that level. An LF representation is a partial representation of the meaning of a sentence; that is, it represents its structural meaning and abstracts away from other aspects of meaning such as word meaning and pragmatics. An LF representation thus represents the aspects of semantic interpretation that are expressed syntactically—that is, the contribution of grammar to meaning.

Any particular proposal concerning the existence of a level of Logical Form ought to characterize the nature of the representations at this level, the algorithm used to generate these representations, and the various principles that constrain them. According to the Extended Standard Theory model (1), LF representations are derived from S-Structure representations.

(1) D-Structure → S-Structure → LF

May (1977) argues that the mapping between S-Structure representations and LF representations is transformational. In the same way that transformations relate D-Structure representations to S-Structure representations, they relate S-Structure representations to representations at LF. Since transformations apply to phrase markers and generate other phrase markers, it follows that LF is a level of phrase structure representations consisting of bracketings labeled with grammatical categories.

The transformational rule that May argues for is quantifier raising (QR), an instance of the movement rule Move α. QR takes quantificational phrases and moves them in the LF component to a nonargument position ($\bar{\text{A}}$-position) where they receive their scope.[1] Like other instances of Move α, QR leaves behind a nonovert category—or trace—bound by the moved quantifier. This nonovert $\bar{\text{A}}$-bound category is referred to as a *variable* by analogy with standard usage in logic. As an illustration, consider sentence (2) and its two possible interpretations (2a) and (2b).

(2) Some man loves every woman.
    a. There is a man x such that, for every woman y, x loves y.
    b. For every woman y, there is a man x, such that x loves y.

After QR applies, two possible LF representations can be generated:

(3) a. [$_{IP}$ some man$_i$ [$_{IP}$ every woman$_j$ [$_{IP}$ x_i loves y_j]]]
    b. [$_{IP}$ every woman$_j$ [$_{IP}$ some man$_i$ [$_{IP}$ x_i loves y_j]]]

In other words, the S-Structure representation of (2) is associated with at least two different LF representations: one in which *some man* c-commands *every woman* and the other in which *every woman* c-commands *some man*. The two LF representations correspond to the two interpretations given in (2a–b).[2]

The grammar thus provides for a specific representation of quantificational structure generated by Move α. As a result, it is possible to assume that the general principles of syntactic well-formedness that regulate the application of Move α in Syntax will regulate its application at LF. In this respect, Kayne (1984), among many others, argues that some version of the Empty Category Principle applying to Move α at LF will account for the distribution and interpretation of negative polarity items in French.[3]

In addition to the characterization of relative scope, postulating an articulated interpretive level such as LF permits the statement of significant grammatical generalizations that cannot be expressed at other syntactic levels. The common example is the weak crossover phenomenon discussed by Chomsky (1976)—that is, the impossibility of construing the pronoun as anaphoric to the *wh*-element or the quantifier in *Who did his mother see?* and *His mother saw everyone*, despite the possibility of construing it this way with a nonquantificational element, as in *His mother saw John*. Assuming the LF representations of these sentences to be as shown in (4),

(4) a. [$_{CP}$ Who$_i$ [$_{IP}$ his mother see x_i]]

b. [$_{IP}$ everyone$_i$ [$_{IP}$ his mother saw x_i]]
c. [$_{IP}$ his mother saw John]

it is possible to state the following descriptive generalization to account for the contrast: A variable cannot be the antecedent of a pronoun to its left. (See Chomsky 1976, Higginbotham 1980, among others.)

As the discussion has illustrated, the choice of a theory of the LF component is based on empirical considerations. Therefore, any particular proposal concerning LF ought to be considered as an empirical proposal. Another clear illustration of the empirical nature of LF is provided by the behavior of pronominals in Mandarin Chinese. For some speakers of Mandarin Chinese, there is a clear discrepancy between the behavior of referential pronouns and that of pronouns bound by a quantificational antecedent (bound pronouns). Whereas a referential pronoun can occur in the object position of an embedded clause, as in (5a), a bound pronoun cannot occur in such a context, as in (5b).

(5) a. Zhangsan$_i$ shuo ta$_i$ dele jiang.
Zhangsan said he got prize
'Zhangsan said that he got the prize.'

b. *Meigeren$_i$ dou shuo ta$_i$ dele jiang.
everyone all said he got prize
'Everyone said that he got the prize.'

To account for such a discrepancy, Aoun and Hornstein (1986) argue that for these speakers, pronominals obey two distinct disjointness requirements:

(6) a. *The A-Disjointness Requirement*
A pronoun must be A-free in the minimal complete functional complex (CFC) in which it occurs.

b. The *$\bar{A}$-Disjointness Requirement*
A pronoun must be $\bar{A}$-free in the minimal CFC containing a c-commanding subject and the pronoun.

As the application of these two requirements is being illustrated, bear in mind that quantificational elements will be in an $\bar{A}$-position at LF. In (5a) the pronoun is $\bar{A}$-free in the embedded clause in which it occurs; the $\bar{A}$-Disjointness Requirement is trivially satisfied since there is no $\bar{A}$-binder. In (5b), on the other hand, the pronoun satisfies the A-Disjointness but not the $\bar{A}$-Disjointness Requirement: at LF the pronoun is not $\bar{\text{A}}$-free in the minimal clause containing a c-commanding subject, namely, the matrix clause. This analysis leads us to expect (correctly) that a bound pronoun interpretation will be possible in the following contexts:[4]

(7) a. Meigeren$_i$ dou shuo Mary xihuan ta$_i$.
   everyone all say Mary like him
   'Everyone said that Mary likes him.'

  b. Meigeren$_i$ dou yiwei ni shuo ta$_i$ dele jiang.
   everyone all think you said he got prize
   'Everyone thought that you said that he got the prize.'

In Aoun and Li 1990 we further argue that the $\bar{\text{A}}$-Disjointness Requirement incorporates a minimality effect:

(8) *The Minimal Disjointness Requirement*
A bound pronoun must be $\bar{\text{A}}$-free from the first available $\bar{\text{A}}$-binder.

The evidence we provide for such a reformulation is that sentences like (5b) improve when a modal or a negative element—both of which are taken to be in $\bar{\text{A}}$-position at the appropriate levels—intervenes between the quantifier and the pronoun, as in (9a–b).

(9) a. Meigeren$_i$ dou *hui* shuo ta$_i$ dele jiang.
   everyone all will say he got prize
   'Everyone would say that he got the prize.'

  b. Meigeren$_i$ dou *mei* shuo ta$_i$ dele jiang.
   everyone all not say he got prize
   'Everyone did not say that he got the prize.'

Once the existence of an $\bar{\text{A}}$-disjointness requirement incorporating a minimality effect is recognized, it can provide a testing ground for various proposals concerning the LF component. For instance, it is generally assumed that (i) a *wh*-element that has not been raised by S-Structure to Spec of Comp (*wh*-in-situ) is subject to such a raising process in the LF component (see Chomsky 1973, Aoun, Hornstein, and Sportiche 1981, Huang 1982, among others) and (ii) that such a *wh*-raising process applies in a successive-cyclic fashion (see Huang 1982; but see Aoun and Li 1993 for an alternative view). Overt *wh*-extraction to Spec of Comp in Mandarin Chinese does not occur. As Huang argues, *wh*-extraction to Spec of Comp, an $\bar{\text{A}}$-position, takes place at LF. We thus expect a normally illicit relation between a quantifier and a (bound) pronoun to become possible when *at LF* a *wh*-element comes to intervene between the quantifier and the bound pronoun. This expectation is fulfilled, as the contrast between (10a) and (10b) indicates.

(10) a. *Meigeren$_i$ dou shuo ta$_i$ dele jiang.
       everyone all said he got prize
       'Everyone said that he got the prize.'
   b. Meigeren$_i$ dou xiang-zhidao ta$_i$ dele shenme jiang.
       everyone all wonder he got what prize
       'Everyone wondered what prize he got.'

The relation between the pronoun and the quantifier in (10a) is not licit because at LF the pronoun is $\bar{\text{A}}$-bound in the minimal clause containing a c-commanding subject, namely, the matrix clause. Like its English counterpart, the verb *xiang-zhidao* 'wonder' selects a *wh*-element. In Mandarin Chinese this selectional requirement is satisfied at LF once the *wh*-element is raised to the Comp of the clause governed by *xiang-zhidao* (see Huang 1982). The LF representation of (10b) is given in (11).

(11) [$_{IP}$ meigeren$_i$ [$_{IP}$ x_i dou xiang-zhidao [$_{CP}$ shenme$_j$ [$_{IP}$ ta$_i$ dele x_j
      everyone   all wonder   what   he got
      jiang]]]]
      prize

Notice that here, the *wh*-element in $\bar{\text{A}}$-position intervenes between the quantifier *meigeren* 'everyone' and the pronoun *ta* 'he'. According to the Minimal Disjointness Requirement in (8), the pronoun ought to be free from the most local $\bar{\text{A}}$-binder, the *wh*-element. This is why it can be bound by the quantifier *meigeren* 'everyone'. The $\bar{\text{A}}$-Disjointness Requirement thus provides direct support for the assumption cited earlier that *wh*-in-situ is subject to Move α at LF: only at LF will the *wh*-element come to intervene between the pronoun and the quantificational antecedent.

The disjointness requirement provides direct evidence for the existence of *wh*-raising at LF. It also bears directly on certain proposals concerning the LF treatment of anaphoric expressions. For various reasons, Chomsky (1986b) and Lebeaux (1983) argue that anaphors are raised to an $\bar{\text{A}}$-position at LF. We thus expect an anaphor in $\bar{\text{A}}$-position to be necessarily disjoint from a pronoun. This indeed is the case with the long-distance anaphor *ziji* 'self' in Chinese:

(12) *Zhangsan$_i$ shuo ziji$_i$ zhidao ta$_i$ hen congming.
      Zhangsan said self know he very clever
      'Zhangsan said that self knew that he was clever.'

After the anaphor is raised to an $\bar{\text{A}}$-position at LF, it will $\bar{\text{A}}$-bind the pronoun:

(13) Zhangsan$_i$ shuo [$_{IP}$ ziji$_i$ [$_{IP}$ x_i renwei [$_{IP}$ ta$_i$ hen congming]]]
     Zhangsan say   self   think   he very clever

The unacceptability of (12) is thus due to the failure of the pronoun to meet the $\bar{\text{A}}$-Disjointness Requirement. Furthermore, since a subject intervenes between the pronoun and the long-distance anaphor, the $\bar{\text{A}}$-Disjointness Requirement is not violated in (14).

(14) Zhangsan$_i$ shuo ziji$_i$ zhidao Mary juede ta$_i$ hen congming.
     Zhangsan said self know Mary feel he very clever
     'Zhangsan said that himself knew that Mary felt that he was clever.'

The interaction of long-distance anaphors with pronouns in Mandarin Chinese indicates that such anaphors must raise at LF. On the other hand, the interaction of short-distance anaphors such as *taziji* 'himself' with pronouns suggests that such anaphors need not raise at LF. This is illustrated by the minimal contrast between (12) and (15).[5]

(15) Zhangsan$_i$ shuo taziji$_i$ zhidao ta$_i$ hen congming.
     Zhangsan said himself know he very clever
     'Zhangsan said that himself knew that he was clever.'

The acceptability of (15) can be accounted for as follows: short-distance anaphors need not raise at LF; they are not necessarily $\bar{\text{A}}$-disjoint from the pronoun.

The behavior of pronominal expressions in Mandarin Chinese thus provides a specific example of the empirical nature of the theory of the LF component: namely, it offers direct evidence for assuming that *wh*-elements raise at LF and that long-distance anaphors, but not short-distance anaphors, necessarily raise at LF. Generally, as Chomsky (1981, chap. 1) indicates, the empirical considerations that enter into the choice of a theory of LF fall into two categories: grammar-internal and grammar-external. Grammar-internal considerations involve the "syntax" of LF and the relation of LF to the rules and principles of grammar. Grammar-external considerations involve the role of LF in explicating the general nature of meaning. Our investigation in this book does not directly bear on the grammar-external considerations. Rather, we will chiefly be concerned with the rules and principles governing the LF component—in particular, with providing a grammar of quantificational phrases. The main features of our proposal are based on a contrastive study of the behavior of quantificational phrases and *wh*-operators in English, Mandarin Chinese, and Japanese. Contrary to standard assumptions, this study reveals that the interaction of quantificational phrases is subject to language variation. For instance, the interaction between quantifier phrases (QPs) in Mandarin Chinese is different from their interaction in English: unlike English active sentences, Chinese active sentences are not ambiguous:

(16) a. Some man loves every woman. (ambiguous)
 b. Every man loves a woman. (ambiguous)
(17) Meige nanren dou xihuan yige nuren.[6] (unambiguous)
 every man all like one women
 'Every man loves a woman.'

On the other hand, the interaction of QPs and *wh*-operators does not seem to be subject to language variation. Consider (18) and (19), discussed by May (1985, 38–39).

(18) What did everyone buy for Max? (ambiguous)

(19) Who bought everything for Max? (unambiguous)

(18), but not (19), is ambiguous. The existence of such a contrast is attributed by May (1985) to the Path Containment Condition (PCC) proposed by Pesetsky (1982). This approach leads us to expect QPs and *wh*-elements to interact differently in languages that do not obey the PCC. This expectation, however, does not appear to be fulfilled: the contrast illustrated in (18) and (19) exists in widely different languages. For example, although Chinese does not seem to obey the PCC, as shown in (20) (discussed in Huang 1982, chap. 4), it nevertheless displays the same contrast illustrated in (18) and (19), as shown in (21) and (22).

(20) Ta xiang-zhidao shei maile shenme?
 he wonder who bought what
 'Who(x), he wonders what(y), x bought y?'
(21) Meigeren dou gei Zhangsan maile shenme? (ambiguous)
 everyone all for Zhangsan bought what
 'What did everyone buy for Zhangsan?'
(22) Shei gei Zhangsan maile meige dongxi? (unambiguous)
 who for Zhangsan bought every thing
 'Who bought everything for Zhangsan?'

The challenge is thus to provide a unified account for both the similarity in the interaction of QPs and *wh*-operators and the difference in the interaction of QPs and other QPs across languages. In this book we argue that the main features of such a unified account will incorporate the following principles:

(23) *The Minimal Binding Requirement (MBR)*
Variables must be bound by the most local potential $\bar{\text{A}}$-binder.

(24) *The Scope Principle*
An operator A may have scope over an operator B iff A c-commands B or an $\bar{\text{A}}$-element in the chain headed by the operator.

The MBR and the Scope Principle, which we take to be interpretive principles constraining the interaction of operators in natural languages, capture the similarities between the various types of operators across languages. As for the cross-linguistic variation affecting the interaction of these operators, it is to be traced back to differences in the constituent structures of the languages under discussion rather than to parametric differences affecting the form and functioning of LF interpretive rules. This theme of *interpretive invariance* will constantly manifest itself throughout this work.

The book is organized as follows. Chapter 1 introduces the MBR and the Scope Principle, which account for cross-linguistic similarities regarding relative quantifier scope. The cross-linguistic variation affecting the interaction of quantifiers is traced back to differences in the constituent structures of the languages under discussion. Chapter 2 discusses the interaction of quantifier phrases with *wh*-operators, and the application of the MBR is extended to account for such an interaction. The empirical considerations uncovered in chapter 3 reveal that only elements in $\bar{\text{A}}$-positions are relevant to the determination of relative scope: only the operator itself and the gaps in $\bar{\text{A}}$-position coindexed with it are relevant for scope interaction. The working of quantifier extraction in the LF component and the formulation of the Scope Principle are refined accordingly. We will argue that quantifiers occurring in nonthematic positions need not undergo raising at LF. Chapter 4 investigates the interaction of operators that occur within simplex noun phrases (NPs), and chapter 5 the interaction of operators that occur within complex NPs. The differences between the interaction of quantificational elements in English and their interaction in Chinese are accounted for in terms of opacity. Essentially, the LF extraction of quantificational elements is subject to a locality effect similar to the one constraining the interpretation of anaphoric elements. Chapter 6 deals with the interaction of *wh*-adjuncts (such as *where*, *when*, *how*, and *why*) with QPs. We will argue that the idiosyncratic behavior of some adjuncts is to be understood in light of their characterization as modifiers. Finally, using the interaction of operators in Japanese as a case study, chapter 7 illustrates how the analysis based on the behavior of operators in English and Chinese extends to other languages.

Chapter 1
Interpretive Invariance: QP/QP Interaction

In this chapter we contrast the behavior of QPs in the basic constituent structures of English and Chinese.[1] We argue that the interpretation of quantificational elements in these two languages can be accounted for by two requirements: the Minimal Binding Requirement (MBR) stated in (I) and the Scope Principle stated in (II).

(I) *The Minimal Binding Requirement*
Variables must be bound by the most local potential $\bar{\text{A}}$-binder.

(II) *The Scope Principle*
A quantifier A may have scope over a quantifier B iff A c-commands a member of the chain containing B.[2]

We start by contrasting the behavior of QPs in English and Chinese in section 1.1. As frequently noted by linguists working on Chinese (see S. F. Huang 1981, C.-T. J. Huang 1982, Lee 1986), a Chinese sentence like (1), contrary to English sentences like (2a–b), is not ambiguous. The subject QP must have scope over the object QP. (The QPs that may have wide scope are italicized.)

(1) *Meigeren* dou xihuan yige nuren.[3] (unambiguous)
    everyone all like   one woman
    'Everyone loves a woman.'

(2) a. *Everyone* loves *a woman*. (ambiguous)
    b. *Some/A woman* loves *everyone*. (ambiguous)

In his important work on the topic, Huang (1982) accounts for such a contrast by postulating the existence of an Isomorphic Principle and assuming a difference in the restructuring possibilities between English and Chinese:

(3) *The Isomorphic Principle*
Suppose A and B are QPs. Then if A c-commands B at S-Structure, A c-commands B at LF.

The essence of the Isomorphic Principle plus restructuring account, to be discussed in some detail later in this chapter, is that restructuring nullifies the effect of the Isomorphic Principle in English but is prohibited by the phrase structure rules in Chinese. The lack of such restructuring in Chinese makes this language display the effect of the Isomorphic Principle in all cases. On the surface, then, English does not exhibit the effect of the Isomorphic Principle but Chinese does.[4]

However, there are instances in English that appear to exhibit an effect of the Isomorphic Principle and instances in Chinese that do not. For example, a passive sentence in Chinese is ambiguous:[5]

(4) Meigeren dou bei yige nuren zhuazoule.   (ambiguous)
    everyone all by one woman arrested
    'Everyone was arrested by a woman.'

An English sentence containing the double object construction [V NP NP], such as the one in (5), is unambiguous, as noted by Larson (1988), who credits D. Lebeaux for this fact.

(5) John assigned someone every problem.   (unambiguous)

Examples such (1), (2), (4), and (5) raise the following questions:

(6) a. Why are active sentences unambiguous in Chinese (1) but ambiguous in English (2)?
    b. Why is the interaction of QPs in an active sentence like (1) in Chinese different from their interaction in the corresponding passive sentence (4)?
    c. Why is the English double object structure in a sentence like (5) unambiguous?

To answer these questions, we show that the traces of QPs raised at LF are subject to the MBR (section 1.2) and that the relative scope of QPs is sensitive to the chains in which the QPs occur—in other words, to the Scope Principle (section 1.3). The MBR and the Scope Principle straightforwardly account for the nonambiguity of active sentences in Chinese, the nonambiguity of double object structures in English, and the ambiguity of passive sentences in Chinese.

As for the ambiguity of active sentences in English, we argue that the different behavior of QPs in Chinese and English active sentences is to be traced back to a difference in the constituent structure of these languages (section 1.4). Specifically, various linguists (see Kitagawa 1986, Koopman and Sportiche 1991, Kuroda 1988, Speas 1986, Zagona 1988) assume that subjects in English are base-generated in the Spec(ifier) of VP and then raised to the Spec of IP. However, we claim that this raising process (subject raising) is not available in Chinese. The existence of subject raising in English but not in Chinese, coupled with the MBR and the Scope Principle, accounts for the contrast between the nonambiguity of active sentences in Chinese such as those in (1) and the ambiguity of active sentences in English such as (2). Our account and Huang's share the same spirit: in both accounts, the variation concerning the interpretation of quantifiers in English and Chinese is traced back to a difference in the constituent structure of the languages under discussion, rather than to parametric differences affecting the form and functioning of LF interpretive rules.

Finally, in section 1.5 we explore some consequences of our analysis and contrast the behavior of QPs in simplex sentences, raising contexts, and, along the lines of Larson 1988, double object constructions.

1.1 Problems

It has repeatedly been noted that English and Chinese differ in the interaction of quantifier scope (see S. F. Huang 1981, C.-T. J. Huang 1982, Lee 1986, among others): the English sentences involving two or more QPs tend to be ambiguous, whereas the Chinese ones tend to be unambiguous. For example, Huang (1982, chap. 3) discusses May's (1977) study of sentences like (7), which is ambiguous.

(7) Every man loves a woman.

In contrast, C.-T. J. Huang (1982) and S. F. Huang (1981) note that the surface word order of QPs tends to reflect their relative scope in Chinese. Thus, (8) is not ambiguous; the subject QP must have wide scope (Huang 1982, 112).

(8) Meige xuesheng dou maile   yiben shu.
    every student all bought one   book
    'Every student bought a book.'

Examples like (9a–b) also support this claim.

(9) a. Meige nanren dou xihuan yige nuren.
    every man   all like one woman
    'Every man loves a woman.'

   b. Meige jingcha   dou kandao yige xiaotou.
      every policeman all see   one thief
      'Every policeman saw a thief.'

The nonambiguity of (9a–b) can be shown by the obligatoriness of a plural expression referring back to the object QP:

(10) a. Meige nanren dou xihuan yige nuren. Tamen xihuan de naxie
       every man   all like   one woman they like   DE those
       nuren dou hen you qian.⁶
       women all very have money
       'Every man loves a woman. The women they love all are rich.'

   b. *Meige nanren dou xihuan yige nuren. Tamen xihuan de nage
      every man   all like   one woman they like   DE that
      nuren hen you qian.
      women very have money
      'Every man loves a woman. The woman they love is rich.'

(11) a. Meige jingcha   dou kandao yige xiaotou. Keshi naxie
       every policeman all see   one thief   but   those
       xiaotou dou tao zou le.
       thief   all run away PAR
       'Every policeman saw a thief. But those thieves ran away.'

   b. *Meige jingcha   dou kandao yige xiaotou. Keshi nage xiaotou
      every policeman all see   one thief   but   that thief
      tao zou le.
      run away PAR
      'Every policeman saw a thief. But that thief ran away.'

This contrasts with (7), for which either plural or singular expressions can refer back to the object QP:

(12) a. Every man loves some/a woman. The women they love are rich.
    b. Every man loves some/a woman. The woman they love is rich.

In order to account for the ambiguity of sentences like (7), May (1977, 1985) assumes that QPs are raised during the mapping from S-Structure to LF so that the interpretations of these QPs are appropriately represented. (7) thus has the LF representations in (13a–b).

(13) a. [$_{IP}$ a woman$_j$ [$_{IP}$ every man$_i$ [$_{IP}$ x_i loves x_j]]]
   b. [$_{IP}$ every man$_i$ [$_{IP}$ x_i [$_{VP}$ a woman$_j$ [$_{VP}$ loves x_j]]]]

In these LF representations the QPs are adjoined to IP or VP (see May 1985, Chomsky 1986b).[7] These representations yield two readings: in (13a) *a woman* has scope over *every man* because it c-commands *every man*, and in (13b) *every man* has scope over *a woman* because it c-commands *a woman*.[8]

As noted earlier, Chinese sentences such as (8) and (9) are not ambiguous: the subject QP must have scope over the object QP. The reading where the object QP has scope over the subject QP is not available. A priori, two possible accounts for the contrast between English and Chinese may be pursued. The first would trace this contrast back to distinct LF rules operating in each language. The second would consider that English and Chinese have the same LF rules and trace the contrast back to a difference in the syntactic representation of the languages under discussion. The first option runs counter to a commonly held view among linguists that considers the LF interpretive component not to be the locus of language variation since the language learner does not have direct access to this component (see Higginbotham 1985).

Huang (1982) accounts for the contrast between English and Chinese in terms of the second option, postulating the existence of the Isomorphic Principle as formuated in (3), repeated here (see also Lee 1986).

(3) *The Isomorphic Principle*
   Suppose A and B are QPs. Then if A c-commands B at S-Structure, A c-commands B at LF.[9]

According to the Isomorphic Principle, the c-command relation holding between QPs at S-Structure must be preserved at LF. Since the subject QP c-commands the object QP at S-Structure in the Chinese sentences (8)–(9), this subject will c-command and have scope over the object at LF. Consequently, there is only one possible reading for (8)–(9). Their English counterpart in (7), however, is ambiguous. Huang argues that this ambiguity is due to a structural ambiguity. Specifically, he assumes the existence of a restructuring process in English. This process can freely and optionally take place in a language as long as it does not violate the language's phrase structure rules. English is essentially a head-initial language. Therefore, a structure such as [$_{IP}$ NP$_1$ [$_{VP}$ V NP$_2$]] can be reanalyzed as [$_{IP}$[$_{IP}$ NP$_1$ [$_{VP}$ V]] NP$_2$] without violating the head-initial pattern in this language. More precisely, an object NP in English can always be analyzed in two ways: either as a sister of V or as a phrase adjoined to IP (restructuring takes place, either via extraposition or simply via rebracketing of the structures). Sentences like (7) thus have two possible structures. When restructuring does not take place, (7) has the structure in (14a); when restructuring does take place, it has the structure in (14b).

(14) a.

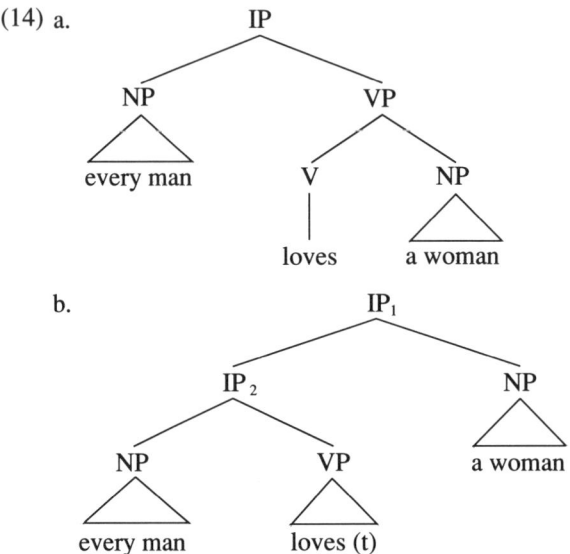

This ambiguity in structure results in ambiguity in interpretation. In (14a) the subject NP c-commands and, according to the Isomorphic Principle, has scope over the object NP. In (14b), after restructuring, the object NP c-commands and has scope over the subject NP.

In Chinese, on the other hand, such a restructuring process is prohibited by the phrase structure constraints in this language. Chinese is essentially a head-final language, with the exception of cases involving a V or a P and their complements (at the V' or P' level). An object that is sister to a V can follow the verbal head. However, when restructuring takes place and adjoins the object NP to IP, this object NP would occur finally under IP. It would be a nonhead occurring in final position of a constituent (IP), a violation of the head-final constraint. In other words, although (1) can have the structure in (15a), it does not have the structure in (15b) derived by restructuring (for details of the phrase structure constraints and their effects on restructuring, see Huang 1982, chap. 2–4).

(15) a.   [$_{IP}$ meigeren dou [$_{VP}$ xihuan yige nuren]]
          everyone all   like   one woman

b. *[$_{IP}$[$_{IP}$ meigeren dou [$_{VP}$ xihuan yige nuren]
   everyone all   like   one woman

(15b) is ruled out by the phrase structure constraint in Chinese. Since there is only one possible structure for (1)—namely, (15a)—this sentence is unambiguous. The subject QP must have wide scope according to the Isomorphic Principle.

In brief, the contrast between the ambiguity of the English sentences (2a–b) and the nonambiguity of the Chinese sentence (1) is due to the difference in the phrase structure constraints in these two languages. The phrase structure constraints in English do not prohibit a restructuring process that alters the c-command relationship between a subject NP and an object NP. The phrase structure constraints in Chinese prohibit such a restructuring process.

Huang's analysis has two components: the Isomorphic Principle, which is taken to apply in both English and Chinese, and the restructuring process, which is responsible for the difference between the two languages under consideration. Since the effect of the restructuring process is not shown in other syntactic processes, we assume for the purpose of our presentation that the Isomorphic Principle manifests itself in the interpretation of QPs in Chinese but not in English. In the remainder of this chapter we discuss this approach and uncover certain empirical problems facing it. In the spirit of Huang's approach, we then offer an analysis of quantifier scope that handles the discrepancy between English and Chinese.

When a wider range of data is examined, it appears that the Isomorphic Principle (and restructuring) cannot exhaustively account for the different behavior of QPs in English and Chinese. Contrary to the observation that the Isomorphic Principle seems to have an effect in Chinese but not in English, there are instances in English that seem to exhibit the effect of the Isomorphic Principle. In addition, there are instances in Chinese that do not exhibit the effect of the Isomorphic Principle, indicating that the Isomorphic Principle may not hold even in Chinese.

Let us consider Chinese first. Contrary to the predictions of an approach that invokes the Isomorphic Principle, the passive counterpart of (1) is ambiguous in Chinese, as indicated in (4), repeated here.

(4) Meigeren dou bei yige nuren   zhuazoule.   (ambiguous)
    everyone all   by one woman arrested
    'Everyone was arrested by a woman.'

In passive sentences like (4) the subject QP c-commands the *by*-QP at S-Structure. According to the Isomorphic Principle, the subject QP must have scope over the *by*-QP at LF. A reading where the *by*-QP has wide scope should thus be impossible. However, this reading is in fact available in (4). The Chinese sentence (4) is ambiguous in the same way that the English sentences (2a–b) and their passive counterparts (16a–b) are ambiguous.[10]

(16) a. Some/A woman is loved by everyone.
   b. Everyone is loved by some/a woman.

Examples such as (4) show that the Isomorphic Principle cannot exhaustively account for the determination of the relative scopes of QPs in Chinese.

Furthermore, contrary to the observation that the IP does not manifest itself in English, we find instances where it indeed does seem to manifest itself:

(17) I assigned someone every problem.

(17) is not ambiguous for the speakers consulted: the indirect object *someone* necessarily has scope over *every problem*, as first pointed out to us by J. Higginbotham and R. Larson (who credits D. Lebeaux for this observation; see Larson 1990, 603). This is surprising given that sentences like (2) and (16) in English are ambiguous. As pointed out by Schneider-Zioga (1988), other sentences illustrating the lack of ambiguity between internal complements are (18a) and (18b).

(18) a. He loaded some truck with every tool.
   b. He sprayed some tree with every chemical.

The lack of ambiguity in (17)–(18) seems to suggest that the Isomorphic Principle may have applied in this instance (or that restructuring is impossible in this instance). Barss and Lasnik (1986) and Larson (1988) argue that in double object structures the indirect object asymmetrically c-commands the direct object at S-Structure. Schneider-Zioga (1988) shows that the same asymmetric c-command relation holds in (18a–b). Assuming that the Isomorphic Principle applies in these cases, it is expected that the first complement following the verb has scope over the second complement in (17)–(18).

In brief, we have found instances in Chinese to which the Isomorphic Principle cannot apply and instances in English that display the effect of the Isomorphic Principle—instances that directly contradict the claim that the Isomorphic Principle exists in Chinese and that a restructuring process nullifies the effect of the Isomorphic Principle in English. Since the Isomorphic Principle and the restructuring process were designed to capture the difference in behavior of the QPs in these two languages, our examples suggest that such an account is not descriptively adequate.[11] Thus, we are left with no explanation for the original problem, stated in (13a), that the Isomorphic Principle and restructuring were designed to account for. In addition, during our discussion of the Isomorphic Principle we uncovered further problems not explained by any analysis of QPs. Our task will be to provide an account for these problems.

1.2 Proper Binding of Variables

We assume in this work that QPs are raised at LF and adjoined to an $\bar{\text{A}}$-position by the rule of QR (see May 1977, 1985). Variables left by QR obey various well-formedness requirements. Thus, as argued by Aoun and Hornstein (1985), Kayne (1981), and others, these variables obey some version of the Empty Category Principle (ECP). In the spirit of Chomsky 1986b (also see Barss 1984 and the references cited there), we would like to suggest that these variables obey the following locality requirement at LF (see Williams 1988 for a similar but different proposal):

(19) *The Minimal Binding Requirement (MBR)*
Variables must be bound by the most local potential antecedent ($\bar{\text{A}}$-binder).[12]

The MBR has the effect of ruling out representations (20a–b) and allowing representation (20c). In these representations the variables x_1 and x_2 are traces generated by the LF raising of QP_1 and QP_2, respectively.

(20) a. $[_{IP} QP_1 [_{IP} QP_2 [_{IP} x_1 [_{VP} \ldots x_2 \ldots]]]]$
 b. $[_{IP} QP_2 [_{IP} QP_1 [_{IP} x_1 [_{VP} \ldots x_2 \ldots]]]]$
 c. $[_{IP} QP_1 [_{IP} x_1 [_{VP} QP_2 [_{VP} \ldots x_2 \ldots]]]]$

In (20a) QP_2 is the first available $\bar{\text{A}}$-binder for x_1 and x_2. According to the MBR, x_1 and x_2 must both be bound by QP_2. This is not the case, however, since x_1 is coindexed with QP_1 by movement. (20a) will therefore be ruled out by the MBR. Notice that (20a) cannot be salvaged by reindexing x_1 with QP_2. After this reindexing process, not only would both variables be bound by a single QP but QP_1 would not bind any variable, thus violating the prohibition against vacuous quantification (May 1977) or, alternatively, the Bijection Principle (Koopman and Sportiche 1982). (20b) is ruled out in the same manner: QP_1 is the most local potential antecedent for both x_1 and x_2. In contrast, the traces in (20c) are properly bound. The most local potential antecedent for x_1 is QP_1; the most local potential antecedent for x_2 is QP_2. Both traces are bound by the most local potential antecedent, obeying the MBR.

Given the MBR, it is expected that sentences where one QP asymmetrically c-commands the other are unambiguous. This expectation is fulfilled in Chinese active sentences like (1) and in English sentences with double complement constructions like (17)–(18).

To see why the active sentence (1) in Chinese is unambiguous, consider its S-Structure representation, given in (21).[13]

(21)

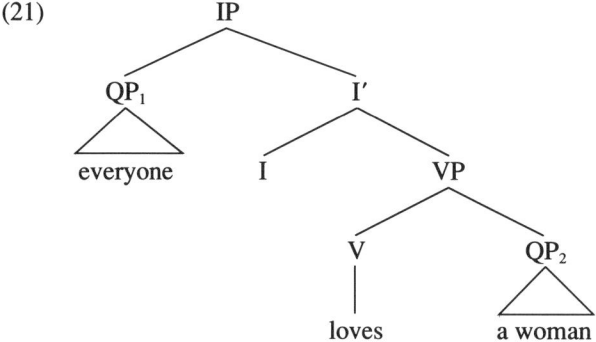

If we adopt Chomsky's (1986a) claim that adjunction is possible only to a maximal projection that is a nonargument, then in (21) QP_1 can adjoin to IP and QP_2 to VP or IP. The MBR, however, allows QP_2 to adjoin to VP only. If QP_2 were to adjoin to IP, the output would be similar to the ill-formed representations (20a) or (20b). Therefore, the only possible LF representation for (1) will be (22).

(22) [$_{IP}$ everyone$_i$ [$_{IP}$ x_i [$_{VP}$ a woman$_j$ [$_{VP}$ loves x_j]]]]

The subject QP_1 *everyone* c-commands the object QP_2 *a woman* after QR, deriving the interpretation where QP_1 has scope over QP_2. The active sentence (1) in Chinese is therefore not ambiguous. The MBR forces sentences like (1) to be unambiguous.

A similar analysis will account for the nonambiguity of English double complement constructions such as those in (17)–(18). Assuming that such constructions form a small clause, as argued by Kayne (1984), these sentences have the structure in (23).

(23) a. I [$_{VP}$ assigned [$_{sc}$ someone [$_{Pred}$ every problem]]]
    b. I [$_{VP}$ loaded [$_{sc}$ some truck [$_{Pred}$ with every tool]]]
    c. I [$_{VP}$ sprayed [$_{sc}$ some tree [$_{Pred}$ with every chemical]]]

According to the MBR, the first QP adjoins to VP (or some higher node), and the second QP can only adjoin to Pred.[14] The first QP thus has scope over the second QP.

The MBR offers a new perspective for the analysis of QPs. However, it clearly cannot account for the whole range of data. For instance, according to the MBR, passive sentences in Chinese ought to behave like active sentences: they should not be ambiguous. As the ambiguity of (4) illustrates, however, this is not the case. We now turn to this problem.

1.3 Chains

The LF structures of an active Chinese sentence such as (1) and its passive counterpart (4) are (24) and (25), respectively.

(24) [meigeren$_i$ [x_i yige nuren$_j$ [dou xihuan/zhuazou x_j]]]
    everyone   one woman   all like/arrest

(25) [meigeren$_i$ [x_i yige nuren$_j$ [dou bei x_j [zhuazoule t$_i$]]]]
    everyone   one woman   all by   arrested

The only structural difference between (24) and (25) is the existence of an NP-trace in (25).[15] This suggests that the NP-trace may play a role in determining QP scopes. In fact, various studies of quantifier lowering (see May 1977, Aoun 1985, and the references cited there) have indicated that NP-traces do play a role in determining the scope of QPs. Consider (26).

(26) Someone$_i$ seems [t$_i$ to love everyone].

(26) is ambiguous. Assuming that the matrix subject QP is interpreted from the position in which the trace occurs, (26) will be ambiguous just as (2b) (*Someone loves everyone*) is ambiguous. Based on such ambiguities, it seems plausible to conclude that the determination of the scope of QPs is sensitive to the chain containing the QP and the empty category with which the QP is coindexed. Specifically, it is possible to suggest a generalization like (27).

(27) *The Scope Principle*
    A quantifier A may have scope over a quantifier B iff A c-commands a member of the chain containing B.[16]

To see how the Scope Principle applies, consider the LF representation (28) of (26).

(28) [$_{IP}$ someone$_i$ [$_{IP}$ x_i [seems [$_{IP}$ everyone$_j$ [$_{IP}$ t$_i$ to love x_j]]]]]

(28) does not violate the MBR: t_i is an NP-trace that needs to be A-bound. In (28a) *someone* c-commands *everyone*. In turn, *everyone* c-commands the NP-trace t_i, which is a member of the chain containing *someone*. According to the Scope Principle, either QP may have scope over the other—hence the ambiguity of (26).

Having introduced the Scope Principle, we now turn to the contrast between the lack of ambiguity in the Chinese active sentence (24) and the ambiguity of its passive counterpart (25). In (24), schematically represented in (29a), both QP$_1$ and the variable it binds, x_1, c-command but are not c-commanded by either QP$_2$ or the variable x_2 in object position. According to the Scope Principle given in (27), (24) should not be ambiguous: QP$_1$ must have scope over QP$_2$. In (25), schematically represented in (29b), the passive subject QP$_2$ c-commands QP$_1$ and QP$_1$ c-commands the NP-trace of the passive subject.

(29) a. QP$_1$ x_1 QP$_2$ x_2 (active)
    b. QP$_2$ x_2 QP$_1$ x_1 t$_2$ (passive)

In a representation like (29b), QP$_2$ has scope over QP$_1$ since it c-commands QP$_1$. QP$_1$ also has scope over QP$_2$ since it (QP$_1$) c-commands a member of the chain containing QP$_2$. The Scope Principle captures the contrast between the ambiguity of passive constructions and the lack of ambiguity of active constructions in Chinese. Moreover, as we will show, it accounts for the contrast between active sentences in English and Chinese.

1.4 Constituency Difference between English and Chinese

In order to offer an account for the contrast between English and Chinese active sentences such as (2) and (1), we must digress somewhat to discuss the basic constituent structures of English and Chinese. We will argue that the difference in the interpretation of quantifiers in English and Chinese active sentences results from structural differences between the two languages rather than from a different functioning of LF interpretive rules.

Recently various syntactic considerations have led several linguists to assume that subjects in English are generated at D-Structure in the Spec of VP position.[17] These subjects are raised to the Spec of Infl position at S-Structure (see the references mentioned in the introduction to this chapter). Under this view, instead of the traditional structure in (30a), an English sentence has the structure in (30b).

(30) a. [$_{IP}$ NP [$_{I'}$ I VP]]
   b. [$_{IP}$ NP$_i$ [$_{I'}$ I [$_{VP_1}$ t$_i$ VP]]]

We would like to suggest, however, that subject raising is not available in Chinese. In fact, the lack of subject raising in Chinese has been independently proposed by Wible (1990), who argues (p. 50) that the constituent structure of a clause in Chinese is as shown in (31). In (31) the subject is base-generated in Spec of VP position and stays in this position at S-Structure (NP$_1$ is subject and NP$_2$ is object in (31)).[18]

(31)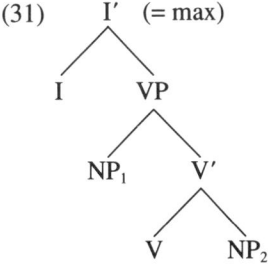

Wible relates the difference between English and Chinese constituent structures to their difference with respect to the presence versus absence of Agr(eement). Aoun and Li (1989) suggest a similar correlation: the lack of subject raising in Chinese is related to the degenerate nature of Infl in this language. In the framework of Chomsky (1986a), raising to subject in general is made possible by a process of V-raising to Infl. V-raising to Infl would make Infl a lexical item, which would then allow VP$_1$ in (30b) not to count as a barrier for subject raising. Aoun and Li suggest that the degenerate nature of Infl in Chinese prevents V-raising from taking place. As a consequence, VP in (31) will always count as a barrier in this language. Alternatively, it is possible to claim that an empty category must be not only properly bound but also lexically governed (see Jaeggli 1982, Stowell 1986, Aoun, Hornstein, Lightfoot, and Weinberg (AHLW) 1987). Subject raising in this case would be impossible because this process will leave a trace not lexically governed, Infl not being a lexical governor.

That there is a distinction between the English and Chinese basic constituent structures has been argued independently by Aoun and Hornstein (1986). The evidence comes from the contrast between the distribution of bound pronouns in English and their distribution in Chinese. As discussed briefly in the introduction to this book, in Chinese the distribution of bound pronouns is not parallel to the distribution of referential pronouns:

(32) a. Zhangsan$_i$ shuo ta$_i$ hele pijiu.
Zhangsan said he drank beer
'Zhangsan said that he drank beer.'
b. *Meigeren$_i$ dou shuo ta$_i$ hele pijiu.
everyone all say he drank beer

Aoun and Hornstein account for this contrast by means of an $\bar{\text{A}}$-disjointness requirement.

With the $\bar{\text{A}}$-Disjointness Requirement, the absence of Agr in Chinese and its presence in English accounts for the contrast between the unacceptability of (32b) and the acceptability of (33).

(33) Everyone$_i$ [x_i said [he Agr is a fool]].

In (33) the domain in which the pronoun must be $\bar{\text{A}}$-free is the embedded clause. It can be $\bar{\text{A}}$-bound by the QP, which occurs outside this domain.

The contrast between (32b) and (33) is thus accounted for by the absence versus presence of Agr. However, the contrast between the English (34a) and the Chinese (34b) is totally unexpected.[19]

(34) a. Everyone's$_i$ friend likes him$_i$.
b. *Meigeren$_i$ de pengyou dou xihuan ta$_i$.
everyone DE friend all like him

If these two sentences have identical LF representations, as in (35), they should be treated on a par under the assumption that the same $\bar{\text{A}}$-Disjointness Requirement holds in English and Chinese, as argued by Aoun and Hornstein (1986).

(35) a. [$_{IP}$ everyone's$_i$ [$_{IP}$ x_i friend [$_{VP}$ likes him$_i$]]]
b. [$_{IP}$ meigeren$_i$ de [$_{IP}$ x_i pengyou [$_{VP}$ dou xihuan ta$_i$]]]
everyone DE friend all like him

In (35a–b) the domain in which the pronoun must be A-free and $\bar{\text{A}}$-free is the whole clause. The unacceptability of the Chinese sentence (35b) is expected since the pronoun is $\bar{\text{A}}$-bound in its domain.[20] On the other hand, the acceptability of the English sentence (34a) comes as a surprise. The problem disappears, however, when the difference in the constituent

Interpretive Invariance   25

structure between Chinese and English discussed in this section is assumed. After QR the LF representation of (34a) will be (36) instead of (35a).

(36) [IP everyone's$_i$ [IP[NP x_i friend]$_j$ [VP$_1$ t$_j$ [VP$_2$ likes him$_i$]]]]

The crucial difference between the representations in (35a) and (36) is that in (36) it is VP$_1$ that contains a subject t_j and so VP$_1$ is the domain in which the pronoun must be $\bar{\text{A}}$-free. Nothing prevents this pronoun from being $\bar{\text{A}}$-bound by the quantifier *everyone* outside its domain.

In brief, the difference in the constituent structure of English and Chinese accounts for the behavior of (bound) pronouns in contexts such as (34a–b). We have brought up these facts because they directly support the analysis of the basic constituent structures of English and Chinese put forward in this section. In the next section we will show that the difference in constituent structure has important consequences for the interpretation of QPs in English and Chinese.

Having outlined the basics of our analysis, we proceed to the details of how QPs are analyzed in English and Chinese. Specifically, we will discuss how the problems listed in (6) are solved and how a wider range of data may be accommodated by this analysis.

1.5 The Analysis

1.5.1 QP Subjects in Simplex Sentences

Consider once again the contrast between the nonambiguity of the Chinese sentence (1) and the ambiguity of the English sentence (2a), represented in (37) and (38).

(37) Meigeren dou xihuan yige nuren.
 everyone all like one woman
 'Everyone loves a woman.'
 a. $\forall(x), \exists(y), x$ loves y
 b. *$\exists(y), \forall(x), x$ loves y

(38) Everyone loves a woman.
 a. $\forall(x), \exists(y), x$ loves y
 b. $\exists(y), \forall(x), x$ loves y

We can now provide a straightforward account for such a contrast by assuming that the basic constituent structures of English and Chinese are different. (37) and (38) are represented in (39) and (40), respectively.

(39) [$_{I'}$ I [$_{VP_1}$ everyone [$_{VP_2}$ loves *a woman*]]]

(40) [$_{IP}$ *everyone$_i$* [$_{I'}$ I [$_{VP_1}$ t$_i$ [$_{VP_2}$ loves *a woman*]]]]

In (39) the subject QP *everyone* can be raised and adjoined to VP$_1$ or higher to IP and the object QP *a woman* to VP$_1$. *Everyone* will then c-command and have scope over *a woman* (the reading represented in (37a)). It is not possible for *a woman* to adjoin to IP to derive the reading in (37b) because either the trace of *a woman* or the trace of *everyone* would not be bound by the most local potential antecedent, thus violating the MBR. In (40) the subject QP *everyone* can adjoin to IP and the object QP *a woman* to VP$_2$ or VP$_1$. The latter possibility, adjunction of the object QP to VP$_1$, is allowed despite the fact that the trace *t* of the subject QP is dominated by VP$_1$. This is because the trace in question is an NP-trace. A *potential* antecedent for an NP-trace is an NP in an A-position, rather than an $\bar{\text{A}}$-position. Therefore, when the object QP adjoins to VP$_1$, this raised QP will not qualify as a potential antecedent for the NP-trace but will qualify as the most local potential antecedent for the variable in the object position. The representation in (41), generated by applying QR to (40), is thus grammatical and yields two readings. In (41) QP$_1$ c-commands and has scope over QP$_2$; this generates the reading (38a). In turn, QP$_2$ c-commands a member of the chain containing QP$_1$, (namely, *t*) and has scope over QP$_2$; this generates the reading (38b).

(41)

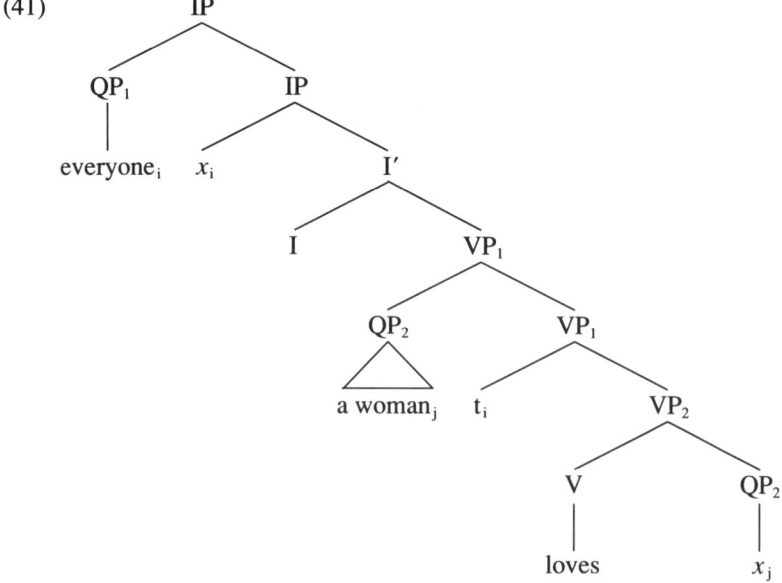

The contrast between Chinese and English active sentences thus is solved. As in Huang's account, the difference in interpretation between Chinese and English is traced back to a structural difference between the two languages and not to a parametric variation affecting the form or functioning of LF interpretive rules.

1.5.2 QP Subjects in Raising Structures

We now would like to point out one direct consequence of our analysis. We have assumed that in Chinese, contrary to English, no subject raising takes place in simplex sentences. The same reasoning leads us to expect the absence of any other subject-raising process in Chinese even in *seem*-type constructions. However, subject-to-subject raising seems to occur in the following sentence, where the matrix subject has been raised from the embedded subject position (see Teng 1977, Hou 1979, Li 1990 for the arguments that *keneng* 'likely' is a raising verb):

(42) [$_{IP}$ Women$_i$ [$_{VP}$ keneng [$_{IP}$ t$_i$ bu lai]]].
     we   likely   not come
     'We are likely not to come.'

If subject raising is not possible at all in Chinese, the derivation in (42) should not be allowed. The existence of such derivations indicates either that the claim regarding the lack of subject raising in Chinese is wrong or that structures like (42) are not standard raising structures. In fact, the behavior of QPs in sentences like (42) demonstrates that the second possibility is correct.

First observe the following sentence:

(43) Meigeren dou keneng kandao yige nuren.
     everyone all likely see   one woman
     'Everyone is likely to see a woman.'

If (43) were a raising structure, its S-Structure representation would be (44). In (44) NP$_3$ *a woman* can adjoin to the embedded IP or VP$_2$ (t_i is an NP-trace; the MBR is not violated) and NP$_1$ *everyone* can adjoin to the matrix IP. If *everyone* adjoins to the embedded IP, it will c-command t_i and be c-commanded by *everyone*. According to the Scope Principle, *a woman* can have either wide or narrow scope with respect to *everyone*, since it is c-commanded by *everyone* and c-commands t_i, a member of the chain containing the QP *everyone*. In brief, (43) should be ambiguous if (44) were a raising structure in Chinese. But in fact it is not ambiguous:

(44)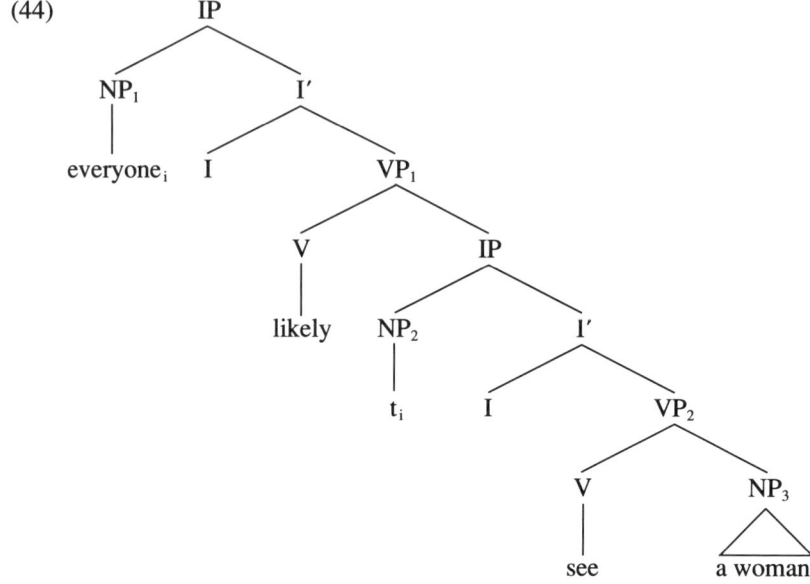

everyone must have scope over *a woman*. In other words, t_i in (44) seems to be invisible for determining scope relations. (43) behaves like a simplex sentence rather than a complex one. The lack of ambiguity in (43) may be accounted for if we assume that a reanalysis process takes place in these structures. As a consequence of this process, the two verbs are reanalyzed into one V and the IP boundary is erased:

(45) Meigeren dou [$_V$ keneng kandao] yige nuren.
 everyone all   likely see   one woman

One may wonder why reanalysis must take place in Chinese. The answer lies in the status of t_i in (44). t_i is an offending trace in (44) (see section 1.4); since V-raising does not occur in Chinese, VP$_1$ is a barrier for t_i. t_i therefore will not meet the ECP. On the other hand, when reanalysis takes place in (44)–(45), the offending trace t_i will not be visible. The sentence therefore becomes acceptable. This amounts to saying that movement takes place freely: *everyone* is moved from NP$_2$ to NP$_1$ position in (44). The output of this movement process will either be ruled out or be salvaged by a reanalysis process. This reanalysis process makes t_i invisible; t_i will not participate in the determination of QP scopes. This is why "raising" structures in Chinese do not display any scope ambiguity.

1.5.3 QP Complements

In the previous discussion we concentrated on the interaction of subject and object QPs. In the following sections we will study the interaction of the complements within VP. In particular, we will study double object constructions of the form [V NP NP] and dative constructions of the form [V NP PP] and adopt an account of the interaction of operators in these constructions based on proposals by Larson (1988, 1990).

1.5.3.1 Double Object and Dative Constructions Various proposals have been made with respect to the structure of dative and double object constructions (see, among others, Stowell 1981, Kayne 1984, Chomsky 1986b, and Larson 1988, 1990). Although the proposals vary, they contribute to understanding and capturing various properties of these constructions. We discuss the contributions of these proposals below.

Kayne (1984) (also see Stowell 1981) notes that in double object constructions [V NP_2 NP_1], NP_2 is interpreted as the possessor of NP_1. According to Kayne, double object constructions have the structure in (46a) and the corresponding dative constructions [V NP_1 *to* NP_2] have the structure in (46b).

(46)

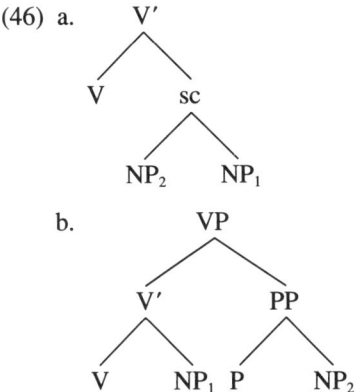

In (46a) the verb selects a small clause: NP_2 is the subject and NP_1 is the predicate. The subject and the predicate bear a possession relation; that is, the predicate assigns a possessor θ-role to the subject. In (46b) the V assigns Case and a θ-role to NP_1 and P assigns Case and a θ-role to NP_2.

Stowell proposes a somewhat different structure. He claims that NP_2 can be incorporated into the V so that the Case Filter will not be violated, as in (47a).

(47) a.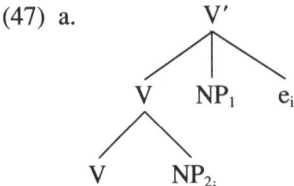

The incorporation of NP_2 into V takes place only when there is a possession relation between NP_2 and NP_1.[21] The incorporated NP_2 has a possessor θ-role; in other words, a possessor θ-role is assigned to the particular position $[_V \text{ V } [_{NP} \underline{}]]$, capturing the semantic requirement of double object structures observed by Kayne.

Alternatively, NP_2 can be realized in e position; in this situation the Case assigner *to* also occurs, as shown in (47b).

(47) b.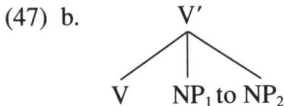

The semantic possession relation and Case assignment thus are the two main properties captured by Stowell's and Kayne's analysis.

In contrast, Larson (1988) proposes a highly articulate structure to capture the hierarchical relation between the two internal complements. Basing his account on proposals by Barss and Lasnik (1986), he argues that the following hierarchical relations hold in double object and dative constructions:

(48) a. In [V NP_2 NP_1], NP_2 asymmetrically c-commands NP_1.
 b. In [V NP_1 P NP_2], NP_1 asymmetrically c-commands NP_2.

Evidence for these c-command relations comes from the facts concerning anaphor binding in (49), quantifier binding in (50), weak crossover in (51), the superiority effect in (52), the distribution of *each...the other* in (53), and the licensing of negative polarity items in (54).

(49) *Anaphor binding*
    a.   I showed Mary herself.
        *I showed herself Mary.
    b.   I showed/presented Mary to herself.
        *I showed/presented herself to Mary.

(50) *Quantifier binding*
    a.   I gave every worker$_i$'s mother his$_i$ paycheck.
        *I gave his$_i$ mother every worker$_i$'s paycheck.

b. I gave/sent every check$_i$ to its$_i$ owner.
??I gave/sent his$_i$ check to every worker$_i$.

(51) *Weak crossover*
   a. Which man$_i$ did you send his$_i$ check?
      *Whose$_i$ pay did you send his$_i$ mother?
   b. Which check$_i$ did you send to its$_i$ owner?
      *Which worker$_i$ did you send his$_i$ check to?

(52) *Superiority*
   a. Who did you give which check?
      *Which paycheck did you give whom?
   b. Which check did you send to whom?
      *Whom did you send which check to?
      (*To whom did you send which check?)

(53) *Each...the other*
   a. I showed each man the other's socks.
      *I showed the other's friend each man.
   b. I sent each boy to the other's parents.
      *I sent the other's check to each boy.

(54) *Negative polarity*
   a. I showed no one anything.
      *I showed anyone nothing.
   b. I sent no presents to any of the children.
      *I sent any of the packages to none of the children.

The contrast in acceptability between the two (a)-sentences in each of (49)–(54) shows that NP_2 asymmetrically c-commands NP_1 in double object constructions [V NP_2 NP_1]. The contrast between the two (b)-sentences in each case shows that NP_1 asymmetrically c-commands the PP, [P NP_2], in dative constructions [V NP_1 P NP_2].

To capture these asymmetric c-command relationships is one of the main goals of Larson's (1988, 1990) analysis. He suggests that the structure underlying dative constructions is (55), where V_2 and PP form a predicate, V'_2, whose subject is NP_1. NP_1 and V'_2 form a VP that is sister to an empty V, V_1. The verb *gave* is base-generated in V_2 position and assigns an inherent Case to its dative complement. This inherent Case is realized as *to*. [*gave to Mary*] is predicated of NP_1 *a book*. In this structure NP_1 is Caseless; therefore, the verb in V_2 position must move to V_1 position in order to assign Case to NP_1, generating (56).

(55)

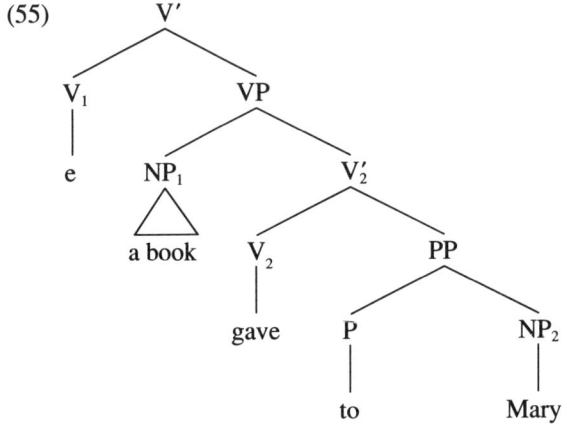

(56) He gave a book to Mary.

In this sentence *a book* asymmetrically c-commands *Mary* (see (55)), capturing the facts in (49)–(54).

As for the corresponding double object construction [V NP_2 NP_1] in (57), Larson derives it from (55) via a process similar to passivization.

(57) John gave Mary a book.

As with passivization, the (inherent) Case of V, realized as *to*, is absorbed. The subject NP_1 is generated in an adjunct position, as in (58).

(58)

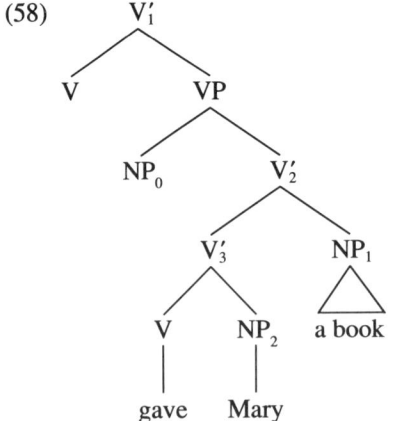

The Caseless *Mary* moves to NP_0 position. As a result, *Mary* asymmetrically c-commands *a book* in NP_1 position. NP_1 is assigned Case by V'_3 via a V'-reanalysis process: V'_3 is reanalyzed as a V, and this reanalyzed V is

Interpretive Invariance 33

able to assign a structural accusative Case to NP_1. (57) is thus the passive counterpart of (56).

We are going to adopt a variant of Larson's analysis of double object constructions. Assume that both objects in double object constructions are internal arguments. Furthermore, assume that assignment of internal θ-roles obeys a directionality requirement, as argued by Koopman (1984) and Travis (1984). All internal arguments of a verb will be base-generated on the same side. If the NP *a book* is indeed an internal argument, a representation compatible with the directionality requirement on θ-role assignment would be one where the internal arguments are on the same side of the θ-role assigner, as in (59).

(59)
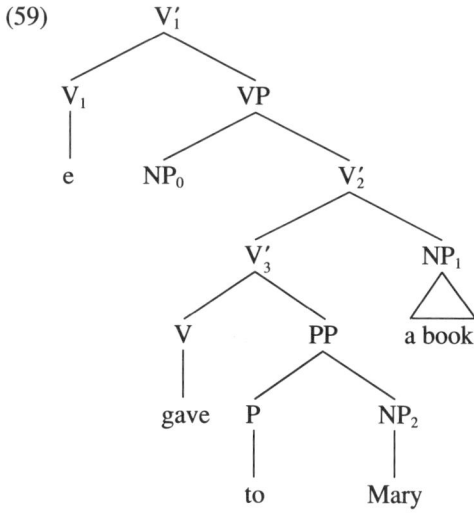

In (59) NP_0 is the Spec of VP, if every VP must have a Spec. NP_1, *a book*, and the dative PP are the internal arguments of V.[22] NP_1, however, cannot stay in place, since it does not receive Case from V'. It raises to the Spec of VP position, NP_0, to be assigned Case by the V that is raised to V_1 position, as in Larson's analysis.

In (59) the Case assigner *to* has been generated. In the event that this element is not generated, NP_2, as in Stowell's account, will have to be incorporated into the verb as in (61) so that it can receive the possessor θ-role and so that the Case Filter will not be violated. When the verb undergoes movement to the higher V position, the incorporated NP_2 will be moved along, deriving the structure in (62).

(60)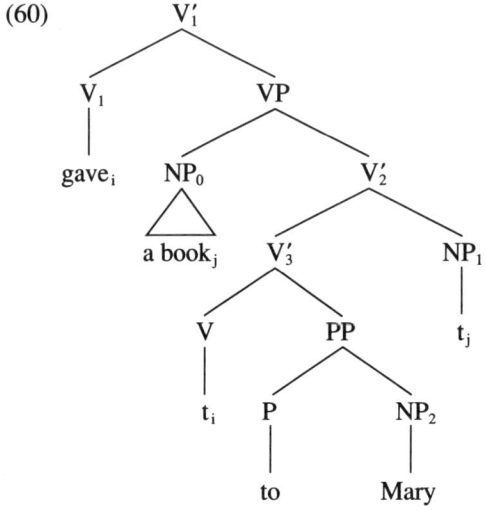

(61)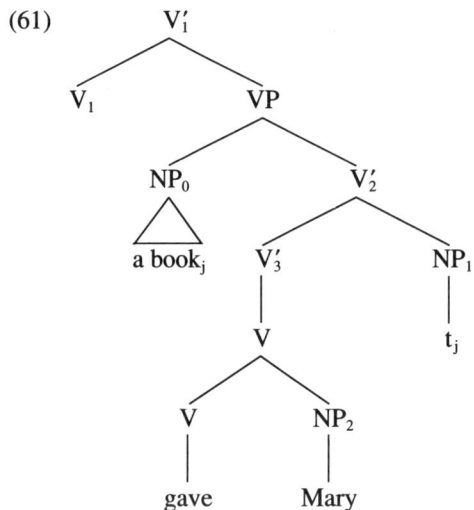

We now turn to the scope interactions of operators in double object and dative constructions.

As mentioned earlier, dative constructions like (63) are ambiguous and double object ones like (64) are not (examples (63)–(64) are from Larson 1990, 604).

Interpretive Invariance   35

(62)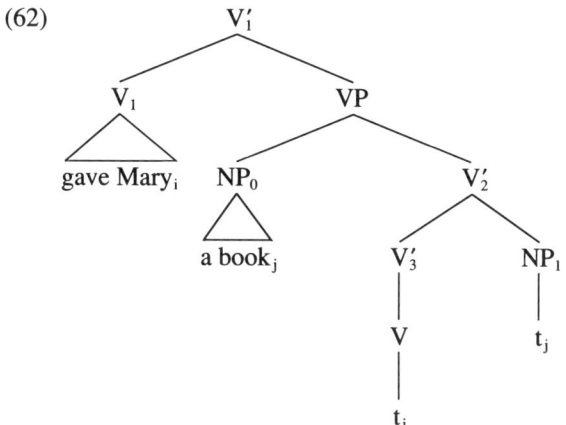

(63) John assigned one problem to every student.   (ambiguous)
(64) John assigned one student every problem.   (unambiguous)

(63) will have the S-Structure representation shown in (65).

(65)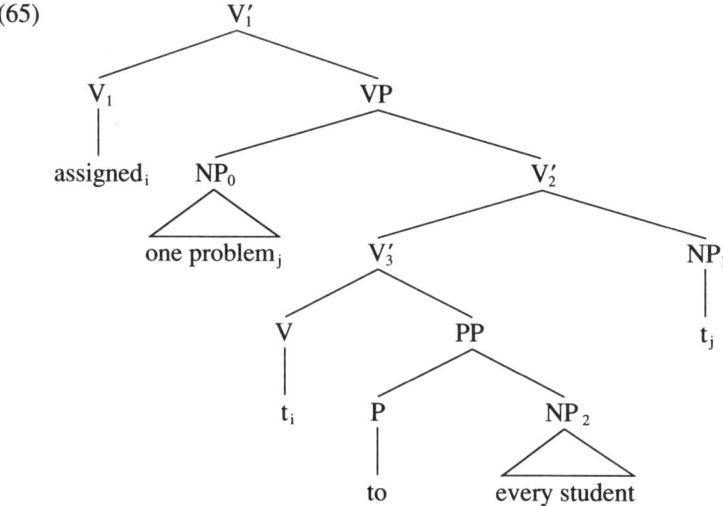

Since *one problem* has been moved from NP_1 position to NP_0 position, the ambiguity of (63) will be accounted for in the same way as the ambiguity of the canonical English active sentence.

(64) has the S-Structure representation shown in (66). In this representation *one student* will adjoin to V'_1 or higher but not to V_1, assuming that X^0 categories are not possible hosts for the adjunction of QPs. *Every*

(66)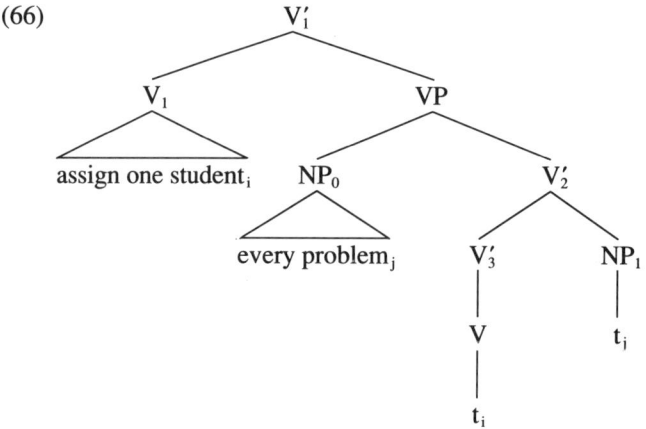

problem can adjoin to VP in (66), but not higher, because of the MBR. Thus, (64) is unambiguous.

1.5.3.2 Load/Spray Constructions As noted by Schneider-Zioga (1988) and Larson (1988, 1990), constructions with *load/spray* verbs exhibit the same behavior with respect to the interaction of quantifiers as do double object and dative constructions. Consider (67) and (68) (from Larson 1990, 604).

(67) a. The worker loaded one box on every truck.
b. The worker loaded one truck with every box.

(68) a. Max sprayed some slogan on every wall.
b. Max sprayed some wall with every slogan.

(67a) and (68a) are ambiguous, with either the theme or the locative taking wide scope. (67b) and (68b) are not ambiguous. This contrast parallels the one between dative and double object constructions.

The ambiguity of (67a) and (68a) thus can be accounted for in exactly the same way as that of the dative construction. (67a), for instance, has the partial S-Structure representation in (69), just like (65). (69) will yield two interpretations, as (65) does. The partial D-Structure representation of (67b) is (70). As in (61), NP_2 must be incorporated into V in (70): this is necessary to allow the possessor θ-role to be assigned and to satisfy the Case Filter. *Every box* is assigned Case by *with*; it does not need to be moved to NP_0 position to receive Case. The partial S-Structure representation of (67b) thus can be (71). Then, in the same way that (62) is unambiguous, (71) derives only the reading on which *one truck* takes wide scope.

Interpretive Invariance

(69)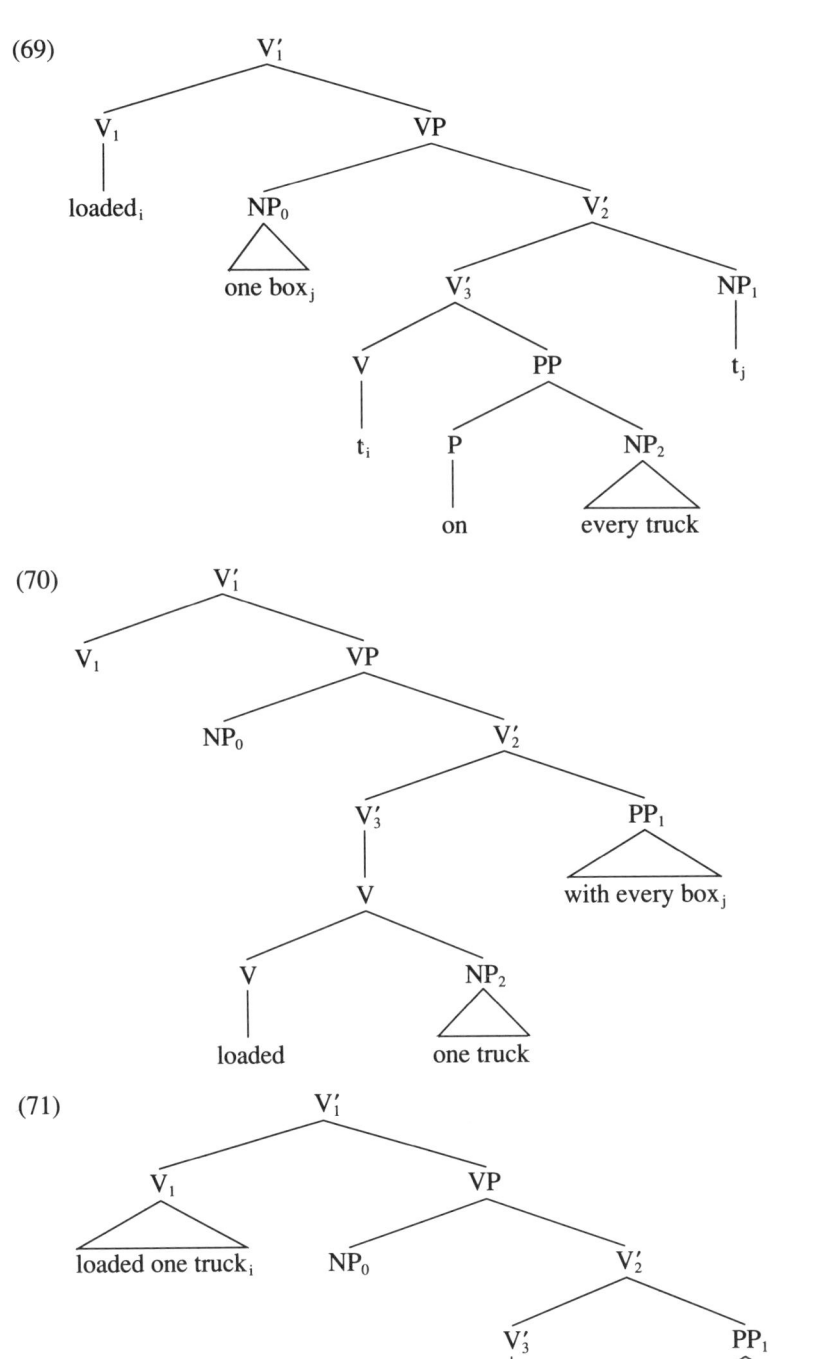

(70)

(71)

In brief, the similar interpretation of *load/spray* constructions and dative/double object constructions is traced back to the similarity of their structures and derivations.

1.6 Conclusion

Recapitulating, the analysis we have presented in this chapter has three main features:

• The Minimal Binding Requirement (19), which requires traces to be bound by the most local potential antecedent
• The Scope Principle (27), which states that the determination of the relative scope of QPs is sensitive to the chain in which they occur
• A structural difference between the basic constituent structures of English and Chinese

This analysis accounts for the following facts:

• The lack of ambiguity of active sentences in Chinese (1)
• The ambiguity of passive sentences in Chinese (4)
• The contrast between the ambiguity of active sentences in English and the nonambiguity of their Chinese counterparts ((1) vs. (2a–b))
• The contrast between the ambiguity of the English sentences in *seem*-type contexts and the nonambiguity of their Chinese counterparts ((26) vs. (43))
• The nonambiguity of double object constructions and the ambiguity of dative constructions.
• The parallelism between *load/spray* constructions and dative/double object constructions

In this chapter we have restricted our discussion to the interaction of quantifier phrases in English and Chinese. In the following chapter we turn to the interaction of quantifier phrases with *wh*-operators in these two languages.

Chapter 2:
Comparative Dimension: QP/*Wh* Interaction

In this chapter we turn to the interaction of QPs with *wh*-operators. Whereas the interaction of QPs with other QPs is subject to language variation, we will show that the interaction of QPs with *wh*-operators is the same in English and Chinese. We will argue that this type of interaction can also be accounted for by the MBR and the Scope Principle. These principles thus provide a unified account for the interaction of QPs with other QPs and for their interaction with *wh*-operators.

As a starting point, we consider the following canonical cases illustrating the interaction of QPs and *wh*-operators, discussed by May (1985):

(1) What did everyone buy for Max?

(2) Who bought everything for Max?

(1) is ambiguous; (2) is not. In his important work on the subject, May relates the existence of such a contrast to the asymmetry governing extraction in English that is to be accounted for by the Path Containment Condition (PCC) proposed by Pesetsky (1982). May's approach leads to the expectation that QPs and *wh*-elements will interact differently in languages that do not obey the PCC. However, this expectation does not appear to be fulfilled. The contrast illustrated in (1) and (2) recurs in widely differing languages such as Chinese and Spanish that do not exhibit the same kinds of effects prescribed by the PCC. On the other hand, such a recurrent contrast in various languages *is* expected in an analysis that incorporates the MBR. The account presented in chapter 1 will provide a unified analysis for the behavior of QP/QP interaction and QP/*wh* interaction in various languages.

We start by providing a detailed discussion of the contrast noted in (1) and (2) and the analysis proposed by May (section 2.1). Then we show that by sharpening the notion "potential antecedent," we are able to account for such a contrast by appealing to the MBR and the Scope Principle (section 2.2). During the course of the discussion, it will become evident that NP-traces seem to be relevant for determining the relative scope of QPs but not for determining the relative scope of *wh*-elements. This will lead us to explore ways of eliminating such a discrepancy in chapter 3.

2.1 QP/*Wh* Interaction

Consider again the contrast between (1) and (2), noted by May (1985). Depending on whether the QP is in subject or object position, the sentences can be ambiguous or unambiguous. When the QP is in subject position, the sentence is ambiguous. *Everyone* in (1) can have either a distributive or a collective reading. In contrast, when the QP is in object position, the sentence is unambiguous. *Everyone* in (2) can only have a collective reading. In terms of scope, when the QP is in subject position, it can have scope over the *wh*-word. When the QP is in object position, however, it cannot have scope over the *wh*-word (see May 1985, 1988, Hoji 1986 for a detailed discussion of scope ambiguity in such cases; also see Williams 1988 for a different viewpoint and analysis).

May attributes the existence of such a contrast to the PCC, which regulates LF representations (as well as D-Structure and S-Structure representations; May 1985, 139). May states the PCC as in (3) and defines *path* and related notions as in (4) (p. 118) (also see Pesetsky 1982).

(3) *Path Containment Condition*
Intersecting $\bar{\text{A}}$-categorial paths must embed, not overlap.

(4) A path is a set of occurrences of successively immediately dominating categorial nodes connecting a bindee to its binder. Each contiguous pair of nodes within a path constitutes a *path segment*, and a path, more precisely, is just a set of such segments.... Paths *intersect* only if they have a common path segment.... If the paths do intersect, then the PCC requires that one of the paths must properly contain all the members of the other.

The application of the PCC in English can be illustrated by the LF extraction of *wh*-elements. For instance, raising *wh*-in-situ out of a *wh*-island displays a subject-object asymmetry (the slight deviance of (5b) is due to Subjacency):

(5) a. ?*[Who$_i$ do you wonder [what$_j$ [x_i saw x_j]]]?
    b. ? [What$_j$ do you wonder [who$_i$ [x_i saw x_j]]]?

To see how the PCC distinguishes (5a) and (5b), compare the LF representations of these two sentences in (6a) and (6b). In (6a), the LF representation of (5a), there are two intersecting paths: the path of *who* is shown in (7a) and the path of *what* is shown in (7b).

(6) a.
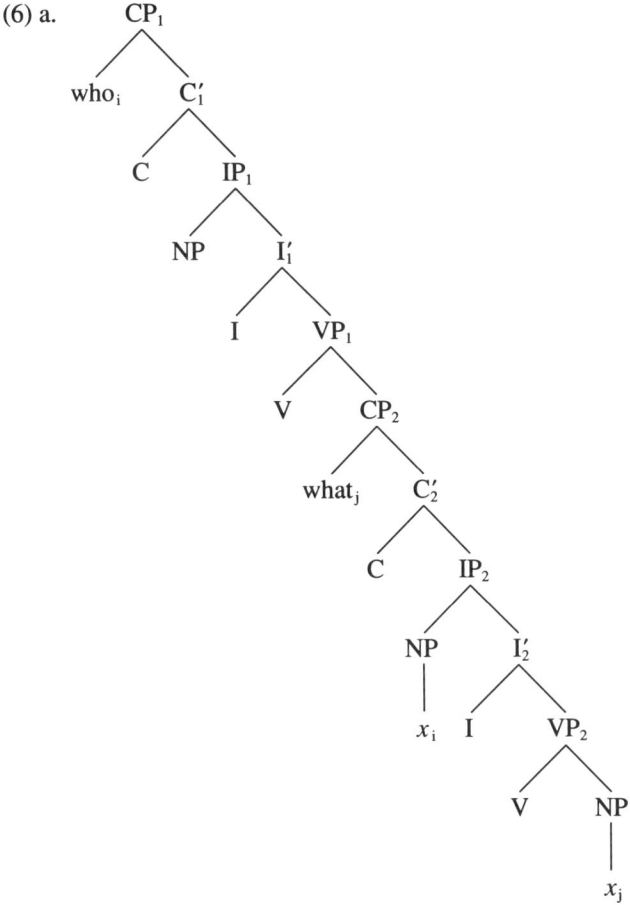

b.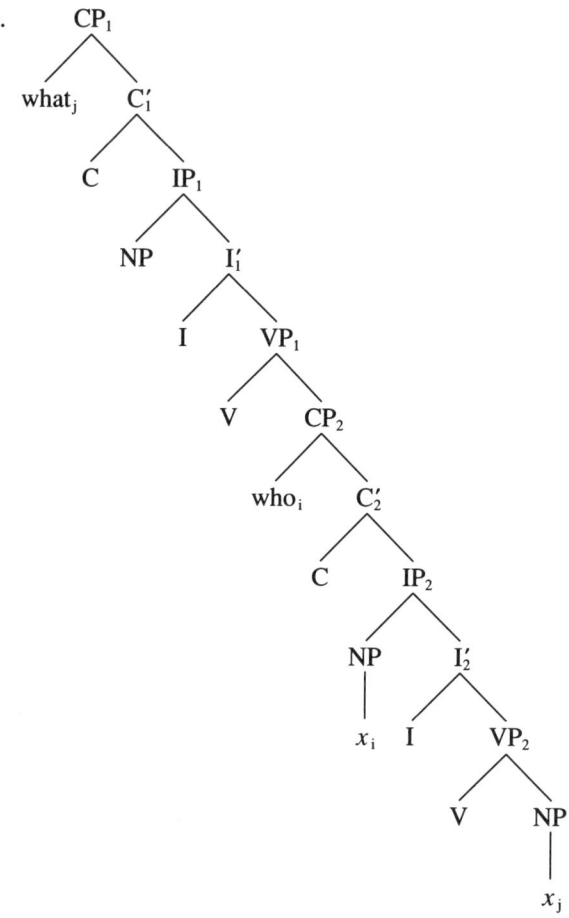

(7) a. $\quad\quad\quad\{IP_2, C'_2, CP_2, VP_1, I'_1, IP_1, C'_1, CP_1\}$
 b. $\{VP_2, I'_2, IP_2, C'_2, CP_2\}$

These two paths overlap, violating the PCC. On the other hand, the two paths in (6b), the LF representation of (5b), do not overlap. Instead, the path of *who* (8a) is embedded in the path of *what* (8b).

(8) a. $\{VP_2, I'_2, IP_2, C'_2, CP_2, VP_1, I'_1, IP_1, C'_1, CP_1\}$
 b. $\quad\quad\quad\quad\{IP_2, C'_2, CP_2\}$

The PCC thus captures the contrast between (5a) and (5b). With this, it is now clear that certain representations would not be allowed for (1)–(2). After the quantifiers are raised at LF, the LF representation for (1) is (9)

Comparative Dimension 43

and the representations for (2) can be (10a–b) (the PP *for Max* is not represented here since it does not play any role):

(9)

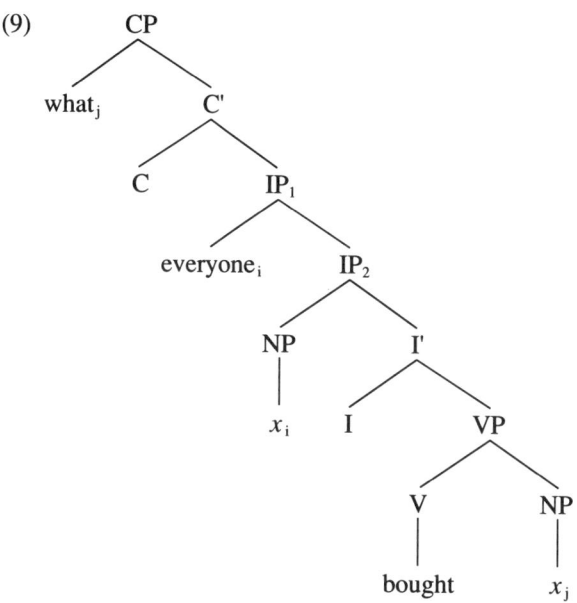

(10) a.

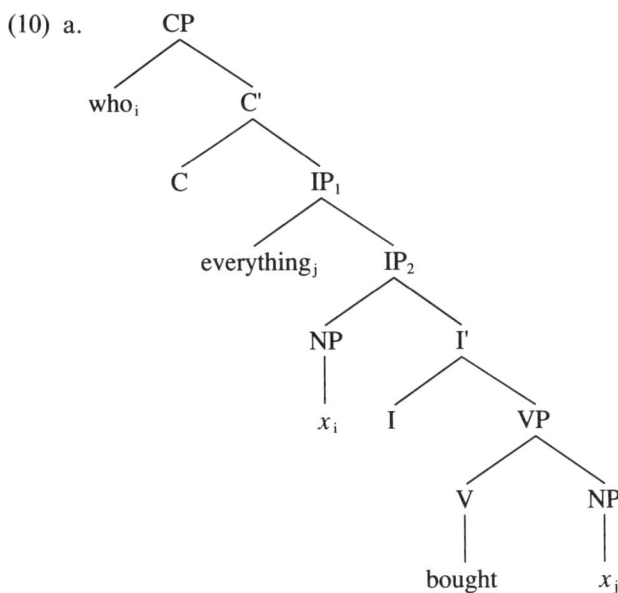

(10) b.

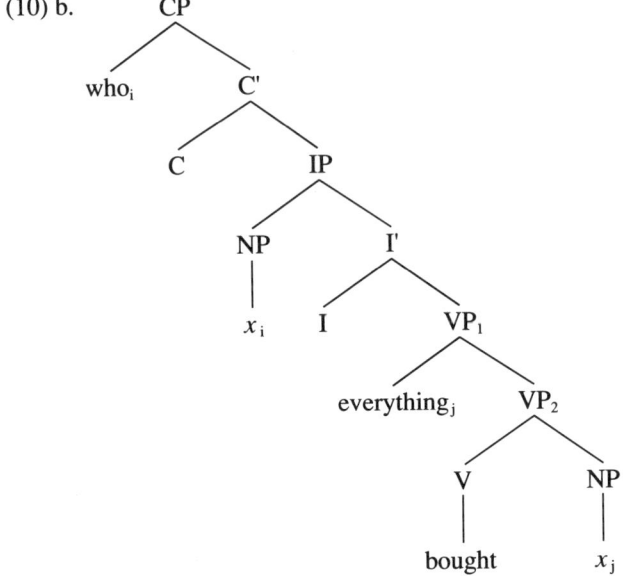

In (9) and (10b) the PCC is satisfied. The relevant paths in (9) and (10b) are (11) and (12), respectively. These paths do not overlap.

(11) *Paths in (9)*
$\{IP_2, IP_1\}$
$\{VP, I', IP_2, IP_1, C', CP\}$

(12) *Paths in (10b)*
$\{VP_2, VP_1\}$
$\{IP, C', CP\}$

In contrast, the two paths in (10a) do overlap:

(13) *Paths in (10a)*
$\{VP, I', IP_2, IP_1\}$
$\{IP_2, IP_1, C', CP\}$

The PCC thus rules out the representation in (10a). The well-formed LF representations for (1) and (2) are (9) and (10b), respectively.

Having determined the LF representations of (1) and (2), May relates the difference in interpretation between the two sentences to the difference in their structures. According to his account, the basic structural difference between the operators in (9) and the operators in (10b) is a government relation: in (9) *what* and *everyone* govern each other, whereas in

(10b) *who* and *everything* do not govern each other. May defines *government* as in (14) (p. 33; see also Aoun and Sportiche 1983).

(14) A governs B iff A c-commands B, and there are no maximal projection boundaries between A and B.

He defines *c-command* as in (15) (p. 34).

(15) A c-commands B iff every maximal projection dominating A dominates B and A does not dominate B.

In (9) *what* and *everyone* govern each other, because there is no maximal projection boundary between the *wh*-operator and the QP *everyone*, IP not being a maximal projection in May's analysis. In contrast, in (10b) a maximal projection boundary does intervene between the *wh*-operator and the raised QP *everything*, namely, VP_1.

Furthermore, in order to derive the contrast in the interpretation of (1) and (2) from their structural difference, May proposes the following Scope Principle (p. 34):

(16) Members of Σ-sequences are free to take on any type of relative scope relation.

Σ-sequence is defined as follows (p. 34):

(17) A class of occurrences of operators O is a Σ-sequence iff for any operator O_i, $O_j \in \Psi$, O_i governs O_j, where "operator" means "phrases in $\bar{A}$-positions at LF."

According to May's Scope Principle, (1), with the LF representation in (9), is ambiguous: the *wh*-operator and the quantifier govern each other, forming a Σ-sequence. They can take on any type of relative scope relation; that is, either operator can have scope over the other. In contrast, the *wh*-operator and the quantifier do not govern each other in (10b), the LF representation of (2). These two operators do not form a Σ-sequence. Therefore, (2) has only a reading where the *wh*-operator has wider scope.

In brief, May argues that the contrast between the ambiguity of (1) and the nonambiguity of (2) is accounted for by the PCC and his Scope Principle. This analysis makes interesting predictions. The PCC component of this analysis leads us to expect that, in a language where extractions need not obey the PCC, the counterparts of the English sentences (1) and (2) may have different LF representations and as a result may have different interpretations. The Scope Principle component predicts that sentences containing two operators forming a Σ-sequence should always be ambiguous. In the following two sections we will discuss the predictions made by each component of this analysis.

2.1.1 The PCC

In this section we will show that the contrast between the ambiguity of sentences like (1) and the nonambiguity of sentences like (2) cannot be attributed to the PCC. We will reach this conclusion by examining data from languages such as Chinese and Spanish.

Recall that May's analysis crucially relies on the PCC to constrain the LF representations of sentences like (1) and (2). This analysis makes the following predictions: if a language does not display the effects of the PCC, the LF representation and the interpretation of sentences corresponding to (1) and (2) are expected to be different from those of the English sentences (1) and (2). We first discuss Chinese, which does not display extraction asymmetries between subjects and objects, and we then turn to Spanish.

2.1.1.1 Chinese A good instance of a language showing no effects of the PCC is Chinese. Huang (1982) has observed that either a subject or an object can be extracted at LF out of a *wh*-island in Chinese:

(18) Ta xiang-zhidao shei mai shenme?
     he wondered   who buy what
    a. 'Who(x), he wondered what(y) x bought y?'
    b. 'What(y), he wondered who(x) x bought y?'

In order to account for the ambiguity of sentences like (18), Huang argues that, without violating grammatical rules, either the subject *who* or the object *what* can be raised at LF out of an embedded clause whose Comp is filled by another *wh*-word (raising out of a *wh*-island). The interpretations in (18a) and (18b) are generated by the LF representations in (19a) and (19b), respectively. Note that these representations are identical to those in (6a–b) for English. The PCC rules out (6a). If the PCC is at work in Chinese, it should also rule out (19a), given that the PCC should apply at all levels, including LF. However, (19a) is acceptable in Chinese, indicating that the PCC is not at work in this language. Other examples illustrating the same point are provided by topicalization structures such as (20a–b), which involve movement at S-Structure.

Comparative Dimension

(19) a.
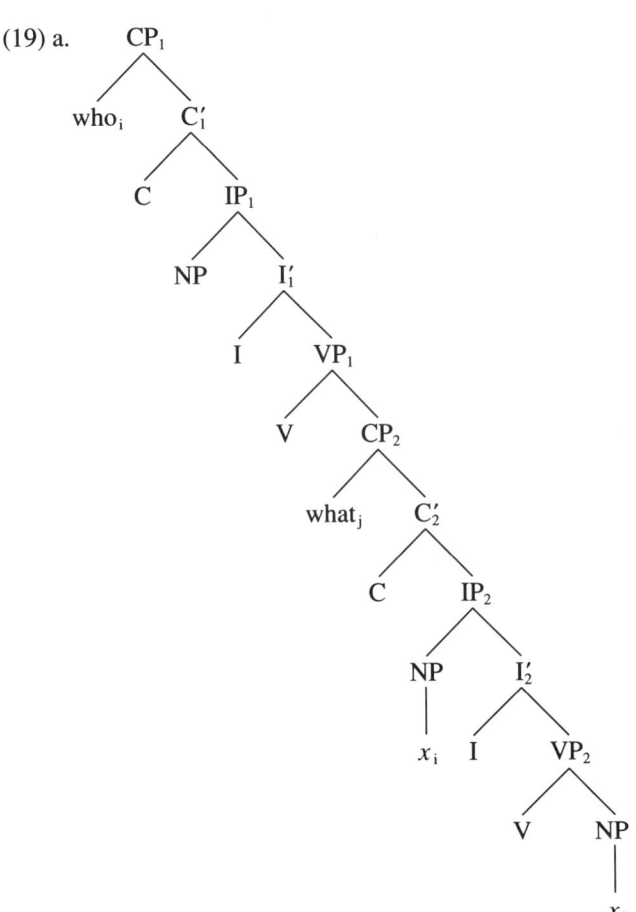

b.

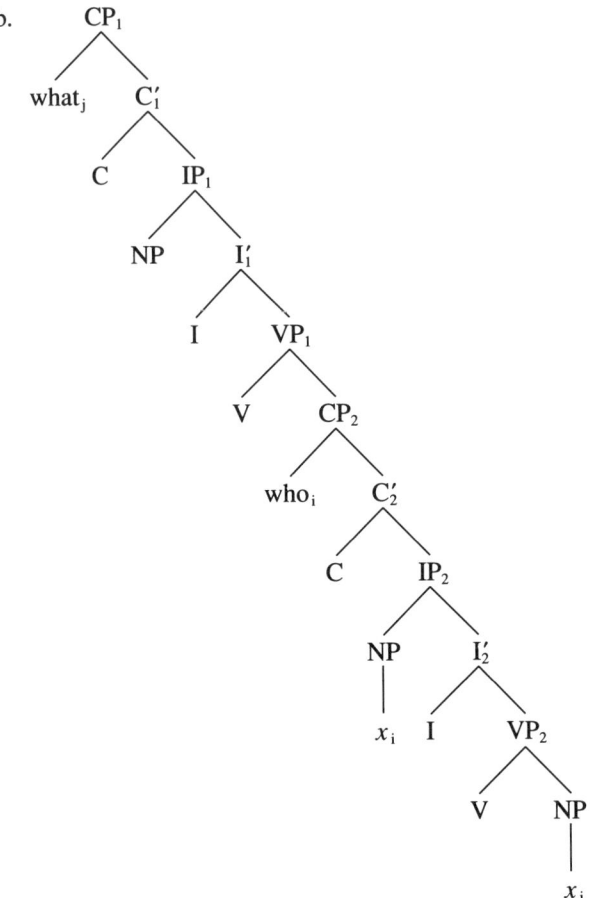

(20) a. Ni renwei zheben shu, shei kanguo?
you think this book who read
'Who do you think this book, has read?'

b. Zhangsan, wo zhidao zhei zhong shu, yiding
Zhangsan I know this kind book certainly
kanbudong.
read-not-understand
'Zhangsan, I know that (he) certainly does not understand this kind of book.'

In (20a) the object NP is topicalized at S-Structure and the *wh*-word undergoes raising at LF. The LF representation of (20a) is given in (21a).

In (20b) both the subject and object NP are topicalized, yielding the representation in (21b). (Assume that topicalization is adjunction to IP.[1] See, among others, Hoji 1985, Lasnik and Saito 1992, Saito 1985, Xu 1986.) In both representations the two paths overlap, even though (20a-b) are well formed.

The cases involving extraction of subject and object in (18) and (20a-b) indicate that the PCC is not relevant in Chinese. With this in mind, we turn to the Chinese sentences (22a-b), which correspond to the English sentences (1) and (2), respectively.

(21) a.

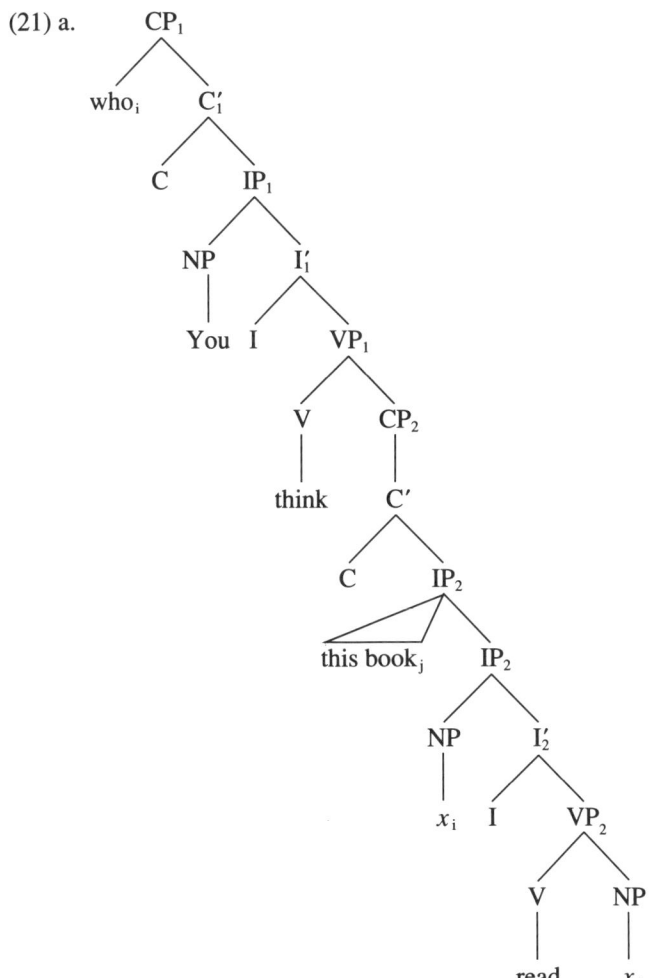

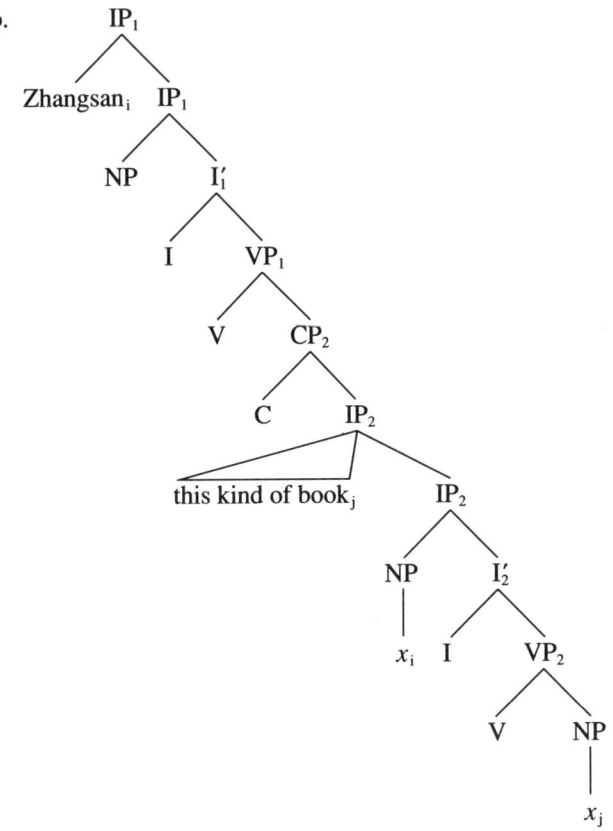

(22) a. Meigeren dou (gei Zhangsan) maile   shenme?
      everyone all   for Zhangsan bought what
      'What did everyone buy (for Zhangsan)?'

   b. Shei (gei Zhangsan) maile   meige dongxi?
      who for Zhangsan bought every thing
      'Who bought everything for Zhangsan?'

Recall that the PCC is not relevant in Chinese. In contrast to their English counterparts, (22a–b) can have the LF representations in (23a–b).

(23) a. [$_{CP}$ shenme$_j$ [$_{IP}$ meigeren$_i$ [$_{IP}$ x_i maile x_j]]]
           what   everyone   bought

   b. [$_{CP}$ shei$_i$ [$_{IP}$ meige dongxi$_j$ [$_{IP}$ x_i maile x_j]]]
          who   every thing   bought

(23a) is similar to the LF representation (9) of the English sentence (1):

just like (1), (22a) should be ambiguous. On the other hand, unlike the representation (10b) of the English sentence (2), the LF representation (23b) of the Chinese sentence (22b) is well formed. The acceptability of (23b) is significant. The two operators govern each other and enter into a Σ-sequence. Thus, if May's analysis of the contrast between (1) and (2) holds true cross-linguistically, it should predict that, unlike the English sentence (2), which is unambiguous, the Chinese sentence (22b) should be ambiguous. In other words, this analysis predicts that both (22a) and (22b) are ambiguous in Chinese. This prediction is not fulfilled: unlike (22a), (22b) is unambiguous.

In brief, the same contrast between the ambiguity of (1) and the nonambiguity of (2) in English exists in the corresponding Chinese sentences (22a) and (22b). The contrast between (22a) and (22b) cannot be captured by the PCC because Chinese does not exhibit the effects of the PCC. Since the same contrast in Chinese cannot be attributed to the PCC, the PCC approach to the contrast in English becomes suspect.

The data from Chinese illustrate a contrast similar to the one existing between (1) and (2) in English. The PCC cannot play a role in accounting for this contrast in such a language. Below, we show that the same contrast as the one existing between the English sentences (1) and (2) exists in Spanish constructions involving V-preposing. In these constructions, too, the PCC cannot account for the interaction of the operators.

2.1.1.2 Spanish Consider first the Spanish sentences (24a–b). (The following examples and discussions rely heavily on Jaeggli 1985 and Torrego 1984.)

(24) a. [Quién$_i$ no sabes   [qué$_j$ compró [x_i [V x_j]]]]?
       who   NEG (you) know   what bought
       'Who don't you know what bought?'

   b. *[Qué$_j$ no sabes   [quién$_i$ compró [x_i [V x_j]]]]?
       what NEG (you) know who   bought
       'What don't you know who bought?'

The LF representations for (24a–b) are (25a–b), respectively. (The postverbal subject is adjoined to VP; V is moved to Comp in Syntax (see Jaeggli 1985; also see Torrego 1984, where it is assumed that V is adjoined to IP). Irrelevant details are omitted in the representations.) The two paths for (24a–b) are shown in (25c–d), respectively.

(25) a. [$_{CP_1}$ quién$_i$ no sabes [$_{CP_2}$ qué$_j$ compró [$_{IP_2}$ x_i [$_{VP_2}$ V x_j]]]]
who NEG (you know) what bought

b. *[$_{CP_1}$ qué$_j$ no sabes [$_{CP_2}$ quién$_i$ compró [$_{IP_2}$ x_i [$_{VP_2}$ V x_j]]]]
what NEG (you know) who bought

c. *Paths for (25a) (overlapping)*
{VP$_2$, IP$_2$, CP$_2$}
{IP$_2$, CP$_2$, CP$_1$}

d. *Paths for (25b) (embedded)*
{VP$_2$, IP$_2$, CP$_2$, CP$_1$}
{IP$_2$, CP$_2$}

According to the PCC, (24a) should be ungrammatical and (24b) should be grammatical. These predictions are not borne out, however. Unlike what happens with the corresponding sentences in English, extracting a subject out of a *wh*-island in (24a) is better than extracting an object out of a *wh*-island in (24b) in Spanish.² Taking this as the starting point of the Spanish structures involving the extraction of a subject and an object, we turn to the Spanish cases corresponding to the English sentences (1) and (2).

Consider the Spanish sentences (26a–b).

(26) a. Quién examinó cada doctor?
who examined every doctor
'Who did every doctor examine?'

b. Quién examinó a cada paciente?
who examined every patient

Let us look first at (26b), which corresponds to the English sentence (2). According to the extraction facts in (24a–b), the only well-formed LF representation of this sentence is (27a).³

(27) a. [$_{CP}$ quién$_i$ [$_C$ examinó [$_{IP}$ a cada paciente$_j$ [$_{IP}$ x_i [$_{VP_2}$ V x_j]]]]]
who examined every patient

In (27a) the *wh*-subject is moved to the Spec of Comp and the V is moved to Comp. The object QP can adjoin to IP (or VP) at LF. Notice that in (27a) the two operators govern each other. According to the Scope Principle, (26b) should be ambiguous. This is not the case, however. In (26b) the *wh*-operator necessarily has scope over the QP.

Let us look next at (26a), the Spanish counterpart of the English sentence (1). The object *wh*-word *quién* is moved to the Spec of Comp and the

V is preposed to the Comp at S-Structure. At LF the subject QP *cada doctor* can adjoin to IP (see notes 2 and 3):

(27) b. [$_{CP}$ quién$_j$ examinó [$_{IP}$ cada doctor$_i$ [$_{IP}$ x_i [$_{VP}$ V x_j]]]]
        who examined every doctor

Compared to (24b), the representation in (27b) should not be well formed. However, (26a) is in fact acceptable. It also is ambiguous: either operator can have scope over the other.

In brief, the account for the contrast between (1) and (2) based on the PCC leads us to expect that in Spanish, (26b) should be ambiguous and (26a) unacceptable. These sentences therefore should not display the same contrast as the one existing between the corresponding English sentences (1) and (2). This expectation is not fulfilled. The Spanish sentences in question display exactly the same contrast as the corresponding English sentences: (26b) is unambiguous and (26a) is ambiguous.

If we follow the logic of the approach based on the PCC, we expect Chinese and Spanish sentences to behave differently from English sentences with respect to interaction of *wh*-words and QPs. However, we have shown that the Chinese and Spanish sentences involving such interaction, (22a–b) and (26a–b), behave exactly like the corresponding English sentences (1) and (2). These facts therefore cast doubt on the plausibility of the PCC account. We argue in the next section that the other component of the analysis that May (1985) proposes for English, the Scope Principle, does not adequately account for the interaction of QPs with other QPs in general.

2.1.2 The Scope Principle

Recall that May's Scope Principle defined in (16) states that when two operators govern each other, either one can have scope over the other. This principle is designed to capture the fact that a sentence like (1) is ambiguous even though it has only one well-formed LF representation. Sentence (1) and its LF representation are repeated here as (28) and (29).

(28) What did everyone buy (for Max)?

(29) [$_{CP}$ what$_j$ [$_{IP}$ everyone$_i$ [$_{IP}$ x_i buy x_j]]]

The Scope Principle (16) also captures the fact that (30), which involves two QPs instead of a QP and a *wh*-word, is ambiguous. The only well-formed LF representation generating this ambiguity is given in (31). In this representation the two QPs govern each other. Thus, according to the Scope Principle, either one can have scope over the other.

(30) Someone saw everyone.

(31) [$_{IP}$ everyone$_j$ [$_{IP}$ someone$_i$ [$_{IP}$ x_i saw x_j]]]

In this section we show that there are many instances involving interaction of two QPs in English and Chinese that do not conform to the Scope Principle as defined in (16).

Consider first the following sentence in English:

(32) John assigned one student every problem.

After QR at LF, (32) has the LF representation in (33).

(33) [$_{IP}$ every problem$_j$ [$_{IP}$ one student$_i$ [$_{IP}$ John assigned t$_i$ t$_j$]]]

In this representation the two operators govern each other. The Scope Principle (16) predicts this sentence to be ambiguous. This prediction, however, is not borne out: as discussed in section 1.5.3, (32) is not ambiguous. *One student* must have scope over *every problem*. The Scope Principle (16) thus fails to explain why sentences like (32) in English are not ambiguous.

Not only does the Scope Principle (16) fail to account for the interaction of QPs with other QPs in English, it also fails to account for such an interaction in Chinese.

Consider first the Chinese counterpart of the English double object structure [V NP$_1$ NP$_2$] (as in (32)), given in (34).

(34) Wo zhidinggei yige xuesheng meige wenti.[4]
    I   assign   one student   every problem
    'I assigned a student every problem.'

Just like (32), (34) is unambiguous. Since the derivation of the Chinese double object structure is the same as that of its English counterpart (see section 1.5.3), (34) should be ambiguous according to the Scope Principle (16). The nonambiguity of (34) thus contradicts the prediction of the Scope Principle in (16).

Next consider the following pair of sentences, of the type discussed in section 1.1:

(35) a. Meigeren dou zhuazou yige nuren.   (unambiguous)
       everyone all arrest   one woman
       'Everyone arrested a woman.'

    b. Meigeren dou bei yige nuren   zhuazou.   (ambiguous)
       everyone all by one woman arrest
       'Everyone was arrested by a woman.'

(35a) is an active sentence containing a QP in subject position interacting with a QP in object position. (35b) is a passive sentence containing a QP in subject position interacting with a QP in the *by*-phrase. As indicated in chapter 1, the active sentence (35a) is unambiguous but the passive sentence (35b) is ambiguous.

Since Chinese does not display any subject-object asymmetry with respect to extraction, there are three possible LF representations corresponding to (35a):

(36) a. [$_{IP}$ meigeren [$_{IP}$ yige nuren [...
       everyone   a   woman

b. [$_{IP}$ yige nuren [$_{IP}$ meigeren [...
    a   woman everyone

c. [$_{IP}$ meigeren ... [$_{VP}$ yige nuren [...
    everyone   a   woman

The Scope Principle (16) would derive two readings for any of the three representations in (36). We thus expect (35a) to be ambiguous. However, contrary to this prediction, (35a) is unambiguous. The contrast between the nonambiguity of the active sentences and the ambiguity of the passive sentences in (35) is not expected.

There are other cases that May's Scope Principle as defined in (16) cannot accommodate—for example, the nonambiguity of the Chinese sentences involving QPs within PPs:

(37) Wo wei yige ren zuo meijian shiqing.   (unambiguous)
    I for one man do every thing
    'I did everything for a man.'

According to the Scope Principle (16), (37) should be ambiguous, because both QPs can be adjoined to IP. However, (37) can only have the reading where the prepositional object has wide scope.[5]

Recapitulating, we have shown that the nonambiguity of the double object structure [V NP$_1$ NP$_2$] in both English and Chinese cannot be accounted for by the Scope Principle defined in (16). This principle also fails to account for certain other phenomena in Chinese: the nonambiguity of active sentences, the contrast between active and passive sentences, and the nonambiguity of instances involving PPs. In fact, the Scope Principle (16), together with the PCC, would lead us to expect that the instances involving QP/QP interaction should be ambiguous in general. This, however, is not the case. Thus, we conclude that the Scope Principle as stated in (16) does not adequately account for the scope properties of quantificational expressions.

2.2 A Unified Account for QP/*Wh* Interaction

We will show in this section how the interaction of QPs and *wh*-operators can be accounted for by the MBR and the Scope Principle. To do so, we need to clarify some differences between the variables bound by QPs and the variables bound by *wh*-operators with respect to the binding theory. We first discuss the distinction between these variables in section 2.2.1 and then give our analysis of QP/*wh* interaction in section 2.2.2.

2.2.1 Variable Types

We showed in chapter 1 that the LF representations of sentences involving QP interaction are constrained by the MBR. The MBR rules out representations like (38a–b), where x_1 and x_2 are derived by raising QP_1 and QP_2, respectively. The only possible representation that is allowed by the MBR is the one in (38c).

(38) a. $[QP_1 \ldots QP_2 \ldots x_1 \ldots x_2]$
 b. $[QP_1 \ldots QP_2 \ldots x_2 \ldots x_1]$
 c. $[QP_1 \ldots x_1 \ldots QP_2 \ldots x_2]$

The variables bound by *wh*-operators, however, do not seem to behave like the variables bound by QPs with respect to the MBR. These variables seem to violate the MBR blatantly. For instance, consider (39), with multiple *wh*-questions. The marginality of (39) is due to a Subjacency violation (see Chomsky 1977).

(39) ?What$_j$ did you wonder who$_i$ x_i bought x_j?

In (39) the variable bound by *what* does not appear to be bound by the first available $\bar{A}$-binder, *who*. How, then, is the MBR satisfied in this case? The answer to this question lies in recognizing an important distinction between variables bound by *wh*-words and variables bound by QPs with respect to the binding theory. Chomsky (1981) assumes that variables coindexed with *wh*-operators are name-like expressions that are subject to Principle C of the binding theory. Moreover, Aoun and Hornstein (1985) argue that variables coindexed with standard QPs (such as *everyone* or *someone*) are *not* subject to Principle C. We discuss some of Aoun and Hornstein's (1985) arguments in chapter 5. For the present discussion, it suffices to assume that variables bound by QPs, contrary to variables bound by *wh*-elements such as *who* and *what*, are not subject to Principle C.

This contrast between variables bound by *wh*-operators and those bound by QPs with respect to Principle C suggests an answer to the question raised by (39) regarding the application of the MBR. The solution to the apparent violation of the MBR lies in sharpening the notion "potential Ā-binder" encoded in the MBR. We assume that:

(40) A qualifies as a potential Ā-binder for B iff A c-commands B, A is in an Ā-position, and the assignment of the index of A to B would not violate Principle C of the binding theory.

The characterization of a potential Ā-binder in (40) disqualifies *who* in the embedded Comp position as a potential Ā-binder for the variable x_j in the object position: assignment of the index of *who* to the object variable would entail that this object variable be coindexed with the variable x_i in subject position. Since the subject variable is in an A-position, such coindexing would create a violation of Principle C with respect to the object variable. Therefore, *what* in the matrix Comp position, but not *who* in the embedded Comp position, qualifies as the most local potential antecedent. Since no other potential antecedents intervene between *what* and the object variable, the object variable is bound by the most local potential antecedent, satisfying the MBR.

Summarizing, we have shown that even though variables bound by *wh*-operators do not obey the MBR in the same way as variables bound by QPs, both types of variables actually obey the MBR. The basic distinction between these two variable types lies in their different status with respect to Principle C: variables bound by *wh*-operators are subject to Principle C but variables bound by QPs are not. This distinction will dictate whether or not an Ā-binder is a potential antecedent as defined in (40).

Having clarified the distinction between QP-variables and *wh*-variables with respect to the application of the MBR, we proceed to extend our analysis of QPs to the cases involving QP/*wh* interaction.

2.2.2 Syntax of *Wh*/QP Scope

In this section we show that the contrast between the English sentences (1) and (2) and the same contrast between their counterparts in Chinese can be uniformly accounted for by the analysis outlined in the previous sections. We consider first the ambiguous sentences such as (1), in section 2.2.2.1. We then turn to the unambiguous sentences such as (2), in section 2.2.2.2.

2.2.2.1 Object *Wh*/Subject QP Interaction First consider the ambiguous English sentence (1), repeated here (again, *for Max* will not be represented for simplicity).

(1) What did everyone buy (for Max)?

At S-Structure, *what* is moved to Spec of Comp, and the subject NP is moved from the Spec of VP position to the Spec of I' position as a result of subject raising. At LF, QR applies, deriving the LF representation in (41).

(41)

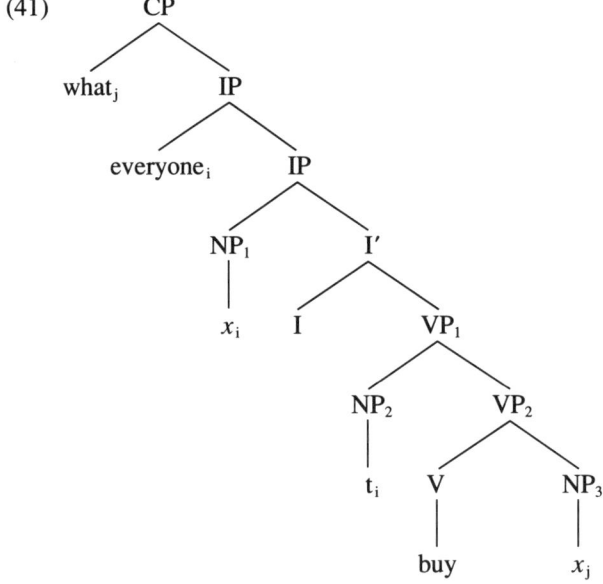

This representation is well formed according to the MBR. The raised QP *everyone* is the most local potential antecedent for x_i. The object variable generated by *wh*-raising must also be bound by its most local potential antecedent. The raised subject QP *everyone* does not qualify as a potential Ā-binder for the variable in object position. Indeed, assignment of the index of *everyone* to the object variable would trigger a Principle C violation since this variable would end up being A-bound by t_i or x_i. In short, *everyone* does not qualify as a potential antecedent for this variable. No other potential antecedent intervenes between *what* and the variable in object position. *What* counts as the most local potential antecedent. Thus, the MBR is satisfied.

Note that (41) yields two readings according to the Scope Principle established in chapter 1 that incorporates the notion of chain. *What* c-commands *everyone* and its variable, yielding the reading where *what* has scope over *everyone*. In turn, *everyone* c-commands the variable bound by *what* in NP_3 position, yielding the reading where *everyone* has scope over *what*. Sentence (1) is thus ambiguous.

The same account directly extends to the Chinese counterpart of (1), the ambiguous (22a), repeated here as (42) (as with (41), the PP is irrelevant).

(42) Meigeren dou (gei Zhangsan) maile   shenme?   (ambiguous)
     everyone all for Zhangsan bought what
     'What did everyone buy (for Zhangsan)?'

This sentence has the LF representation given in (43). This representation is generated by the LF movement of the *wh*-word *shenme* to the Spec of Comp and the LF movement of the subject QP to IP.

(43) $[_{CP}$ shenme$_j$ $[_{IP}$ meigeren$_i$ $[_{IP}$ x_i $[_{VP}$ maile x_j]]]]
          what   everyone   bought

The MBR is satisfied in (43) as in (41). *Everyone* is the most local potential antecedent for the subject variable x_i. The object variable generated by *wh*-raising is properly bound by its most local potential antecedent *what*. This well-formed representation yields two readings since *what* c-commands *everyone* and *everyone* c-commands x_j, a member of the chain containing *what*. (42) is therefore ambiguous.

The relevant sentence in Spanish, (26a) (repeated here as (44)), is accounted for in the same way.

(44) Quién examinó cada doctor?   (ambiguous)
     who   examined every doctor
     'Who did every doctor examine?'

Since the subject NP can be extracted from postverbal position, a partial S-Structure representation for (44) is (45a) (recall that V is preposed in this type of *wh*-question). At LF the subject QP adjoins to VP_1 (or IP), as shown in (45b).

(45) a. $[_{CP}$ quién$_j$ $[_{C'}$ examinó $[_{IP}[_{VP_1}$ $[_{VP_2}$ V x_j] cada doctor]]]]
            who   examined   every doctor

     b. $[_{CP}$ quién$_j$ $[_{C'}$ examinó $[_{IP}[_{VP_1}$ cada doctor$_i$ $[_{VP_1}[_{VP_2}$ V x_j] x_i]]]]]
            who   examined   every doctor

In this representation both the QP-trace and the *wh*-variable meet the MBR (see the relevant discussion of (1) and (42)). *Who* c-commands and has scope over the subject QP. In turn, the raised subject QP c-commands the *wh*-variable. According to the Scope Principle of chapter 1, either operator may have scope over the other. (44) is therefore ambiguous.

In this section we have illustrated how the MBR and the Scope Principle introduced in chapter 1 offer a unified account for the interaction of QP/*wh* scope in the ambiguous English sentence (1) and its counterparts in Chinese and Spanish. The MBR constrains the possible LF representations. The Scope Principle, which crucially makes use of the chain containing the operators and their variables, derives the scope relations.

Next we show how the same analysis accounts for the nonambiguity of the English sentence (2) and its counterparts in Chinese and Spanish. Since the account for Chinese is more straightforward, we discuss the Chinese case first.

2.2.2.2 Subject *Wh*/Object QP Interaction The Chinese counterpart of the unambiguous English sentence (2) is (22b), repeated here as (46).

(46) Shei (gei Zhangsan) maile meige dongxi?   (unambiguous)
     who for Zhangsan bought every thing
     'Who bought everything (for Zhangsan)?'

At LF *who* is moved to the Spec of Comp and the QP *everything* undergoes QR. VP and IP are both possible adjunction sites for QR, as illustrated in (47a–b).

(47) a. [$_{CP}$ shei$_i$ [$_{IP}$ x_i [$_{VP_1}$ meige dongxi$_j$ [$_{VP_2}$ maile x_j]]]]
        who   every thing   bought

   b. [$_{CP}$ shei$_i$ [$_{IP}$ meige dongxi$_j$ [$_{IP}$ x_i [$_{VP}$ maile x_j]]]]
        who   every thing   bought

The MBR, however, only allows (47a). In (47a) both x_i and x_j are bound by the most local potential $\bar{\text{A}}$-binder, thus obeying the MBR. In contrast, (47b) is ruled out by the MBR: the most local potential antecedent for both x_i and x_j is *everything*. Thus, (47a) is the only well-formed LF representation for (46). This representation yields only one interpretation where *who* has scope over *everything*. Therefore, (46) is unambiguous.

The same analysis can be extended to the relevant sentence in Spanish, (26b) (repeated here as (48)), without any modifications.

Comparative Dimension

(48) Quién examinó a cada paciente?   (unambiguous)
    who   examined every patient

The partial S-Structure representation of (48) is (49).

(49) $[_{CP}$ quién$_i$ [examinó $[_{VP_1}[_{VP_2}$ V a cada paciente] x_i]]]
     who   examined   every patient

In (49) *every patient* can only adjoin to VP_2, according to the MBR. The chain containing the *wh*-operator and its variable c-commands both the raised QP and its variable in object position. Therefore, (48) is unambiguous according to the Scope Principle in chapter 1.

In brief, the nonambiguity of the Chinese sentence (46) and the Spanish sentence (48) follows straightforwardly from the MBR and the Scope Principle in chapter 1. We thus are able to offer a unified account for a recurring set of facts in these two languages even though their subject and object positions behave differently with respect to the PCC. We show in the next section that the nonambiguity of the English sentence (2) can also be accounted for by the same analysis, provided that we clarify the nature of the chain entering into scope relations.

2.2.2.3 NP-Traces and Scope Assignment   As mentioned earlier, the English sentence (2) is unambiguous.

(2) Who bought everything (for Max)?

This sentence has the S-Structure representation in (50) (see section 1.4).

(50)

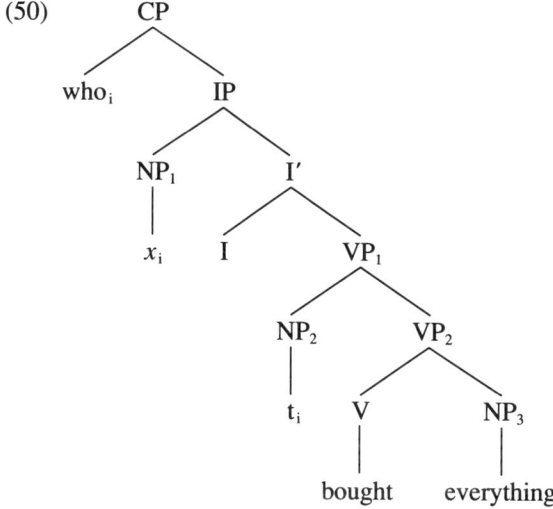

In (50) the object QP *everything* can adjoin to VP_2 or VP_1:

(51) a. [who$_i$ [x_i [$_{VP_1}$ t$_i$ [$_{VP_2}$ everything$_j$ [$_{VP_2}$ V x_j]]]]]
  b. [who$_i$ [x_i [$_{VP_1}$ everything$_j$ [$_{VP_1}$ t$_i$ [$_{VP_2}$ V x_j]]]]]

(51a) yields one reading: *who* has scope over *everything* because the chain [*who*$_i$, x_i, t_i] c-commands both *everything* and its trace x_j. (51b) should yield two readings: *who* c-commands and has scope over *everything*, and *everything* c-commands *t*, a member of the chain containing *who*. According to the Scope Principle in chapter 1, *everything* must also have scope over *who*. However, this is not the case: (50) is unambiguous. It has the reading where *who* has wide scope but not the reading where *everything* has wide scope. Note that this impossible reading is derived because *everything* c-commands *t*, the NP-trace coindexed with *who*. This seems to indicate that the NP-trace *t* in (50) should not play a role in determining scope relations. This conclusion conflicts with the one reached in chapter 1, where we indicated that NP-traces play a role in determining scope relations between QPs in sentences like (52), which has the structure in (53).

(52) Someone saw everything. (ambiguous)

(53)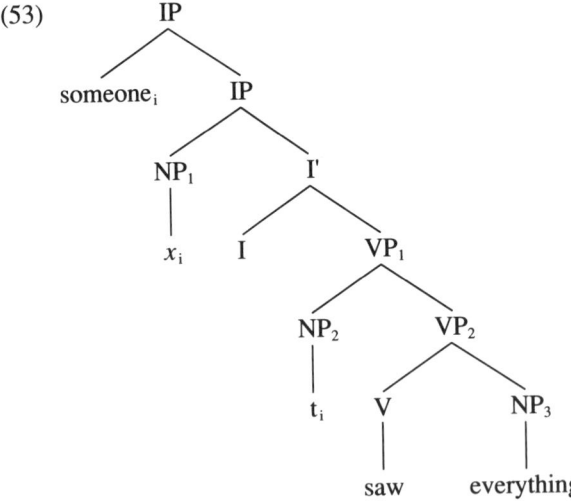

In (52) *everything* can have scope over *someone*. We have accounted for this interpretation by adjoining *everything* to VP_1 in (53). *Everything* would then c-command the NP-trace coindexed with the subject QP *someone*. This means that the NP-trace in NP_2 position must interact with the object QP *everything*.

Comparative Dimension 63

In brief, it seems that NP-traces play a role in the determination of relative scope between two QPs but not between a QP and a *wh*-word:

(54) In the representation [$wh_i \ldots x_i \ldots t_i$]

where x_i is a variable coindexed with wh_i and t_i is an NP-trace coindexed with x_i,

t_i does not constitute a member of the chain relevant to the determination of scope;

whereas in the representation [$QP_i \ldots x_i \ldots t_i$]

where x_i is a variable coindexed with QP_i and t_i is an NP-trace coindexed with x_i,

t_i constitutes a member of the chain relevant to the determination of scope.[6]

The generalization in (54) seems to be necessary not only to account for the contrast between (2) and (52) but also to account for a wider range of examples in English. Consider the following passive constructions in English:

(55) a. Someone$_i$ is loved t$_i$ by everyone. (ambiguous)
 b. Who$_i$ is loved t$_i$ by everyone? (unambiguous)

(55a) is ambiguous. However, (55b) is unambiguous. This contrast is captured by the generalization in (54) as shown below.

After QR at LF, (55a) has the LF representation in (56a). In this representation both QPs undergo QR: the subject *someone* adjoins to IP and the *by*-QP adjoins to VP$_1$. t_1 is the NP-trace generated by subject raising and t_2 is the NP-trace generated by passivization. Two chains are formed: [$someone_i, x_1, t_{1_i}, t_{2_i}$] (see note 6) and [$everyone_j, x_j$].

(55b) has the LF representation in (56b). In (56b) the subject *who* moves to the Spec of Comp. Two chains are formed: [$who_i, x_i, t_{1_i}, t_{2_i}$] and [$everyone_j, x_j$] (see note 6).

Notice that in (56a) *someone* c-commands and has scope over *everyone*; *everyone* c-commands t_1 and t_2 and thus has scope over the QP coindexed with t_1 and t_2, *someone*. Therefore, (55a) is ambiguous. The LF representation (56b), in contrast, does not generate any ambiguity: *everyone* does not have scope over *who*, even though it c-commands the NP-traces t_1 and t_2, which are bound by *who*. The nonambiguity of (55b) thus shows that NP-traces bound by *wh*-operators are not relevant for the determination of relative scope. The generalization in (54) captures the contrast between

(56) a.
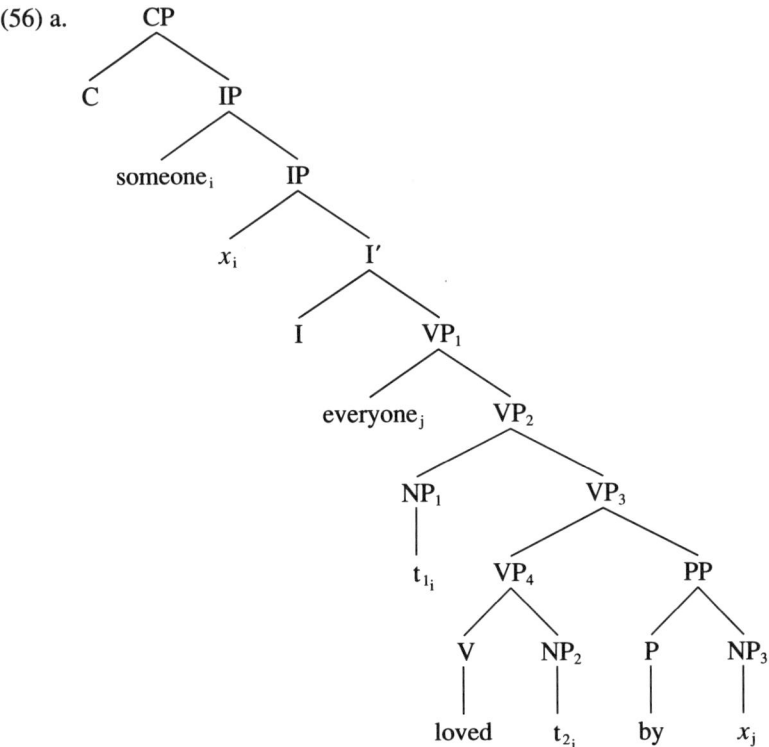

(56) b.
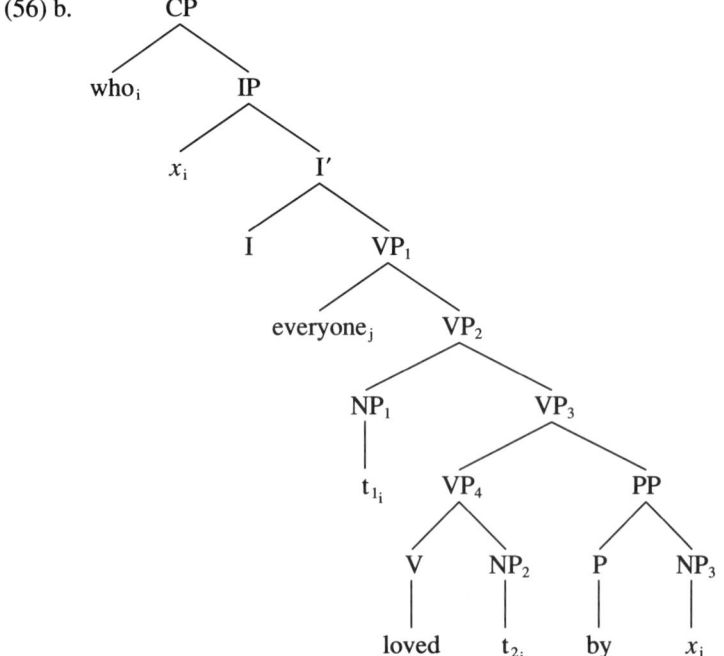

the ambiguity of (55a) involving QP/QP interaction and the nonambiguity of (55b) involving QP/*wh* interaction.

This discrepancy between the role of NP-traces coindexed with *wh*-words and the role of NP-traces coindexed with QPs just noted for English also exists in Chinese, as the following passive sentences illustrate:

(55) c. (Yaoshi) yige nuren bei meigeren ma...[7]   (ambiguous)
     if   a   woman by everyone scold
    '(If) a woman was scolded by everyone...'

   d. Shei bei meigeren ma?   (unambiguous)
     who by everyone scold
    'Who was scolded by everyone?'

The interaction of QPs in (55c) results in an ambiguous sentence, in contrast to (55d), an instance of QP/*wh* interaction, which is unambiguous. The NP-trace in the object position of (55d), which is coindexed with the *wh*-operator, cannot play a role in determining scope relations. If it did, the sentence would be ambiguous because this NP-trace is c-commanded by the QP after QR applies, as in (56b). The contrast between the Chinese passive constructions in (55c) and (55d) reveals that the generalization in (54) is valid for both English and Chinese passive constructions.

Other instances involving NP-traces also confirm the generalization in (54). Consider, for instance, the raising constructions in (55e–f).

(55) e. Someone seems to [t love everyone].   (ambiguous)
   f. Who seems [t to love everyone]?   (unambiguous)

In (55e–f) there is an NP-trace generated by subject-to-subject raising. (55e) is ambiguous but (55f) is unambiguous. This contrast can be captured by assuming that NP-traces play a role in determining relative scope for QPs but not for *wh*-elements. Consider first (55e). After the subject QP *someone* in (55e) is raised by QR, as in (57a), *everyone* can have scope over *someone* by adjoining to VP_3 or IP_3 of the embedded clause. In either case *everyone* c-commands the NP-trace t_i, which is a member of the chain containing *someone* and thus has scope over *someone*. Notice that the wide scope reading for *everyone* can be derived if the NP-trace in NP_3 or NP_4 position is relevant for determining scope. Next consider (55f). This sentence has the structure in (57b). Once again, *everyone* can adjoin to VP_3 or IP_3 of the embedded clause and c-command the NP-trace coindexed with *who*. However, (55f) is unambiguous. The wide scope reading of *everyone* must be barred. The nonambiguity of this sentence supports the

(57) a.

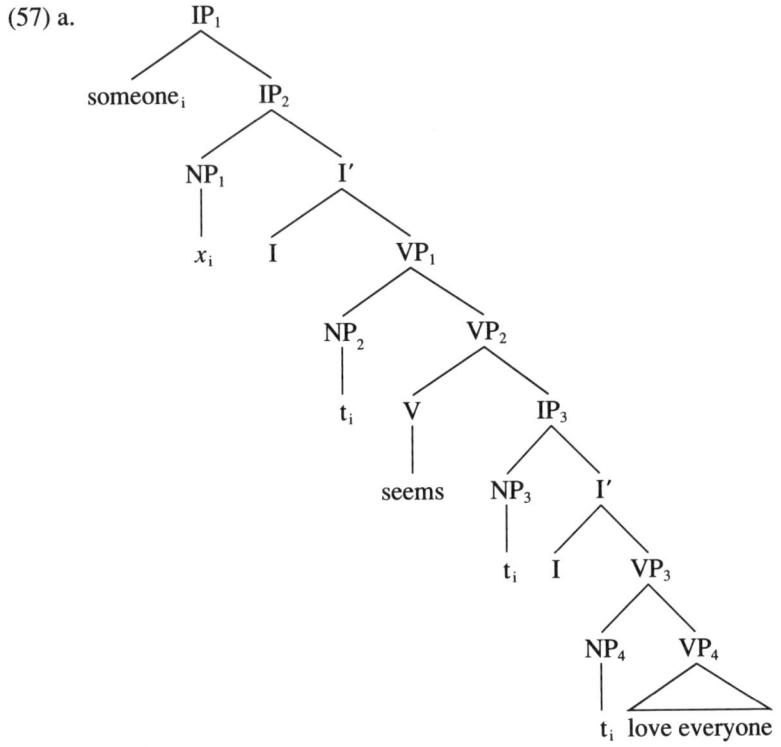

claim that NP-traces do not play a role in determining the relative scope of *wh*-elements.

In brief, the contrast between the ambiguity of (57a) and the nonambiguity of (57b) can be captured if an NP-trace coindexed with a QP enters into scope relations but an NP-trace coindexed with a *wh*-operator does not. The generalization in (54) once again captures such a contrast.

Recapitulating, our analysis based on the MBR and the Scope Principle in chapter 1 uniformly accounts for the scope relations between *wh*-operators and QP operators in the English sentences (1) and (2), the Chinese sentences (42) and (46), and the Spanish sentences (44) and (48). Furthermore, the sentences in (55) are accounted for in the same manner. We repeat these sentences here:

(1) What did everyone buy (for Max)? (ambiguous)

(2) Who bought everything (for Max)? (unambiguous)

(42) Meigeren dou (gei Zhangsan) maile shenme? (ambiguous)
    everyone all   for Zhangsan bought what
    'What did everyone buy (for Zhangsan)?'

(57) b.

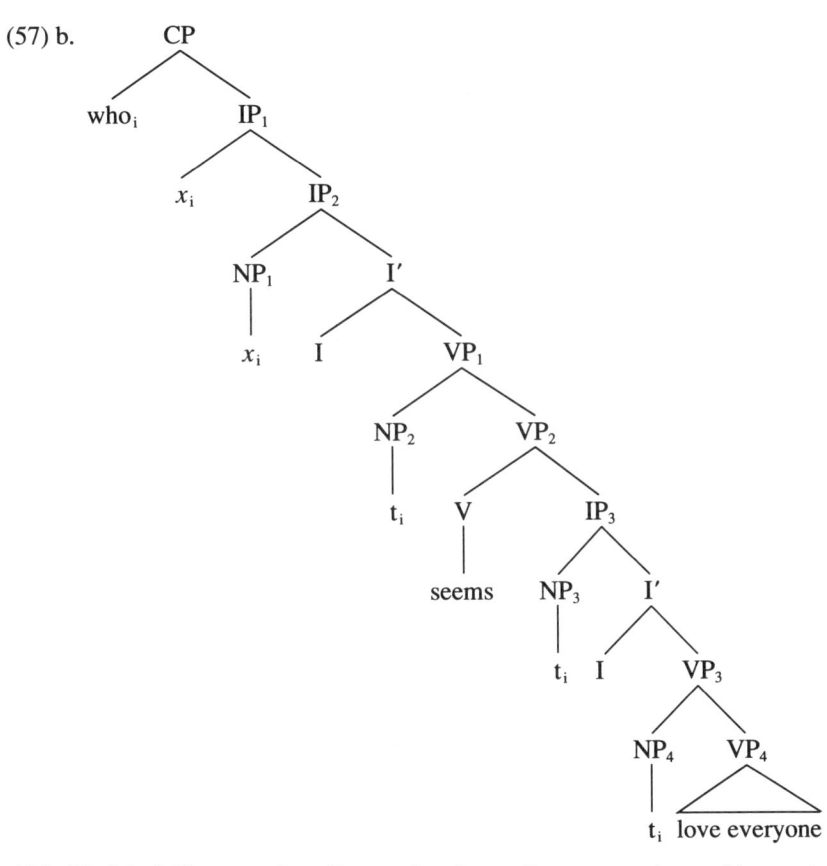

(46) Shei (gei Zhangsan) maile meige dongxi? (unambiguous)
who for Zhangsan bought every thing
'Who bought everything (for Zhangsan)?'

(44) Quién examinó cada doctor? (ambiguous)
who examined every doctor
'Who did every doctor examine?'

(48) Quién examinó a cada paciente? (unambiguous)
who examined every patient
'Who examined every patient?'

(55) a. Someone is loved by everyone. (ambiguous)

b. Who is loved by everyone? (unambiguous)

c. (Yaoshi) yige nuren bei meigeren ma... (ambiguous)
if a woman by everyone scold
'(If) a woman was scolded by everyone...'

d. Shei bei meigeren ma? (unambiguous)
   who by everyone scold
   'Who was scolded by everyone?'

e. Someone seems to love everyone. (ambiguous)

f. Who seems to love everyone? (unambiguous)

The analysis presented in this chapter makes certain predictions regarding the interpretation of a wide range of data involving QP/*wh* interactions. We now turn to these predictions.

2.2.2.4 Scope and Configurations A main feature of the analysis presented so far is the distinction between variables bound by QPs and variables bound by *wh*-elements. Following Chomsky (1981), we assumed that the latter type of variable is subject to Principle C of the binding theory, and, following Aoun and Hornstein (1985), we assumed that the former is not subject to such a binding principle. This distinction played a role in determining what counts as a potential antecedent. For instance, consider LF representation (58).

(58) $[_{CP}\ wh_j\ [_{IP}\ QP_i\ [_{IP}\ x_i\ [_{VP} \ldots x_j \ldots]]]]$

Here the QP is not a potential antecedent for the variable x_j in object position because coindexing QP with x_j would trigger a Principle C violation: x_j would be c-commanded by and coindexed with x_i; it would end up A-bound by x_i. It is clear from this that the structural configuration in which variables and operators occur plays a role in determining the possible LF representations—hence, the interpretation—of these elements. In particular, the notion of c-command plays a role in determining what counts as a possible antecedent: in the configuration $[wh_j \ldots QP_i \ldots x_i \ldots x_j]$, the fact that x_i c-commands x_j prevents QP_i from counting as a possible antecedent for x_j.

Since in our analysis, structural considerations play a role in determining the interaction of QPs and *wh*-elements, it is useful to discuss various configurations where QPs and *wh*-elements occur and to see whether our analysis successfully applies in these configurations. Because of the complexity of the structures and the close relation between QP/QP interaction and QP/*wh* interaction, we will discuss only a subset of the data in this chapter and discuss other structures in subsequent chapters.

Our analysis makes the following predictions concerning the interaction of *wh* and QP operators: in a language with overt *wh*-movement

Comparative Dimension

(such as English), if at S-Structure a QP c-commands a variable bound by a *wh*-operator in a sentence S, this sentence will be ambiguous. On the other hand, if a QP is c-commanded by the variable bound by a *wh*-operator, S will not be ambiguous. These predictions are schematically represented in (59).

(59) *English, a language with overt* wh-*movement*
    a. QP c-commands the variable bound by *wh*   (ambiguous)
       [$wh_i \ldots QP \ldots x_i$]
    b. The variable bound by *wh* c-commands QP   (unambiguous)
       [$wh_i \ldots x_i \ldots QP$]

Similarly, in a language without overt *wh*-movement (such as Chinese), if at S-Structure a QP c-commands a *wh*-word in a sentence S, this sentence will be ambiguous. If a QP is c-commanded by a *wh*-word at S-Structure, S will not be ambiguous. These predictions are schematically represented in (60).

(60) *Chinese, a language without overt* wh-*movement*
    a. QP c-commands *wh*   (ambiguous)
       [$QP \ldots wh$]
    b. *wh* c-commands QP   (unambiguous)
       [$wh \ldots QP$]

Let us see why the possible interpretations are as indicated. After *wh*-raising applies to (60), the LF representations of these Chinese sentences will be exactly like the LF representations of (59). Consider first sentences with the representations (59a) and (60a). After QR applies, the only well-formed LF representation corresponding to these sentences will be (61a).

(61) a. [$wh_i \ldots [QP_j \ldots [x_j \ldots x_i \ldots]]$]

In this representation the *wh*-operator c-commands the QP, which in turn c-commands x_i, a member of the chain containing the *wh*-word. Therefore, sentences with this representation are ambiguous.

Consider now sentences with the representations (59b) and (60b). For these sentences, QP can only adjoin to a node c-commanded by the variable coindexed with the *wh*-operator, as in (61b). Otherwise, the MBR will be violated (see (61c)).

(61) b. [$wh_i [x_i [QP_j [x_j]]]$]
    c. *[$wh_i [QP_j [x_i [x_j]]]$]   (ruled out by the MBR)

According to the Scope Principle in chapter 1, sentences with the form (61b) will be unambiguous because the chain $[wh_i, x_i]$ c-commands both the QP and its trace.

In brief, our analysis predicts sentences of the form (59a) and (60a) to be ambiguous and sentences of the form (59b) and (60b) to be unambiguous. This prediction seems to be fulfilled, as evidenced by a wide range of constructions containing a QP and a *wh*-word. We now discuss some of these constructions.

Subject and object A subject NP necessarily c-commands an object NP. The possible interactions are schematically represented in (62).

(62) a. subject QP...object *wh*   (ambiguous)

　　b. subject *wh*...object QP   (unambiguous)

Examples illustrating this construction are (1) and (2) in English and (22a–b) in Chinese.

Subject and a PP A subject NP necessarily c-commands an NP in a PP. The possible interactions are schematically represented in (63).

(63) a. [subject QP... [P *wh*]]   (ambiguous)

　　b. [subject *wh*... [P QP]]   (unambiguous)

Examples illustrating this construction are shown in (64).

(64) a. Who did everyone buy the books for?   (ambiguous)

　　b. Who bought the books for everyone?   (unambiguous)

　　c. Meigeren dou wei shei　maile　shu?   (ambiguous)
　　　 everyone all　for whom bought book

　　d. Shei wei meigeren maile　shu?   (unambiguous)
　　　 who for　everyone bought book

Double object constructions $[V\ NP_1\ NP_2]$ As argued by Larson (1988), NP_1 asymmetrically c-commands NP_2 in double object constructions (see section 1.5.3). The possible interactions are as shown in (65).

(65) a. [V NP_1(QP) NP_2(*wh*)]   (ambiguous)

　　b. [V NP_1(*wh*) NP_2(QP)]   (unambiguous)

Examples illustrating this construction are given in (66).

(66) a.　What did you assign everybody?   (ambiguous)

　　b. ??Who did you assign every problem?   (unambiguous)[8]

c. Ni zhidinggei meigeren shenme wenti?   (ambiguous)
   you assign   everyone   what   problem
   'What problem did you assign everyone?'

d. Ni zhidinggei shei meige wenti?   (unambiguous)
   you assign   who every problem
   'Who did you assign every problem?'

In brief, our analysis predicts that sentences that contain a QP c-commanded by a *wh*-word and in which the variable is bound by a *wh*-word are unambiguous. On the other hand, sentences that contain a QP c-commanding a *wh*-word or in which the variable is bound by a *wh*-word are ambiguous. As indicated in (62)–(66), such predictions are attested in a wide range of structures.

2.3 Conclusion

Our purpose in this chapter was to account for the interaction of QP and *wh*-operators. Our starting point was the discussion of sentences such as (1) and (2) in English.

(1) What did everyone buy (for Max)?   (ambiguous)

(2) Who bought everything (for Max)?   (unambiguous)

We indicated that the contrast between these English sentences recurs in widely differing languages such as Chinese and Spanish. We argued that this recurring contrast can be uniformly accounted for by the MBR and the Scope Principle stated in (I) and (II).

(I) *The Minimal Binding Requirement*
    Variables must be bound by the most local potential $\bar{A}$-binder.

(II) *The Scope Principle*
    A quantifier A may have scope over a quantifier B in case A c-commands a member of the chain containing B.

In order to establish the main features of our analysis, we constantly contrasted the behavior of operators in English and Chinese. This contrastive study was illuminating. The results of the investigation presented in this chapter and in chapter 1 revealed that the interaction between QPs in Chinese differs from their interaction in English. On the other hand, the interaction of QPs with *wh*-operators is identical in Chinese and English. The analysis incorporating the MBR and the Scope Principle provides a unified account for these differences and similarities.

In the course of the discussion, interesting results were reached. We have shown that the elements that enter into scope relations are operators and variables but not NP-traces. The relevance of operators and variables in determining scope relations may be illustrated by (1), the LF representation of which is given in (67).

(1) What did everyone buy?

(67) [$_{CP}$ what$_j$ [$_{IP}$ did everyone$_i$ [$_{IP}$ x_i buy x_j]]]

(1) is ambiguous. The reading where *what* has scope over *everyone* can only be accounted for if operators play a role in determining scope relations: *what*, but not its variable, c-commands the QP *everyone* and thus may have scope over this QP. Furthermore, the reading where *everyone* has scope over *what* can be accounted for if variables play a role in determining scope relations. *Everyone* c-commands the variable bound by *what*, but not the operator *what*, and thus may have scope over *what*.

We have also uncovered a basic difference between QPs and *wh*-words. This difference lies in the role that an NP-trace plays in determining QP and *wh* scopes. An NP-trace coindexed with a QP enters into scope relations, but an NP-trace coindexed with a *wh*-word crucially must not enter into scope relations. In the LF representation (69) of sentence (68), *every problem* cannot have scope over the *wh*-element despite the fact that it c-commands an NP-trace bound by this *wh*-element.

(68) Who was assigned every problem?

(69) [$_{CP}$ who$_i$ [$_{IP}$ x_i [$_{IP}$ every problem$_j$ [$_{VP}$ was assigned t$_i$ x_j]]]]

Obviously, the most radical way to account for such a discrepancy is to deny that NP-traces play a special role in determining the relative scope of QPs. If we succeed in showing that NP-traces do not play such a role, then there will be no difference between the determination of the relative scope of QPs and the determination of the relatives scope of *wh*-elements. Only the operators and the variables they bind will be relevant to determining the relative scope of QPs and *wh*-elements. In chapter 3 we explore various models that allow us to reach this conclusion.

Chapter 3
Syntax of Scope

The interaction of quantifiers with *wh*-operators discussed in chapter 2 revealed that NP-traces are not relevant for such an interaction even though they are relevant to the interaction of quantifiers with other quantifiers. In this chapter we provide an account for the interaction of quantifiers that does not refer to NP-traces and thus helps us to eliminate the observed discrepancy (section 3.1). This account leads us to reconsider the working of quantifier extraction in the LF component. We argue that such an extraction is not a unitary process (section 3.2). Rather, it is to be factored into two processes: a process of NP-adjunction that applies to the whole quantificational phrase and adjoins it to a nonargument position, and a process of Q-adjunction that applies to the bare quantifier and adjoins it to a position governing its restriction. The existence of these two processes eliminates the relevance of NP-traces in the determination of relative scope and thus the observed discrepancy.

The Scope Principle adopted in chapter 1 refers to the notion of chain: a quantifier A has scope over a quantifier B iff it c-commands B or a member of the chain containing B. Chains contain the operator itself, the intermediate traces in $\bar{\text{A}}$-position coindexed with the operator, the variable bound by the operator, and NP-traces coindexed with the operator. The elimination of NP-traces invites us to reconsider the role of the other members of the chain in determining relative scope (section 3.3). The empirical evidence uncovered, in this connection, will indicate that variables cannot be assumed to play a role in determining relative scope. Only elements in $\bar{\text{A}}$-positions—the operator itself and its intermediate traces—will be shown to be relevant to this process.

3.1 NP-Traces and Quantifier Raising

We noted in section 1.3 that the instances where NP-traces must play a role in determining scope relations are English active, passive, and raising constructions and Chinese passive constructions. We suggest in this section that NP-traces may in fact be disregarded in determining the relative scope of QPs in these constructions. By suggesting that NP-traces do not play a role in determining the scope of QPs, it is possible to provide a unified account for the relative scope of QPs and *wh*-words.

In order to eliminate the role NP-traces play in determining relative scope, we will entertain two distinct analyses. The first assumes that only bare Qs are raised at LF by QR. We will see that this assumption eliminates the need to refer to NP-traces when relative scope is computed. However, it will turn out that raising bare Qs only, although empirically adequate for determining relative scope, is not compatible with other LF phenomena indicating that QR has the option of pied-piping the whole phrase containing the quantifier. This will force us to reconsider the process of quantifier raising at LF and to characterize it as a process applying in two steps: the first step raises the whole phrase containing the quantifier and the second step raises the bare quantifier.

Before we discuss these alternatives, we need to carefully consider the prohibition against adjunction to argument positions. Recall that we assumed with Chomsky (1986a) that it is only possible to adjoin to a non-argument. According to Chomsky, the prohibition against adjunction to arguments may be made to follow from the θ-Criterion. In the following adjunction structure, $\alpha = \beta$ and β is an argument (1986a, 16):

(1) $[_\gamma \alpha [_\beta \ldots]]$

Chomsky indicates that β in (1) is invisible to θ-marking. This is why it is not possible to adjoin to an argument like β. This reasoning clearly indicates that the distinction in adjunction possibility is to be made between θ-position and non-θ-position ($\bar{\theta}$-position). It is not possible to adjoin to a θ-position; otherwise, a θ-Criterion violation would occur. On the other hand, nothing prevents adjunction to a $\bar{\theta}$-position. With this in mind, we proceed to discuss the properties of QR.

3.1.1 Bare Q-Raising

Let us assume that QR raises only bare Qs. This assumption, coupled with the one that considers that adjunction is to a $\bar{\theta}$-position only, allows us to dispense with any reference to NP-traces in determining scope relations.

Syntax of Scope 75

An important difference between raising a bare Q and raising a QP is that raising a bare Q allows one more adjunction site for QR: the QP containing the Q. Consider the representation in (2).

(2)
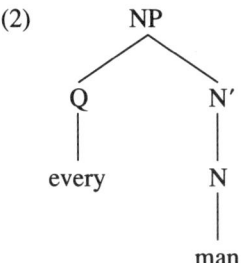
```
        NP
       /  \
      Q    N'
      |    |
    every  N
           |
          man
```

In this representation, assuming that QR can raise bare Qs, Q can adjoin to a node higher than the NP or to the NP itself if this NP is in a $\bar{\theta}$-position. In other words, when the NP is in a θ-position, the bare Q cannot adjoin to it. In contrast, when the NP is in a $\bar{\theta}$-position, this NP will be an available adjunction site for Q-raising.

This difference in adjunction possibilities provides an account for the nonambiguity of Chinese active sentences versus the ambiguity of English active, passive, and raising sentences and of Chinese passive sentences. As pointed out in section 3.1, an important distinction between the former and the latter types of sentences has to do with the characterization of the subject position: the subject position of Chinese active sentences is a θ-position, whereas the subject position of Chinese passive sentences and of English active, passive, and raising structures is a $\bar{\theta}$-position. With this in mind, consider active sentences in Chinese, as in (3).

(3) $[_{IP}[_{VP_1}[_{NP_1}$ Meigeren] $[_{VP_2}$ dou zhuazou $[_{NP_2}$ yige nuren]]]].
everyone   all   arrest   one woman
'Everyone arrested a woman.'

In (3) the subject NP containing the quantifier *one* is in a θ-position. This quantifier cannot adjoin to the subject NP; rather, it must adjoin to VP_1 or IP. The object quantifier cannot adjoin to VP_1 (or IP); if it does, the MBR will be violated. It cannot adjoin to the object NP either because objects are in a θ-position. It must therefore adjoin to VP_2, as in (4).

(4) $[_{IP}[_{VP_1}$ meige$_i$ $[_{VP_1}[_{NP_1}$ ren] $[_{VP_2}$ yige$_j$ $[_{VP_2}$ zhuazou $[_{NP_2}$ x_j nuren]]]]]]
every-   one   one   arrest   woman

In (4) the subject Q c-commands the object Q and thus has scope over it.

Next we turn to English active sentences like the one in (5) and Chinese passive sentences like the one in (6), with the S-Structure representations in (7) and (8), respectively.

(5) Everyone loves a woman.

(6) Meigeren dou bei yige nuren zhuazoule.
    everyone all by one woman arrested
    'Everyone was arrested by a woman.'

(7) [$_{IP}$[$_{NP_1}$ everyone] [$_{VP_1}$ t [$_{VP_2}$ loves [$_{NP_2}$ a woman]]]]

(8) [$_{IP}$[$_{VP_1}$[$_{NP_1}$ meigeren] [$_{VP_2}$ dou bei [$_{NP_2}$ yige nuren] zhuazoule]]]
        everyone   all by   one woman arrested

Consider first active sentences in English. In (7) *every* can adjoin at LF to NP$_1$ or IP and *a* to VP$_1$ (see (9a)): NP$_2$ is not a possible adjunction site because this object occupies a θ-position. *A* can also adjoin to IP. The latter possibility is available only when *every* adjoins to NP$_1$ because of the MBR (see (9b)).

(9) a. [$_{IP}$ every$_i$ [$_{IP}$[$_{NP_1}$ $x_i$one] [$_{VP_1}$ a$_j$ [$_{VP_1}$ t [$_{VP_2}$ loves [$_{NP_2}$ x_j woman]]]]]]

   b. [$_{IP}$ a$_j$ [$_{IP}$[$_{NP_1}$ every$_i$ [$_{NP}$ $x_i$one]] [$_{VP_1}$ t [$_{VP_2}$ loves [$_{NP_2}$ x_j woman]]]]]

In (9a) *every* c-commands but is not c-commanded by *a*. This representation yields the reading where *every* has scope over *a*. In (9b) *a* c-commands but is not c-commanded by *every*. It thus has scope over *every*. This accounts for the ambiguity of active sentences in English.

Consider now passive sentences in Chinese. In (8) *every* can adjoin to the subject NP or VP$_1$ or IP. *A* can adjoin to VP$_2$ (see (10a)) or to VP$_1$, IP (see (10b)). The latter possibility is available when *every* adjoins to the subject NP.

(10) a. [$_{IP}$ every$_i$ [$_{IP}$[$_{VP_1}$ [$_{NP}$ $x_i$one] [$_{VP_2}$ a$_j$ [$_{VP_2}$ was arrested by [$_{NP_2}$ x_j woman]]]]]]

    b. [$_{IP}$ a$_j$ [$_{IP}$[$_{VP_1}$ [$_{NP}$ every$_i$ [$_{NP_1}$ $x_i$one]] [$_{VP_2}$ was arrested by [$_{NP_2}$ x_j woman]]]]]

In (10a) *every* asymmetrically c-commands *a* and thus has scope over *a*. In (10b) it is *a* that asymmetrically c-commands *every* and has scope over it. This takes care of the ambiguity of passive sentences in Chinese. The same analysis accounts for the ambiguity of passive sentences in English.

Finally, consider raising sentences in English such as (11).

(11) Someone$_i$ seems [$_{IP}$ t$_i$ [$_{VP_1}$ t$_i$ [$_{VP_2}$ to love everyone]]].

Syntax of Scope

At LF, since *someone* is lowered to the subject position of the embedded IP (see May 1985), the representation of (11) will be (12).

(12) e seems [$_{IP}$ someone$_i$ [$_{VP_1}$ t$_i$ [$_{VP_2}$ to love everyone]]]

Since Spec of I' in English is a $\bar{\theta}$-position, the bare Q of the lowered *someone* in (12) can adjoin to this Spec position and the object quantifier can adjoin to the embedded IP as in (13).

(13) a. e seems [$_{IP}$ every$_j$ [$_{IP}$[$_{NP_1}$ some$_k$ [$_{NP_1}$ $x_k$one]]$_i$ [$_{VP_1}$ t$_i$ [$_{VP_2}$ to love [$_{NP_2}$ $x_j$one]]]]]

In (13a) the object quantifier *every* c-commands and thus has scope over the subject quantifier *some*. Alternatively, the subject quantifier may adjoin to IP and the object quantifier to VP$_2$, deriving the reading shown in (13b), where the subject quantifier has wide scope.

(13) b. e seems [$_{IP}$ some$_k$ [$_{NP_1}$ $x_k$one]$_i$ [$_{VP_1}$ t$_i$ [$_{VP_2}$ every$_j$ [$_{VP_2}$ to love [$_{NP_2}$ $x_j$one]]]]]

In brief, by assuming that QR raises bare Qs only and that the adjunction sites of QR are $\bar{\theta}$-positions, we do not need to refer to NP-traces in determining the relative scope of QPs. In this way, we are able to offer a unified account for both QP/QP and QP/*wh* interaction: only operators and variables but not NP-traces determine relative scope.

3.1.2 A Mixed Solution: Q- and QP-Raising

The option of raising bare Qs only amounts to saying that there is no pied-piping at LF. However, there is evidence indicating that the raising of the whole phrase containing the quantifier is at work at LF. The main evidence for the existence of this option is provided by the so-called antecedent-contained deletion illustrated in (14). This construction has been discussed by Larson (1987), May (1985), Sag (1976), Williams (1977), and Clark (1992) among others.

(14) Dulles suspected everyone who Angleton did.

As pointed out by Williams (1977), VP-deletion involves a reconstruction of the missing VP in the place of the pro-form. If this interpretive reconstruction process were to apply at S-Structure or at LF before QR applies, then the result of VP-copying will be an infinite LF representation:

(15) a. Dulles [$_{VP}$ suspected everyone who Angleton did]
    b. Dulles [$_{VP}$ suspected everyone who Angleton [$_{VP}$ suspected everyone who Angleton [$_{VP}$ suspected everyone who Angleton...]]]

If, on the other hand, the reconstruction of the missing VP applies at LF, as argued by Williams (1977), and if QR is assumed to raise the whole quantifier phrase, as argued by May (1985), then the post-QR representation of (14) would be (16).

(16) [$_{IP}$[everyone who Angleton did]$_i$ [$_{IP}$ Dulles [$_{VP}$ suspected x_i]]]

Interpretation of the pro-form yields (17).

(17) [$_{IP}$[everyone who Angleton suspected x_i]$_i$ [$_{IP}$ Dulles [$_{VP}$ suspected x_i]]]

The above derivation, which involves pied-piping of the whole quantifier phrase, avoids the regress illustrated in (15). Note that if, as entertained earlier, QR involves raising of bare Qs only, the regress surfaces again. We thus take the working of antecedent-contained deletion to provide evidence for the existence of pied-piping at LF. QR can raise the whole phrase containing the quantifier and not the bare quantifier alone.

We now face the following problem. The discrepancy between the role of NP-traces in determining the relative scope of quantifiers and their role in determining the relative scope of *wh*-operators led us to introduce the option of Q-raising. On the other hand, the antecedent-contained deletion facts indicate that the option of raising the whole QP is also at work. It thus seems that we need to incorporate the two options in the grammar. At this point, we can maintain the existence of the two options side by side and allow them to apply randomly. The disadvantage of this solution is the proliferation of LF derivations accounting for the interaction of operators. For instance, to a standard active sentence in Chinese with the structure in (18) would correspond at least the eight possible LF derivations shown in (19).

(18) QP$_1$ V QP$_2$

(19) a. [$_{VP_1}$ QP$_{1_i}$ [$_{VP_1}$ x_i [$_{VP_2}$ QP$_{2_j}$ [$_{VP_2}$ ...x_j]]]] (QP-raising)
b. [$_{VP_1}$ Q$_{1_i}$ [$_{VP_1}$ x_i [$_{VP_2}$ Q$_{2_j}$ [$_{VP_2}$ ...x_j]]]] (Q-raising)
c. [$_{VP_1}$ Q$_{1_i}$ [$_{VP_1}$ x_i [$_{VP_2}$ QP$_{2_j}$ [$_{VP_2}$ ...x_j]]]] (Q$_1$-, QP$_2$-raising)
d. [$_{VP_1}$ QP$_{1_i}$ [$_{VP_1}$ x_i [$_{VP_2}$ Q$_{2_j}$ [$_{VP_2}$ ...x_j]]]] (QP$_1$-, Q$_2$-raising)
e. [$_{VP_1}$ QP$_{1_i}$ [$_{VP_1}$ Q$_{2_j}$ [$_{VP_1}$ x_i [$_{VP_2}$ ...x_j]]]] (QP$_1$-, Q$_2$-raising)
f. [$_{VP_1}$ Q$_{1_i}$ [$_{VP_1}$ QP$_{2_j}$ [$_{VP_1}$ x_i [$_{VP_2}$ ...x_j]]]] (Q$_1$-, QP$_2$-raising)
g. [$_{VP_1}$ Q$_{2_j}$ [$_{VP_1}$ QP$_{1_i}$ [$_{VP_1}$ x_i [$_{VP_2}$ ...x_j]]]] (Q$_2$-, QP$_1$-raising)
h. [$_{VP_1}$ QP$_{2_j}$ [$_{VP_1}$ Q$_{1_i}$ [$_{VP_1}$ x_i [$_{VP_2}$ ...x_j]]]] (QP$_2$-, Q$_1$-raising)

Syntax of Scope

Given the nonambiguity of sentence (1), we must disallow derivations (19e–h). In order to do so, we can entertain the possibility that XP and X^0 categories do not interact with respect to scope. As a consequence of this proposal, the only representations in (19) that would be relevant for scope would be (19a–b). In these representations the subject quantifier has scope over the object quantifier.

This proposal faces a certain number of difficulties, however. For instance, it is well known that negation, which is generally considered to be an X^0 category (but see Rizzi 1990), interacts with a *because*-phrase that is an XP category. For example, in (20) the negative element may have scope over or be in the scope of the *because*-clause.

(20) He did not go because he was sick.

Another possibility that comes to mind in order to rule out derivations (19e–h) would be to assume a rigid interpretation of the minimality requirement encoded in the MBR. According to this interpretation, an intervening $\bar{\text{A}}$-binder would count as a potential binder for a variable regardless of the categorial nature of the elements involved.[1] Derivations (19e–h) would violate this rigid interpretation of the MBR.

Notice, however, that even after eliminating derivations (19e–h), we are left with four distinct derivations yielding the same reading for (18).

3.1.3 Two Processes of LF Adjunction

In light of the above discussion and the necessity of Q-raising as well as QP-raising, we would like to entertain a mixed alternative that preserves the advantages of both Q-raising and QP-raising. Along lines suggested by Heim (1982), we would like to propose that the LF raising of quantifiers applies in two steps. The first, which we will refer to as *NP-adjunction*, raises the whole nominal phrase whose specifier is quantificational (henceforth, the *quantificational phrase*) to an $\bar{\text{A}}$-position. For reasons that will become clear, we assume that this rule applies obligatorily to a quantificational phrase in a θ-position and is optional otherwise. The obligatory application of NP-adjunction can be understood in light of θ-theory (θ-Criterion). Since quantificational phrases, like other operators, are not referential expressions, these elements cannot remain in a θ-position at LF; otherwise, the θ-Criterion would be violated. On the other hand, nothing either forces or prevents the application of NP-adjunction when the quantificational phrase occurs in a θ-position. The second process of QR—*Q-adjunction*—raises the bare quantifier and adjoins it to an $\bar{\text{A}}$-position *governing* the whole NP whose specifier is quantificational:[2]

(21) *LF extraction of quantificational elements*[3]
    a. NP-adjunction to an $\bar{\text{A}}$-position
    b. Q-adjunction to a position governing the whole NP whose specifier is quantificational

To illustrate the application of these processes, consider once again a standard active sentence in Chinese with the structure in (22), where NP_1 and NP_2 are quantificational expressions. First, NP-adjunction will adjoin the object NP_2 to VP_2 and the subject NP_1 to VP_1 (or to IP), as in (23). Since the subject position, like the object position, is a θ-position in Chinese, NP-adjunction must obligatorily apply in (22).

(22) NP_1 V NP_2

(23)

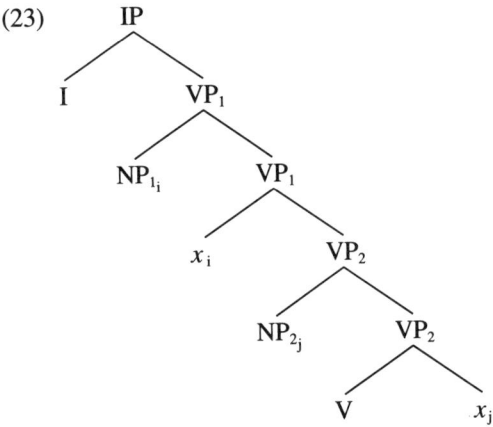

Notice that this is the only application of NP-adjunction that satisfies the MBR. As discussed in chapter 1, adjunction of NP_2 to VP_1 (or IP) as in (23) would be ruled out by this requirement. After NP-adjunction, Q-adjunction applies. Given (21b), this process can only adjoin the bare quantifier to the raised NP in (22), thus generating (25). We assume the scope of a quantifier to be the c-commanding domain of this quantifier or of the minimal NP in $\bar{\theta}$-position dominating this quantifier and its restriction (NP_1 for Q_1 and NP_2 for Q_2).[4] Thus, the LF representation (25) yields the reading where the subject quantifier has scope over the object quantifier.

Notice that as a consequence of the government requirement (see note 3), the raised Q and its restriction end up in a sisterhood relation. In a

(24)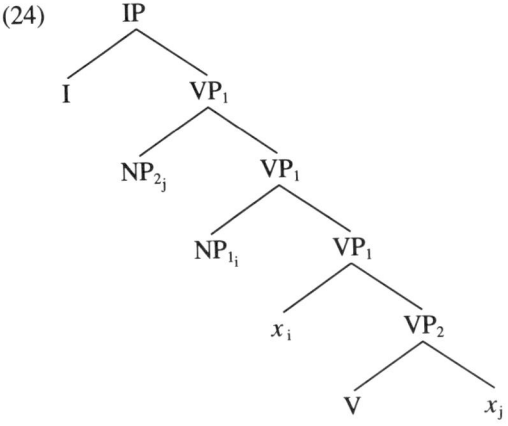

(25)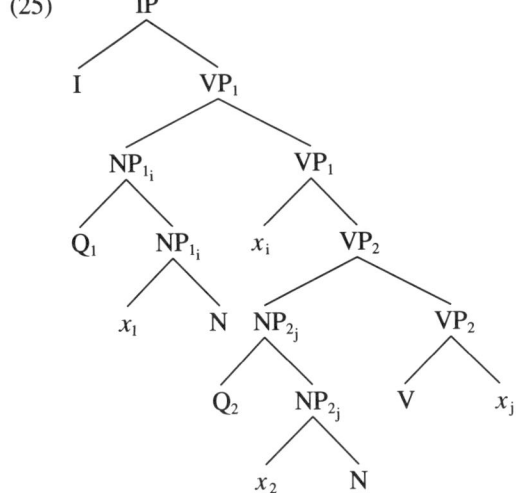

representation such as (25), the NP governed by the quantifier corresponds to the restriction of the quantifier.[5]

Consider, now, how the ambiguity of an active sentence in English (26a) or of a passive sentence in English (26b) (similarly, a passive sentence in Chinese) can be derived without reference to NP-traces.

(26) a. [$_{IP}$ Someone$_i$ [$_{VP_1}$ t$_i$ [$_{VP_2}$ loves everyone]]].
    b. [$_{IP}$ Someone$_i$ [$_{VP_1}$ t$_i$ [$_{VP_2}$ is loved t$_i$ by everyone]]].

In these sentences the subject NP is in a $\bar{\theta}$-position at S-Structure. As a result, NP-adjunction can optionally apply to the subject. In case it applies to the subject, this subject will have scope over the object. For illustrative purposes, the various derivations of an active sentence in English are considered. (Irrelevant details will be omitted in (27)–(28).)

(27) a. *NP-adjunction*
 $[_{IP}$ someone$_m$ $[_{IP}$ x_m $[_{VP}$ everyone$_n$ $[_{VP}$ loves $x_n]]]]$
 b. *Q-adjunction*
 $[_{IP}[_{NP}$ some$_i$ $[_{NP}$ $x_i$one$]]_m$ $[_{IP}$ x_m $[_{VP}[_{NP}$ every$_j$ $[_{NP}$ $x_j$one$]]_n$ $[_{VP}$ loves $x_n]]]]$

In case we choose not to apply NP-adjunction to the subject, the object NP can adjoin to IP without violating the MBR. It will end up c-commanding the subject and thus will have scope over it:

(28) a. *NP-adjunction of object only*
 $[_{IP}$ everyone$_n$ $[_{IP}$ someone $[_{VP}$ loves $x_n]]]$
 b. *Q-adjunction*
 $[_{IP}[_{NP}$ every$_j$ $[_{NP}$ $x_j$one$]]_n$ $[_{IP}[_{NP}$ some$_i$ $[_{NP}$ $x_i$one$]]$ $[_{VP}$ loves $x_n]]]$

In the previous paragraphs we have illustrated the interaction of quantifier phrases. We now consider the interaction of quantifier phrases with *wh*-operators. The main cases to be considered are the following sentences (irrelevant details are omitted throughout):

(29) a. What did everyone buy?
 b. Who bought everything?

Consider (29a) first. Its S-Structure representation is given in (30a). At LF, after NP-adjunction and Q-adjunction, (30a) will have the LF representation in (30b).

(30) a. $[_{CP}$ what$_j$ did $[_{IP}$ everyone$_i$ $[_{VP_1}$ t$_i$ buy $x_j]]]$
 b. $[_{CP}$ what$_j$ did $[_{IP}[_{NP}$ every$_k$ $[_{NP}$ $x_k$one$]_i]$ $[_{IP}$ x_i $[_{VP_1}$ t$_i$ buy $x_j]]]]$

In the latter representation the *wh*-operator c-commands the subject quantifier; the NP immediately dominating the quantifier and its restriction c-commands the variable bound by the *wh*-operator. (29a) thus is ambiguous.

The S-Structure representation of (29b) is (31a). Because of the MBR, NP-adjunction can raise the object to VP$_1$ or VP$_2$ but not to IP, as shown in (31b). In (31b) Q-adjunction can adjoin the bare Q only to the raised NP, deriving (31c), which yields the reading where the *wh*-operator has scope over the object QP.

(31) a. $[_{CP}$ who$_i$ $[_{IP}$ x_i $[_{VP_1}$ t$_i$ $[_{VP_2}$ saw everything$]]]]$

b. [$_{CP}$ who$_i$ [$_{IP}$ x_i [$_{VP_1}$ everything$_j$ [$_{VP_1}$ t$_i$ [$_{VP_2}$ saw x_j]]]]
c. [$_{CP}$ who$_i$ [$_{IP}$ x_i [$_{VP_1}$[$_{NP}$ every$_k$ [$_{NP}$ x_k thing]]$_j$ [$_{VP_1}$ t$_i$ [$_{VP_2}$ saw x_j]]]]]

In general, under the assumption that LF extraction of quantificational elements applies in two steps, the results reached in the previous chapters can be preserved. For instance, as illustrated in (29)–(31), a quantificational phrase cannot c-command the variable bound by a *wh*-operator unless the empty category bound by the quantificational phrase also c-commands this variable; otherwise, the MBR would be violated:

(32) a. *[wh$_i$ [QP$_j$ [x_i [V x_j]]]]   (ruled out by the MBR)
b. [wh$_i$ [QP$_j$ [x_j [V x_i]]]]

To sum up, in chapter 2 we uncovered a discrepancy between the role NP-traces play in determining the relative scope of quantifiers vis-à-vis other quantifiers and the role they play in determining the relative scope of quantifiers vis-à-vis *wh*-operators. In order to eliminate this discrepancy, we were led to reconsider the characterization of the raising processes applying to quantificational phrases at LF. We essentially suggested that the raising of these phrases at LF operates in two steps: NP-adjunction and Q-adjunction. We also suggested that NP-adjunction applies optionally to a quantificational phrase in a $\bar{\theta}$-position and obligatorily to such a phrase in a θ-position. This is the major innovation that distinguishes the application of QR in our framework from its application in the standard framework, where it is usually assumed that QR applies obligatorily. As for the process of Q-adjunction, it does not play any direct role per se in the derivation of relative scope since the bare quantifier always adjoins to the phrase dominating it. We adopted Q-adjunction for general theory-internal reasons (see Heim 1982; also see section 4.2.2.2).[6] In brief, it is the assumption that NP-adjunction optionally applies to the whole QP in a $\bar{\theta}$-position that allows us not to refer to NP-traces in the determination of relative scope.[7]

3.2 Chains and Scope Interaction

As formulated in chapter 1, the Scope Principle refers to chains: an operator A may have scope over an operator B in case it c-commands a member of the chain containing B. The elements of a chain headed by an operator include the operator itself, its intermediate trace(s) in $\bar{A}$-position, the variable, and the NP-trace(s) coindexed with it. The elimination of NP-traces in the determination of scope relations invites further questions concerning the relevance of each element of the chain in the determination of relative scope. In the following subsections we examine the role of variables, operators, and intermediate traces in this process.

3.2.1 Variables

The discussion in the previous chapters assumed that operators and variables play a role in determining scope relations. This is illustrated by the contrast between the sentences in (29a–b), repeated here.

(29) a. [What$_j$ did [everyone [buy x_j]]]?
 b. [Who$_i$ [x_i [bought everything]]]?

Note that the ambiguity of (29a) can be accounted for only if variables play a role in determining scope relations (see the LF representation (30b) of (29a), repeated here).

(30) b. [$_{CP}$ what$_j$ did [$_{IP}$ everyone$_i$ [$_{IP}$ x_i [$_{VP}$ buy x_j]]]]

It is not clear, however, why variables, but not NP-traces, should play a role in determining scope relations. In fact, there exists some evidence suggesting that it is undesirable to consider variables in determining relative scope. Consider the following unambiguous sentence (also mentioned in Lasnik and Saito 1992):

(33) ?What$_j$ do you wonder [whether everyone (unambiguous) bought x_j]?

This sentence can have the following well-formed LF representation (the slight deviance of (33) is due to a Subjacency violation at S-Structure):

(34) [$_{CP}$ what$_j$ do [$_{IP}$ you wonder [$_{CP}$ whether [$_{IP}$ everyone$_i$ [$_{IP}$ x_i [$_{VP}$ bought x_j]]]]]]

In this representation the raised QP c-commands the variable bound by the *wh*-operator. It should yield the reading where the quantifier has wide scope. This reading, however, is unavailable: only the *wh*-operator has scope over the quantifier. The same facts occur in Chinese, as illustrated by the nonambiguity of (35), which has an LF representation similar to (34).

(35) Ni xiang-zhidao meigeren shi-bu-shi dou kandao shenme?
 you wonder everyone be-not-be all saw what
 'What do you wonder whether everyone saw?'

We mention the Chinese sentence in this context because it does not involve a Subjacency violation (see Huang 1982).

Syntax of Scope

The problem raised by (33) is compounded by the ambiguity of (36a-b) (see May 1985, 45, regarding the ambiguity of this type of sentence).

(36) a. [$_{CP}$ What$_j$ do [$_{IP}$ you think [$_{CP}$ t$_j$ [$_{IP}$ everyone bought x_j]]]]?

b. [$_{CP}$ Ni xiang [$_{CP}$ meigeren dou maile shenme]]?
you think everyone all bought what
'What do you think everyone bought?'

The contrast between the nonambiguity of the sentences in (33), (35) and the ambiguity of the sentences in (36a-b) cannot be accounted for in case variables play a role in determining relative scope.

We thus face the following paradox. Certain facts indicate that variables play a role in determining relative scope (see the discussion of (29a), (36a-b)). Other facts indicate that variables do not play such a role (see the discussion of (33), (35)).

In order to solve this paradox, we take the nonambiguity of (33), (35) to suggest that variables do not play a role in determining relative scope relations. This move requires us to find another account for the ambiguity of (29a) or for the contrast between (33), (35) on the one hand and (36a-b) on the other. To provide such an account, we must consider whether operators alone can be used to determine relative scope in (29a).

3.2.2 Operators
Under the assumption that only operators are relevant to determining relative scope, we expect (29a), repeated here as (37), to be unambiguous. The LF representation of (29a)—namely, (30b)—is repeated here as (38).

(37) What did everyone buy?

(38) [$_{CP}$ what$_j$ did [$_{IP}$ everyone$_i$ [$_{IP}$ x_i [$_{VP}$ buy x_j]]]]

Similarly, the ambiguity of (36a-b), with the LF representations in (39a-b), cannot be accounted for if only operators are relevant to determining relative scope.

(39) a. [$_{CP}$ what$_j$ do [$_{IP}$ you think [$_{CP}$ t$_j$ [$_{IP}$ everyone$_i$ [$_{IP}$ x_i bought x_j]]]]]

b. [$_{CP}$ shenme$_j$ [$_{IP}$ ni xiang [$_{CP}$ t$_j$ [$_{IP}$ meigeren$_i$ [$_{IP}$ x_i dou maile
what you think everyone all bought
x_j]]]]]

The ambiguity of (36a-b), (37) thus rules out the option under which only operators determine relative scope. We are therefore left with one option: operators and intermediate traces in $\bar{\text{A}}$-position are relevant to determining relative scope. We will now show that this option can account for the interaction of operators.

3.2.3 Operators and Intermediate Traces

In order to establish the empirical adequacy of this option, we need to show that it yields desirable results for both QP/QP interaction and QP/ *wh* interaction. Consider first the interaction of QPs with other QPs. Notice that the MBR rules out the LF representation (40), where QP_2 c-commands the intermediate trace left by QP_1. Here the variable x_1 is not bound by the first available $\bar{A}$-binder QP_2.

(40) *[QP_1... [QP_2... [t_1... [...x_1... [...x_2...]]]]]

In other words, in the case of QP/QP interaction, intermediate traces do not occur and thus cannot play a role in determining relative scope. Only QPs play a role in this process, as illustrated in the previous chapters.

Let us next turn to the interaction of QPs and *wh*-operators and see whether the option of assuming that only operators and intermediate traces determine relative scope is empirically adequate. We start by considering the interaction of QPs and *wh*-operators such as *who* and *what* that bind an argument variable (*wh*-argument):

(41) a. Who bought everything? (unambiguous)
     b. What did everyone buy? (ambiguous)

The LF representation of (41a) is (42) (irrelevant details are omitted).

(42) [$_{CP}$ who$_i$ [$_{IP}$ x_i [$_{VP}$ everything$_j$ [$_{VP}$ bought x$_j$]]]]

Under the assumption that only operators and intermediate traces are relevant for determining relative scope, (42) yields only the reading where who has scope over the QP, since *who* c-commands it.

As for (41b), note that in addition to the LF representation in (43a), (41b) can have the LF representation in (43b), where the *wh*-operator is first adjoined to VP and then moved to the Spec of Comp, leaving an intermediate trace t_j (as discussed in Chomsky 1986a).

(43) a. [$_{CP}$ what$_j$ [$_{IP}$ everyone$_i$ [$_{IP}$ x_i [$_{VP}$ buy x_j]]]]
     b. [$_{CP}$ what$_j$ [$_{IP}$ everyone$_i$ [$_{IP}$ x_i [$_{VP}$ t$_j$ [$_{VP}$ buy x_j]]]]]

Since by assumption both operators and intermediate traces in $\bar{A}$-position play a role in determining scope relations, (43b) will yield two interpretations: the raised QP is c-commanded by the *wh*-operator in the Spec of Comp and c-commands the intermediate trace generated by

Syntax of Scope

wh-movement, t_j. Thus, the ambiguity of (41b) can be accounted for without resorting to variables.

The assumption according to which operators and intermediate traces, but not variables, are relevant to determining relative scope may also capture the nonambiguity of (33), repeated here, which has the LF representation in (44).

(33) ?What$_j$ do you wonder [whether everyone bought x_j]?

(44) [$_{CP}$ what$_j$ do you wonder [$_{CP}$ whether [$_{IP}$ everyone$_i$ [$_{IP}$ x_i [$_{VP}$ bought x_j]]]]]

As stated earlier, (33) does not have the interpretation where the quantifier has wide scope. This nonambiguity can be accounted for in case the LF representation of (33) does not contain an intermediate trace coindexed with the *wh*-operator:

(45) *[$_{CP}$ what$_j$ do [$_{IP}$ you wonder [$_{CP}$ whether [$_{IP}$ everyone$_i$ [$_{IP}$ x_i [$_{VP}$ t$_j$ [$_{VP}$ bought x_j]]]]]]]

In (45) the intermediate trace t_j is not properly bound. In a formulation of the ECP such as the one given by Lasnik and Saito (1984), this intermediate trace would not be properly governed. In a binding approach, the domain within which the intermediate trace ought to be bound is the embedded clause (see Aoun 1986, AHLW 1987). In the embedded clause this intermediate trace does not have an antecedent. In either approach, the LF representation of (33) would not contain an intermediate trace. As a result, (33) is unambiguous: only the *wh*-operator *what* c-commands the quantifier.

On the other hand, (36a)—repeated here as (46), with the LF representation (47)—is correctly expected to be ambiguous (irrelevant details omitted).

(46) What$_j$ do you think everyone bought x_j?

(47) [$_{CP}$ what$_j$ do [$_{IP}$ you think [$_{CP}$ t$_j$ [$_{IP}$ everyone$_i$ [$_{IP}$ x_i [$_{VP}$ t$_j$ [$_{VP}$ bought x_j]]]]]]]

In (47) each intermediate trace is properly bound. In this LF representation the *wh*-operator c-commands the quantifier. In turn, this quantifier c-commands the intermediate trace coindexed with *what*.

Further support for the role of intermediate traces in determining the relative scope is provided by the interaction between negation and *wh*-operators: sentences like (48), in contrast to the corresponding positive sentence (41b), are unambiguous.

(48) What didn't everyone buy? (unambiguous)

The LF representation of (48) cannot contain an intermediate trace bound by the *wh*-operator, because negation would be the first $\bar{\text{A}}$-binder for this intermediate trace:

(49) *[$_{CP}$ what$_j$ [didn't [$_{IP}$ everyone$_i$ [$_{IP}$ x_i [$_{VP}$ t$_j$ [$_{VP}$ buy x_j]]]]]]

If the intermediate trace is illicit, the quantifier does not have scope over the *wh*-operator. (48) is therefore unambiguous.[8]

3.3 Conclusion

Our goal in this chapter was to eliminate the discrepancy uncovered in chapter 2 between the role NP-traces played in determining the relative scope of QPs interacting with other QPs and their role in determining the relative scope of QPs interacting with *wh*-operators. This led us to reconsider the application of quantifier extraction in the LF component and to factor it into two processes: NP-adjunction and Q-adjunction.

Having eliminated the role of NP-traces, we were forced to reconsider the role of each element of the chain in determining relative scope. We showed that variables, too, do not play a role in this process and established the necessity of considering only operators and intermediate traces when computing relative scope. The picture that emerges is now the following: only elements in $\bar{\text{A}}$-positions are relevant for scope interaction. The Scope Principle must be reformulated as follows:[9]

(50) *The Scope Principle*
An operator A may have scope over an operator B iff A c-commands B or an $\bar{\text{A}}$-element coindexed with B.

In some sense, the fact that only $\bar{\text{A}}$-elements are relevant to determining relative scope is not surprising. The difference between Syntax and LF may be characterized as a distinction between the domains where distinct structural relations are checked. Essentially, Syntax may be viewed as the domain where A-relations are checked and LF as the domain where $\bar{\text{A}}$-relations are checked. Several proposals in the literature can be viewed as embodying some version of this characterization. For instance, based on the approach of Chomsky (1982), Aoun (1985, 116) suggests that, at LF, the relevant indexing is $\bar{\text{A}}$-indexing only: elements in A- or $\bar{\text{A}}$-positions may only be indexed with elements in $\bar{\text{A}}$-positions. A more extreme distinction between the two kinds of relation is embodied in the

NP-model of Van Riemsdijk and Williams (1981). Their NP-Structure is exclusively the domain of A-relations and A-movement, and their *Wh*-Structure, the domain of Ā-relations. Assuming that S-Structure is the locus of A-relations and LF the locus of Ā-relations, the fact that only Ā-elements are relevant to determining relative scope is a further manifestation of the preeminence of Ā-relations at LF.

Chapter 4
Nominal Structures and Scope

A central thesis underlying the analysis we have presented so far is that of interpretive invariance. According to this thesis, logical (LF) interpretation is not the locus of language variation. We have argued that the interpretation of quantificational elements in English and Chinese is subject to identical requirements: the Minimal Binding Requirement and the Scope Principle. The variation in the interpretation of quantifiers in English and Chinese was traced back to a difference in the constituent structure of the languages under discussion, rather than to parametric differences affecting the form and functioning of LF interpretive rules.

In this and the following two chapters, we test the validity of the thesis of interpretive invariance in a variety of constructions in English and Chinese, many of which have not been discussed in the relevant literature. We show that the interaction of operators in these constructions can be understood in light of the MBR and the Scope Principle and that intricate differences affecting the interpretation of quantificational phrases in these structures highlight the intimate relation between structure and interpretation: difference in interpretation is due to difference in structure.

In this chapter we concentrate on the endocentric and exocentric behavior of operators:

(1) a. *Exocentric behavior of operators (Op)*
Interaction of an Op within an NP with another Op outside the NP:

$[_{NP} \ldots Op_1 \ldots] \ldots Op_2$

b. *Endocentric behavior of operators (Op)*
Interaction of an Op within an NP with another Op within this NP:

$[_{NP} \ldots Op_1 \ldots Op_2 \ldots]$

We first discuss the exocentric behavior of operators in section 4.1, including the interaction of QPs with other QPs in section 4.1.1 and the interaction of QPs and *wh*-operators in section 4.1.2. We then turn to the endocentric behavior of operators in section 4.2.

4.1 Exocentric Behavior of Operators

4.1.1 Exocentric Behavior of QPs

The interaction of QPs in pattern (1a) is illustrated in (2).

(2) a. Every woman's mother loves a man. (ambiguous)

    a'. A man's mother will love every woman. (ambiguous)

    b. Meige nuren de mama dou xihuan yige (unambiguous)
every woman DE mother all like one
nanren.
man
'Every woman's mother loves a man.'

    b'. Yige nanren de mama hui xihuan meige (unambiguous)
one man DE mother will like every
nuren.
woman
'A man's mother will love every woman.'

The English sentences in (2a–a') are ambiguous. In contrast, the Chinese sentences in (2b–b') are unambiguous: the QP generated in the Spec of NP has scope over the object QP. The contrast between (2a–a') and (2b–b') parallels the contrast between the English sentences (3a–b), which are ambiguous, and the Chinese sentences (4a–b), which are unambiguous (see the discussion of the relevant sentences in chapter 1).

(3) a. Every man loves a woman. (ambiguous)

    b. A woman will love every man.

(4) a. Meige nanren dou xihuan yige nuren. (unambiguous)
every man all like one woman
'Every man loves a woman.'

    b. Yige nuren hui xihuan meige nanren. (unambiguous)
one woman will like every man
'A woman will love every man.'

We now turn to an account for the contrast between (2a) and (2b).

Nominal Structures and Scope

Consider first representation (5a) of a canonical Chinese sentence, with the gloss given in English.

(5) a.
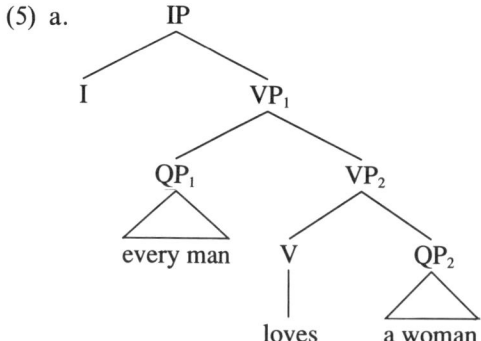

In (5a), since the subject position is a θ-position in Chinese, NP-adjunction must apply to QP_1 and adjoin it to VP_1 (or IP), and QP_2 will adjoin to VP_2. QP_1 will thus c-command and have scope over QP_2.[1]

Now consider the representation (5b) of the Chinese sentence (2b).

(5) b.
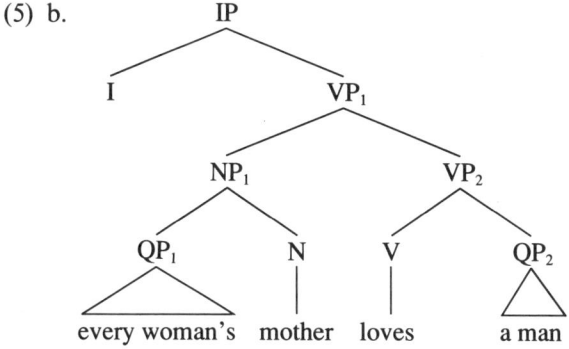

In (5b) NP_1 is not a possible adjunction site for QP_1 since it is a θ-position. QP_1 must adjoin to VP_1 (or IP), and QP_2 to VP_2. QP_1 will c-command and have scope over QP_2. Thus, just like (4), (2b) is unambiguous.

Next we discuss the English sentence (2a). Consider first the LF representation (6a) of a canonical English sentence such as (3a). In (6a) QP_1 adjoins to IP, and QP_2 to VP_1 or VP_2, deriving the reading where QP_1 has wide scope. Alternatively, since QP_1 is in a $\bar{\theta}$-position, NP-adjunction need not apply to it; in that case QP_1 would stay in situ. QP_2 would then adjoin to IP without violating the MBR. This second derivation yields the reading where the object quantifier has wide scope.

(6) a.

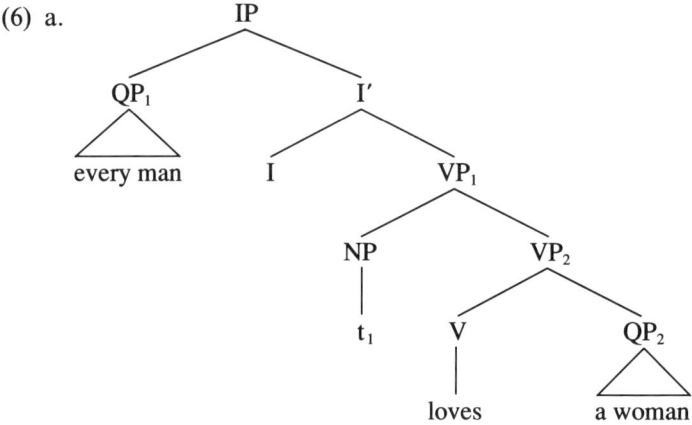

Consider now the S-Structure representation (6b) of sentence (2a).

(6) b.

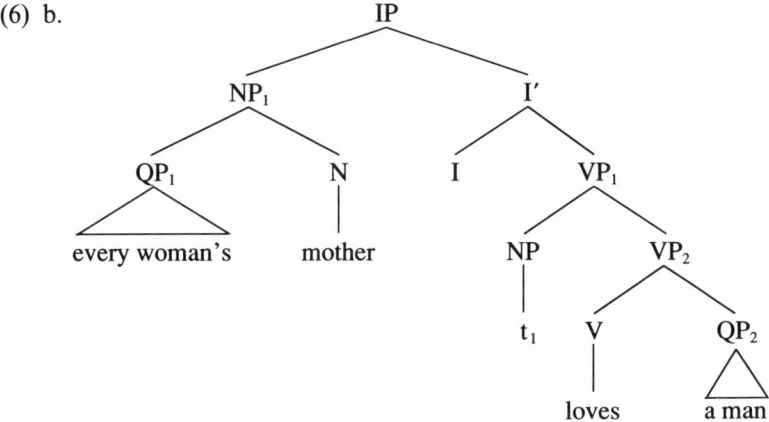

In (6b) QP_1 must undergo NP-adjunction. The reason is that QP_1 is in the Spec of NP position, which is generally taken to be a θ-position.[2] Since NP_1 is in a $\bar{\theta}$-position, QP_1 has the option of adjoining either to NP_1 or to IP. In case QP_1 is adjoined to IP, QP_2 can only adjoin to the VP (VP_1 or VP_2), as in (7). This LF representation derives the reading where QP_1 has scope over QP_2.

In case QP_1 is adjoined to NP_1, QP_2 can adjoin to the IP, as in (8): This LF representation derives the reading where the object QP has scope over the subject. The existence of derivations (7)–(8) thus accounts for the ambiguity of (2a).

Before closing this section, we would like to make the following clarifications concerning the process of NP-adjunction. This process applies to NPs whose specifier is quantificational.[3] These considerations provide

Nominal Structures and Scope

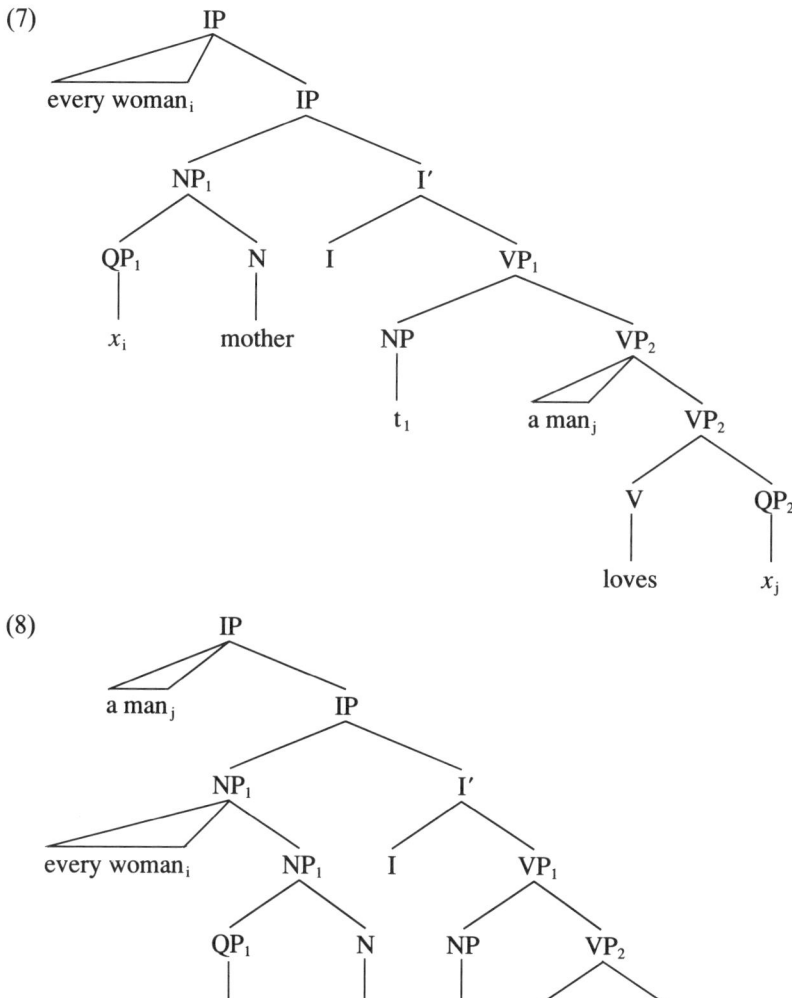

(7)

(8)

more derivations for the English sentence (2a). In (2a) the whole NP will be the target of NP-adjunction. If NP-adjunction applies and adjoins this NP to IP, we derive the reading where the subject quantifier has wide scope, as illustrated in (9). Alternatively, since *every woman's mother* is in a $\bar{\theta}$-position, NP-adjunction need not apply. In this case the object *a man* can adjoin to IP as in (10).[4] This derives the reading where the object quantifier has scope over QP_1.

(9)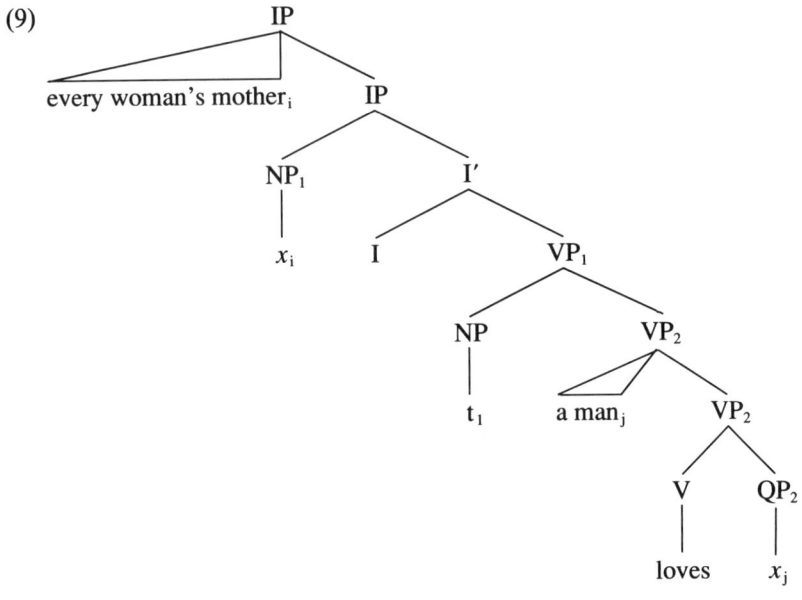

(10)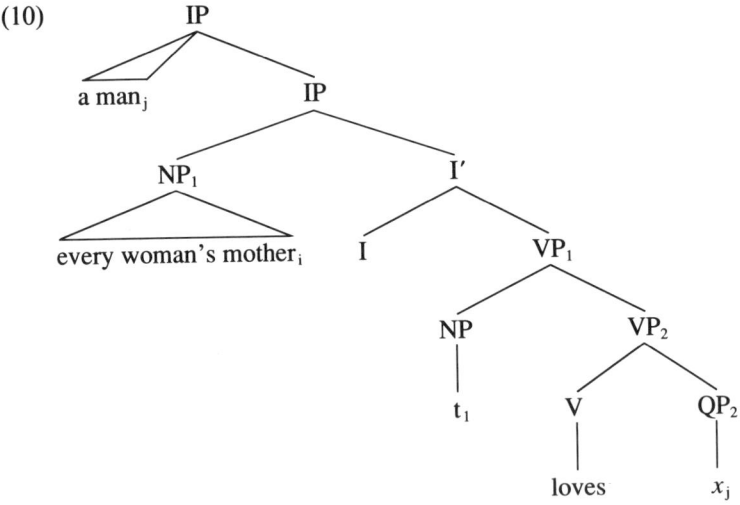

In brief, then, the contrast between the English sentence (2a) and the Chinese sentence (2b) is parallel to the contrast between the canonical active sentences in these two languages. Once again, this contrast can be traced back to the fact that the S-Structure position of a subject in English, but not in Chinese, is nonthematic. The discussion of the contrast between (2a) and (2b) led us to clarify the working of NP-adjunction, allowing NPs whose specifier is quantificational to undergo this process

Nominal Structures and Scope   97

(see note 3). In the following section we show that this assumption is necessary to account for the exocentric behavior of QPs interacting with *wh*-operators.

4.1.2 Exocentric Behavior of QP/*Wh*-Operators

Having discussed the exocentric behavior of QPs occurring in the pattern (1a), we now take up the interaction of QPs and *wh*-operators occurring in this pattern. Two major cases need to be discussed. One is case (11), where a QP within an NP interacts with a *wh*-element outside this NP. This case is illustrated in (12).

(11) [[$_{NP}$ QP...]...*wh*...]

(12) a. What$_i$ did everyone's mother buy x_i? (ambiguous)

b. Meigeren de mama maile shenme? (ambiguous)
everyone DE mother bought what
'What did everyone's mother buy?'

The other is case (13), where a *wh*-element within an NP interacts with a QP occurring outside this NP. This case is illustrated in (14).[5]

(13) [[$_{NP}$ *wh*...]...QP...]

(14) a. Whose mother bought everything? (unambiguous)

b. Sheide mama maile meige dongxi? (unambiguous)
whose mother bought every thing

We first consider the form in (13), using the English sentence (14a) for the purpose of illustration. The S-Structure representation of this sentence is given in (15).

(15) [$_{CP}$ whose mother$_i$ [$_{IP}$ x_i [$_{VP_1}$ t$_i$ [$_{VP_2}$ bought everything]]]]

At LF the QP cannot be adjoined to a position c-commanding the variable x_i bound by the *wh*-operator; if it were, the MBR would be violated. The QP can only be adjoined to VP$_1$ or VP$_2$. The representation in (16) illustrates the adjunction of QP to VP$_1$.

(16) [$_{CP}$ whose mother$_i$ [$_{IP}$ x_i [$_{VP_1}$ everything$_j$ [$_{VP_1}$ t$_i$ [$_{VP_2}$ bought x_j]]]]]

Recall the generalization, established in sections 2.2.2.3 and 3.2.3, that operators and intermediate traces in $\bar{A}$-position, but not NP-traces or variables, play a role in determining the relative scope of a *wh*-operator. That is to say, even though the QP in (16) c-commands the NP-trace coindexed with the variable x_i and the *wh*-operator, it does not have scope over this *wh*-operator. In other words, (14a) is correctly expected to be unambiguous. The same analysis can be extended to the Chinese sentence (14b). After the *wh*-operator moves to the Spec of Comp at LF, as in (17), the QP in the object position cannot be adjoined to a position higher than the variable x_i bound by the *wh*-operator. (14b) is thus unambiguous.

(17) [$_{CP}$ sheide mama$_i$ [$_{IP}$ I [$_{VP_1}$ x_i [$_{VP_2}$ maile   meige dongxi]]]]
       whose mother   bought every thing

Next we turn to the form in (11), exemplified in (12). The S-Structure representations of (12a–b) are (18a–b), respectively.

(18) a. [$_{CP}$ what$_j$ [$_{IP}$[$_{NP}$ everyone's mother]$_i$ [$_{VP}$ t$_i$ [$_{VP}$ buy x_j]]]]

      b. [$_{CP}$[$_{IP}$ I [$_{VP_1}$[$_{NP}$ meigeren de mama] [$_{VP_2}$ maile   shenme]]]]
                              everyone DE mother   bought what

We first consider (18a). NP-adjunction may apply either to *everyone* or to *everyone's mother*. Consider the representations involving NP-adjunction of *everyone*. In order for this derivation to satisfy the MBR, *everyone* must not be adjoined to IP as in (19a).

(19) a. [$_{CP}$ what$_j$ [$_{IP}$ everyone$_k$ [$_{IP}$[$_{NP}$ x_k's mother]$_i$ [$_{VP}$ t$_i$ [$_{VP}$ buy x_j]]]]]

If *everyone* is instead adjoined to the subject NP as in (19b), the *wh*-operator will asymmetrically c-command the QP and have scope over it.

(19) b. [$_{CP}$ what$_j$ [$_{IP}$[$_{NP}$ everyone$_k$ [$_{NP}$ x_k's mother]$_i$] [$_{VP}$ t$_i$ [$_{VP}$ buy x_j]]]]

Consider now the derivation where *everyone's mother* undergoes NP-adjunction, as in (20a).

(20) a. [$_{CP}$ what$_j$ [$_{IP}$ everyone's mother$_i$ [$_{IP}$ x_i [$_{VP}$ t$_i$ buy x_j]]]]

This LF representation satisfies the MBR: the coindexing of the object variable x_j with the raised *everyone's mother* would create a Principle C violation because the variable x_i in subject position c-commands the object variable. (20a) generates the reading where the *wh*-operator has scope over the quantificational expression because the *wh*-operator c-commands it. Note also that in a representation such as (20a), the *wh*-operator may leave an intermediate trace adjoined to VP, as in (20b).

(20) b. [$_{CP}$ what$_j$ [$_{IP}$ everyone's mother$_i$ [$_{IP}$ x_i [$_{VP}$ t$_j$ [$_{VP}$ t$_i$ buy x_j]]]]]

This representation generates the reading where the QP has scope over the *wh*-operator since it c-commands the intermediate trace coindexed with the *wh*-operator. The English sentence (18a) therefore is ambiguous.

Nominal Structures and Scope

This analysis of the English sentence (18a) straightforwardly captures the ambiguity of its Chinese counterpart (18b). (18b) has the LF representation in (21).

(21) [$_{CP}$ Shenme$_j$ [$_{IP}$ I [$_{VP_1}$ meigeren de mama$_i$ [$_{VP_1}$ x_i [$_{VP_2}$ t$_j$ [$_{VP_2}$ maile
what   everyone DE mother   bought
x_j]]]]]]

(21) derives two readings: the quantificational expression is c-commanded by the *wh*-operator and c-commands the intermediate trace bound by the *wh*-operator.

To summarize, in sections 4.1.1 and 4.1.2 we have discussed the interaction of an operator occurring within a simplex NP with an operator occurring outside this NP (see pattern (1a)). The behavior of operator interaction in this pattern follows straightforwardly from the analysis presented in the previous chapters. We also made more precise the application of NP-adjunction. NP-adjunction applies to any quantificational NP or any NP whose specifier is quantificational:

(22) An NP whose specifier is quantificational may undergo NP-adjunction.

Notice that, as formulated, this generalization does not specify whether it must be satisfied at S-Structure or LF, that is, whether the specifier should be quantificational at S-Structure or at LF. The contrast between the ambiguous (23) and the nonambiguous (24) suggests that LF is the appropriate level where (22) must be satisfied ((23) and (24) are from Bowers 1987).

(23) What$_i$ did [pictures of everyone] show x_i?   (ambiguous)

(24) What$_i$ did [those/John's pictures of everyone]   (unambiguous)
     show x_i?

In (23) the QP has the option of moving to the Spec position. If it does, the whole NP [*pictures of everyone*] will be the target of NP-adjunction. In this case (23) is expected to be parallel to (18a), repeated here.

(18) a. What$_i$ did everyone's mother buy x_i?   (ambiguous)

This expectation is fulfilled: (23), like (18a), is ambiguous.

On the other hand, as (25) illustrates, in (24) the Spec position is already filled. The QP *everyone* cannot move to this position. The MBR prevents QR from raising *everyone* to a position c-commanding the variable generated by *wh*-movement. (24) thus cannot have the interpretation

(25)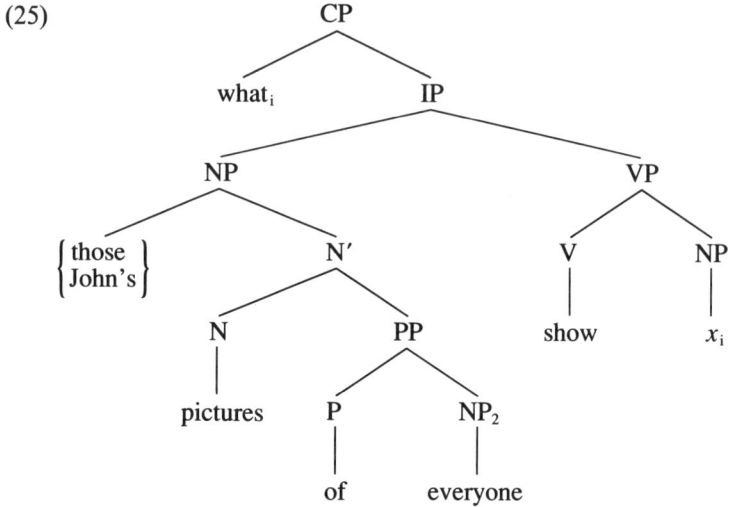

where the QP has scope over the *wh*-operator. The contrast between (23) and (24) thus indicates that LF is the domain where (22) is to be satisfied.

4.2 Endocentric Behavior of Operators

Having discussed the interaction of operators occurring inside an NP with other operators occurring outside this NP (exocentric behavior), we now turn to the endocentric behavior of operators—that is, the interaction of operators inside an NP with other operators inside the same NP. The contrastive study of operator interaction on a sentential level in English and Chinese highlighted an important dimension along which these languages differ, namely, that of subject raising. The presence of subject raising in English accounted for the ambiguity of the canonical active sentences in this language. On the other hand, the absence of this process in Chinese accounted for the nonambiguity of the canonical active sentences in this language. The contrast between the two languages documented at the sentential level resurfaces at the NP level.

Huang (1982) notes that English and Chinese differ in their QP scope interaction within NPs . Thus, he compares the English (26a–b) and the Chinese (27a–d). He notes that (26a–b) admit an inversely linked interpretation (see May 1977), according to which the more inclusive QP has wider scope than the less inclusive possessive QP. On the other hand, (27a–d) cannot have such an interpretation (Huang 1982, 189–90).

(26) a. [Some people from [every walk of life]] like jazz.

Nominal Structures and Scope 101

   b. [Every senator on [a key congressional committee]] voted for the amendment.

(27) a. Wo maile [meiben sange ren de shu].
      I bought every three men DE book
      'I bought every book that belongs to three men.'
   b. Wo maile [sanben meige ren de shu].
      I bought three every man DE book
      'I bought three books, each of which belongs to everybody.'
   c. Wo maile [sange ren de meiben shu].
      I bought three men DE every book
      'For three men x, I bought every one of x's books.'
   d. Wo maile [meige ren de sanben shu].
      I bought every man DE three book
      'For every x, I bought three of x's books.'

For these sentences "while the English (8)–(9) [our (26a–b)] are each ambiguous, neither (1)–(2) [our (27c–d)] nor (10)–(11) [our (27a–b)] are ambiguous" (p. 192).

Huang's observation concerning the contrast between the ambiguous (26a–b) and the unambiguous (27a–d) reveals a tight parallelism between the structure of sentences and the structure of nominal expressions within each language. In order to capture this parallelism, it will be necessary to reconsider the standard structure of noun phrases adopted so far. In particular, we will assume that determiners are to be treated as heads of the phrases in which they occur. Once this assumption is established, it will be possible to capture the parallelism between operator interaction in sentences and operator interaction in nominal expressions. In the same way that the presence versus absence of subject raising on a sentential level accounted for the contrast between active sentences in English and active sentences in Chinese, the presence versus absence of NP-raising on a nominal level will account for contrasts such as the one illustrated in (26a–b) and for inversely linked quantification.

4.2.1 NP Structures in English and Chinese
Various syntactic and theoretical considerations have led several linguists to assume that determiners are to be treated as heads of the phrase in which they occur (see, among others, Abney 1987, Hudson 1989, Kuroda 1988, Stowell 1991). Under this view, the phrase (28) is to be represented

as in (30) rather than as in (29). In (30) the determiner is the head of the Determiner Phrase (DP) and takes a Spec and an NP complement.

(28) John's picture of Bill

(29)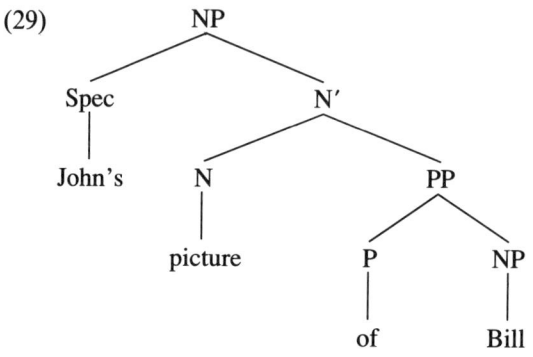

(30)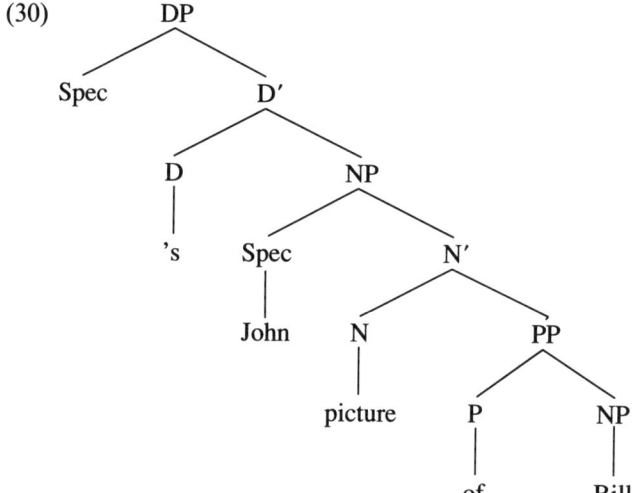

In (30) *John* must be raised to the Spec of D' in order to receive Case, yielding (28).

Assuming that a DP exists in English, the null hypothesis is to assume that Chinese also has a DP structure. As a matter of fact, Bowers (1987) suggests that the Chinese phrase in (31), where a possessive noun occurs with a demonstrative, provides evidence for a DP analysis in this language.

(31) Zhangsan de naben shu
    Zhangsan DE that + CLASSIFIER book
    'that book of Zhangsan's'

In this phrase the possessive noun is generated under the Spec of D′. As for the demonstrative, it is possible to assume that it is generated under D, as suggested by Bowers (1987) (see (32)), or under the Spec of N′, as suggested by Hudson (1989) (see (33)).

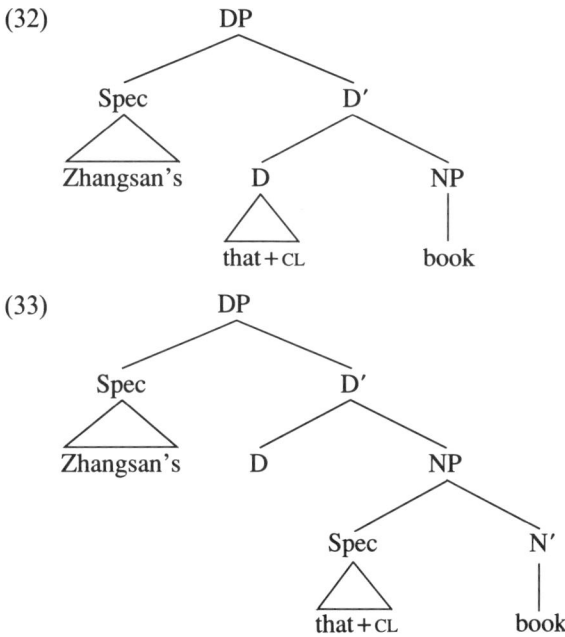

(32)

(33)

Phrases such as (31) in Chinese are naturally generated by the DP analysis. On the other hand, the traditional NP structure in (29) cannot straightforwardly generate this phrase. Within the context of standard X-bar theory (Chomsky 1970) and the traditional NP structure analysis shown in (29), *that* + CLASSIFIER occurs in the Spec of N′ position, as in (34), since it cannot be a complement of *book*.

(34)

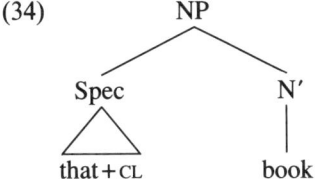

However, *Zhangsan* does not behave like an adjoined element, if an adjoined element is considered to be in an Ā-position. For instance, *Zhangsan* can function as an A-binder for a lexical anaphor:

(35)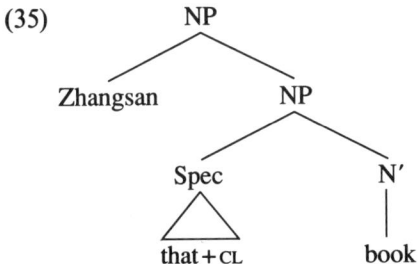

(36) Zhangsan$_i$ de naben   tazij$_i$ shu
     Zhangsan DE that + CL himself book
     'that book of himself of Zhangsan's'

Moreover, *Zhangsan* receives the same possessor interpretation as the noun *John* that is in the Spec position of the English expression *John's pictures of Bill*. Thus, the NP structure in (35) does not accurately characterize the noun phrase *Zhangsan*. The DP analysis in (32)–(33), where *Zhangsan* occurs in Spec position, allows *Zhangsan* to be analyzed as an A-element that receives a possessor θ-role.

Examples such as (36) illustrate the plausibility of extending a DP analysis for English nominal expressions to their Chinese counterparts. English DPs and Chinese DPs do not have identical structures, however, for instance, Chinese, but not English, allows two possessor NPs to occur in a nominal expression:

(37) *John's Bill's books

(38) Zhangsan de Lisi de shu
     Zhangsan DE Lisi DE book
     'Zhangsan's book of Lisi'

The expression in (38) can mean 'the book about Lisi that is owned or written by Zhangsan'. It can also mean 'the book that is owned by Lisi and is borrowed or sold by Zhangsan'. The interpretation of such NPs suggests that (38) has the structure in (39). The existence of a structure like (39) suggests that both Spec of D' and Spec of N' position are Case positions, in contrast to the English structure (30), which has only one Case position (Spec of D'). The fact that Spec of N' is not a Case position in English but is a Case position in Chinese accounts for the contrast between (37) and (38). The claim that both Spec of D' and Spec of N' are Case positions in Chinese entails that there should be no movement from Spec of N' to Spec of D' position: *Zhangsan's book* simply has the struc-

Nominal Structures and Scope 105

(39)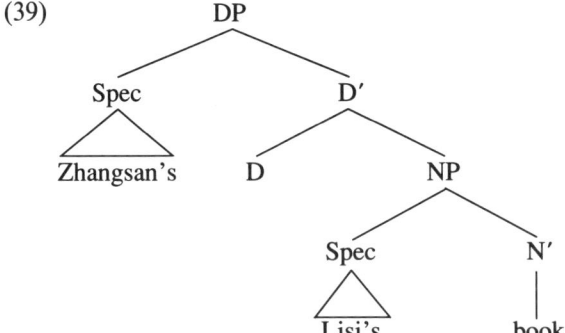

ture in (40) or (41). *Zhangsan* can be base-generated in either the Spec of D′ or the Spec of N′ position. No Spec-to-Spec raising occurs.

(40)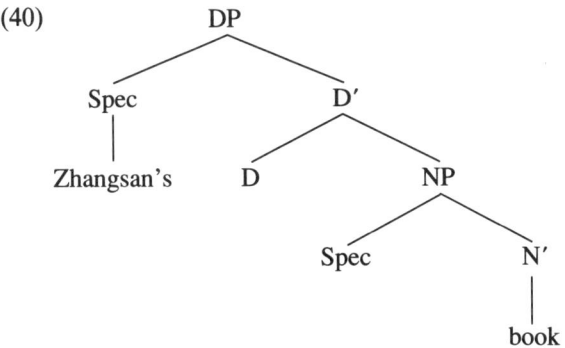

(41)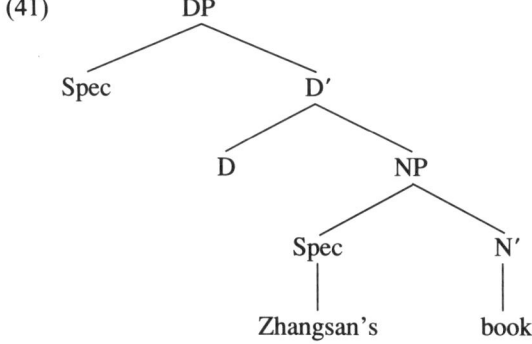

The contrast between the English and Chinese nominal structures with respect to subject raising is reminiscent of the contrast between clausal structures in these two languages.[6] In Aoun and Li 1989 (also see chapter 1), we entertained the possibility that the absence of subject raising in Chinese is to be traced back to the degenerate nature of Infl in Chinese. It is interesting to note in this respect that Ds are also degenerate in Chinese. English nominal expressions generally require articles and force agreement between determiners and nominal heads. Chinese nominal expressions do not require articles and do not have any agreement:

(42) a. He read a/the book.

　　b. *He read book.

　　c. He read three books.

　　d. *He read three book.

(43) a. Ta kan shu.
　　　 he read book

　　b. Ta kan san ben shu.
　　　 he read three CL book

Assuming that within DPs, Agr and articles occur in D(eterminer) position (see Abney 1987), the D position is much more impoverished in Chinese than in English. In DPs, too, it is possible to link the absence of subject raising to the degenerate nature of D.

In brief, the internal structures of nominal expressions in English and Chinese are dissimilar: Chinese, but not English, allows multiple specifiers. The distinction between the two languages may be related to the absence versus presence of subject raising. Just as movement from Spec to Spec is allowed in a clausal structure in English, so it is also possible in a nominal structure. In Chinese, on the other hand, movement from Spec to Spec is unavailable in IPs and DPs. With this in mind, let us turn to the interaction of QPs within nominal expressions.

4.2.2 Endocentric Behavior of QPs

As noted earlier, English and Chinese differ not only with respect to the interaction of QPs in canonical sentences but also with respect to the interaction of QPs within nominal expressions. We briefly discussed Huang's (1982) work on this contrast and quoted his examples in (26)–(27), repeated here as (44)–(45).

(44) a. [Some people from [every walk of life]] like jazz.

　　b. [Every senator on [a key congressional committee]] voted for the amendment.

(45) a. Wo maile [meiben sange ren de shu].
    I bought every three men DE book
    'I bought every book that belongs to three men.'

  b. Wo maile [sanben meigeren de shu].
    I bought three everyone DE book
    'I bought three books, each of which belongs to everybody.'

  c. Wo maile [sange ren de meiben shu].
    I bought three men DE every book
    'For three men x, I bought every one of x's books.'

  d. Wo maile [meigeren de sanben shu].
    I bought everyone DE three book
    'For every x, I bought three of x's books.'

According to Huang, English and Chinese differ in the interaction of these QPs: (44a–b) are ambiguous and (45a–d) are unambiguous. The following examples illustrate the same contrast:

(46) a. a woman's pictures of everyone (ambiguous)

  b. yige nuren de meigeren de zhaopian (unambiguous)
    one woman DE everyone DE picture
    'a woman's pictures of everyone'

The NP in (46a) can have two readings: either *a woman* or *everyone* has wide scope. For (46b), however, only the interpretation where *a woman* has wide scope is possible. Just as the contrast between the ambiguity of the English canonical active sentence and the nonambiguity of the Chinese canonical active sentence is due to the difference in the basic constituent structures of these two languages, we show below that the difference in interpretation of the expressions in (46) is due to the structural difference between English and Chinese nominal expressions discussed in the previous section. We will first discuss the English cases and then turn to their Chinese counterparts.

4.2.2.1 QP/QP Interaction within English Nominal Expressions The interaction of two QPs occurring within a nominal expression such as (46a) in English, *a woman's pictures of everyone*, accounts for its ambiguity. *Everyone* in (46a) can have a narrow or a wide scope interpretation.

In the traditional analysis, a nominal expression like (46a) has the structure in (47).

(47)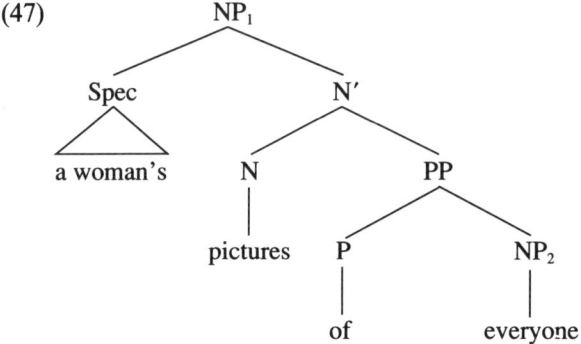

The DP analysis presented in the previous section suggests that this phrase can have the D-Structure representation in (48) instead.

(48)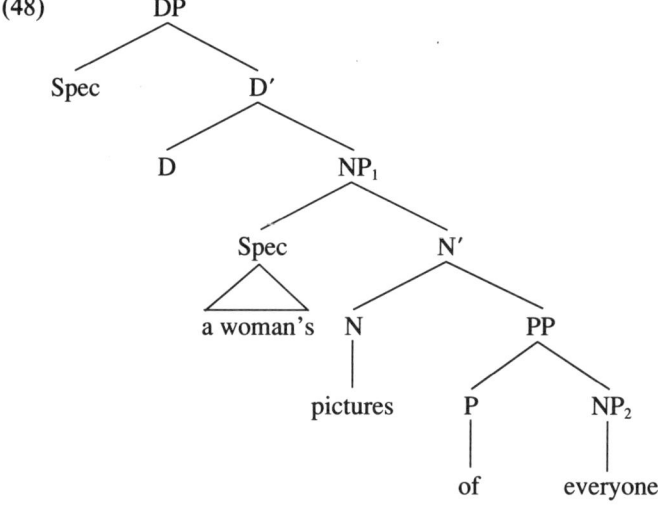

Since Spec-to-Spec movement is allowed in the nominal structure in English, *a woman* in (48) can move to Spec of D', deriving the structure shown in (49). In this structure *everyone* can undergo NP-adjunction at LF and adjoin to NP_1, and *a woman* can adjoin to some node outside the DP. *Everyone* cannot adjoin to DP or any other higher node; if it did, the MBR would be violated. *A woman* would then c-command and have scope over *everyone*:

(49)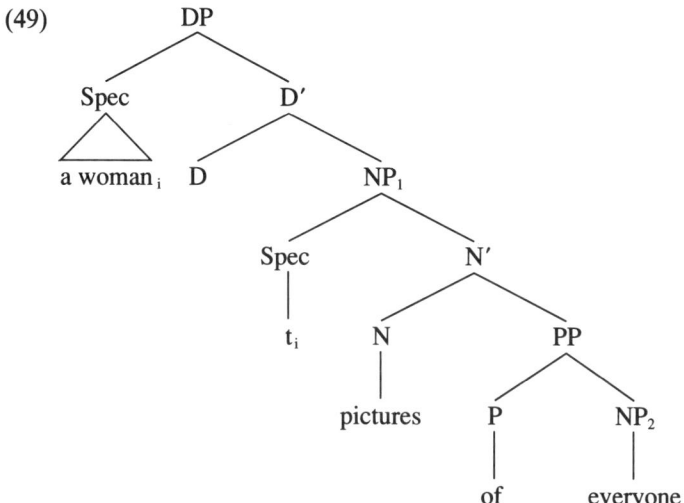

(50) [a woman$_i$ ... [$_{DP}$ x_i ... [$_{NP_1}$ everyone$_j$ [$_{NP_1}$ pictures of x_j]]]]

Other derivations are available. In what follows, we discuss the relevant ones.

Since *a woman* is in a $\bar{\theta}$-position, it need not undergo NP-adjunction. When *a woman* is not raised, *everyone* can adjoin to a node c-commanding *a woman* without violating the MBR. In other words, *everyone* may adjoin to DP or a node higher than DP. Adjunction to a node higher than DP, however, will be ruled out by the locality condition on NP-adjunction. As will be discussed in chapter 5, NP-adjunction is subject to a locality condition that can be subsumed under Principle A of the binding theory: Traces generated by NP-adjunction must be $\bar{A}$-bound within their governing category. Since the Spec of NP$_1$ in (49) is a subject, *everyone* must be bound within NP$_1$. *Everyone* thus cannot be adjoined outside the DP. In the same constructions, NP-adjunction of *everyone* to DP itself may also be impossible: for instance, in (51) the DP is in a θ-position and thus is not a possible adjunction site.

(51) He [$_{VP}$ saw [$_{DP}$ a woman's$_k$ [$_{NP}$ t$_k$ pictures of everyone]]].

Note, however, that in (51) the whole DP may undergo NP-adjunction, since its specifier is a quantificational element. After the DP is raised, it ends up in a $\bar{\theta}$-position and becomes a possible adjunction site:

(52) he [$_{VP}$[$_{DP}$ a woman's$_k$ [$_{NP}$ t$_k$ pictures of everyone]]$_i$ [$_{VP}$ saw x_i]]

Everyone in (52) can then adjoin to the raised DP. This generates the LF representation in (53).

(53) he [$_{VP}$[$_{DP}$ everyone$_j$ [$_{DP}$ a woman's$_k$ [$_{NP}$ t$_k$ pictures of x_j]]]$_i$ [$_{VP}$ saw x_i]]

This representation yields the reading where *everyone* has scope over *a woman*.

Expression (46a) therefore is ambiguous because the QP *everyone* can adjoin to a node inside the DP (NP$_1$ in (49)) or to the DP. Adjunction to DP is possible because the whole DP, whose specifier is quantificational, can undergo NP-adjunction first and ends up in a $\bar{\theta}$-position.

The analysis presented in this section also accounts for the contrast between May's (1977) cases involving inversely linked quantification, (26a–b), which are discussed in great detail by Huang (1982, chap. 4). We will just illustrate briefly here how Huang's discussion of these ambiguous cases can be recast in this analysis.

The ambiguity of these examples,[7] repeated here as (54)–(55), parallels the ambiguity of (46a). The S-Structure representation of (55), for instance, is (56), after Spec-to-Spec movement takes place.

(54) [Some people from [every walk of life]] like jazz.

(55) [Every senator on [a key congressional committee]] voted for the amendment.

(56)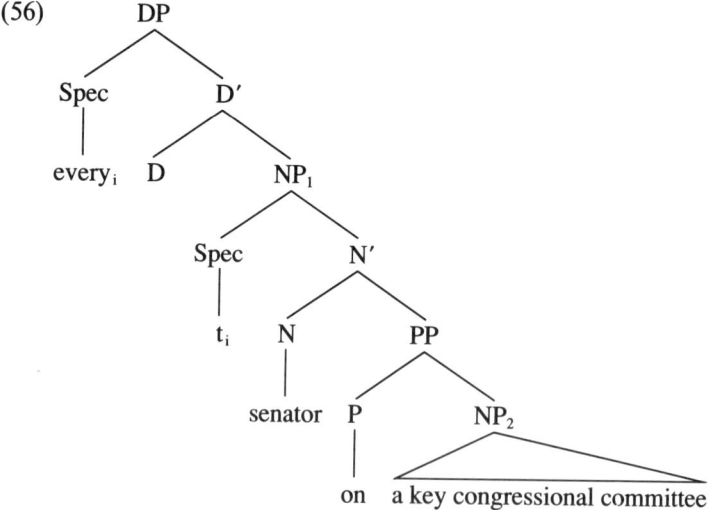

The analysis suggested to account for the ambiguity of (46a) straightforwardly accounts for the ambiguity of (55) (as well as (54)) and will not be repeated here.

4.2.2.2 QP/QP Interaction within Chinese Nominal Expressions Let us now turn to the behavior of QPs in Chinese nominal expressions. As indicated by Huang (1982, chap. 4), Chinese does not have inversely linked quantification. In fact, NPs containing two interacting QPs in this language are always unambiguous. For example, the Chinese counterpart of the ambiguous English phrase (46a) is unambiguous (see (46b)), as are Huang's examples in (27a–d), repeated here as (57a–d).

(46) b. yige nuren   de meigeren de zhaopian   (unambiguous)
     one woman DE everyone DE picture
     'a woman's pictures of everyone'

(57) a. Wo maile [meiben sange ren de shu].   (unambiguous)
       I   bought every   three men DE book
       'I bought every book that belongs to three men.'

   b. Wo maile [sanben meigeren de shu].   (unambiguous)
      I   bought three   everyone DE book
      'I bought three books, each of which belongs to everybody.'

   c. Wo maile [sange ren de meiben shu].   (unambiguous)
      I   bought three men DE every   book
      'For three men x, I bought every one of x's books.'

   d. Wo maile [meigeren de sanben shu]   (unambiguous)
      I   bought everyone DE three book
      'For every x, I bought three of x's books.'

The fact that (46b) and (57a–d) are unambiguous is due to the absence of Spec-to-Spec movement in Chinese nominal expressions. Recall that the DP structures for nominal expressions in English and Chinese differ in a significant way: movement from Spec of N' to Spec of D' occurs in English but not in Chinese. The absence of Spec-to-Spec movement in Chinese correlates with the fact that this language allows both Spec positions to be filled and assigned Case. In other words, the D- and S-structure representations of (46b) can be as shown in (58). In contrast to its English counterpart, *a woman* in (58) is in a θ-position: both Spec of D' and Spec of N' position in Chinese are Case positions; no NP-movement occurs from Spec of N' to Spec of D'. Since both Spec of D' and Spec of N' are base-generated NPs with thematic relations to the head N (possessor or agent or theme), Spec of D' is a θ-position. Being in a θ-position, *a woman* cannot stay in situ. It must adjoin to some node outside the DP. *Everyone* will adjoin to NP. This derives the reading where *a woman* has wide scope. The possibility of taking the whole DP as the target of NP-adjunction

(58)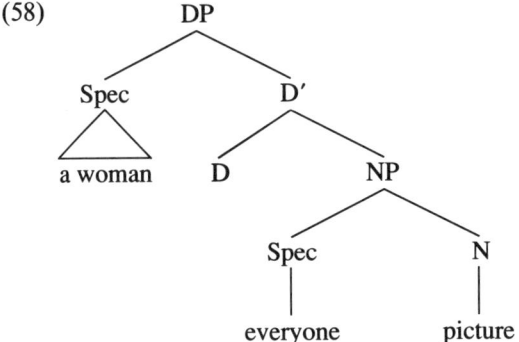

does not generate the reading where *everyone* has scope over *a woman*. After NP-adjunction raises the whole DP to a $\bar{\theta}$-position, *everyone* may adjoin to NP, as in (59a), or to the raised DP, as in (59b).

(59) a.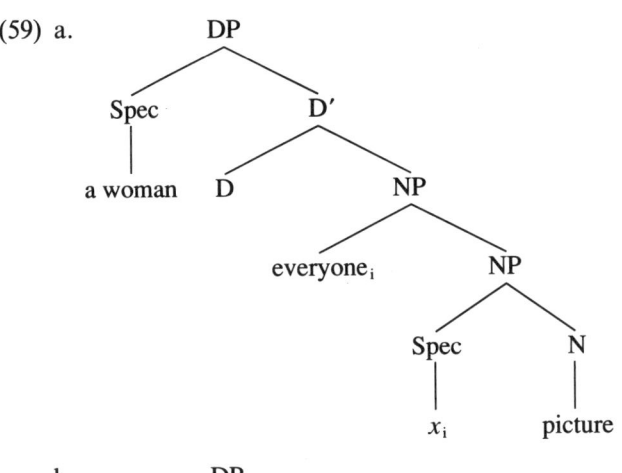

b.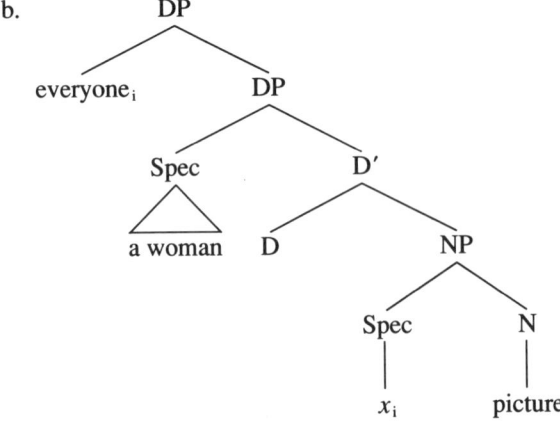

Nominal Structures and Scope

The representation in (59a) does not derive the reading where *everyone* has scope over *a woman*. *A woman* is still in a θ-position (Spec of D′) and must undergo NP-adjunction. The raised *a woman* c-commands *everyone*. Next consider (59b). In this representation *a woman* is also in a θ-position, the Spec of D′ position. Not being able to stay in a θ-position, this QP undergoes NP-adjunction, adjoining to DP. The adjunction of this QP to DP, however, results in an MBR violation: either the trace of *everyone* or the trace of *a woman* will not be bound by the first $\bar{\text{A}}$-binder. (46b) is therefore unambiguous.

The nonambiguity of the expressions in (57a–d) is accounted for in the same way. (57a) has the structure in (60).

(60)
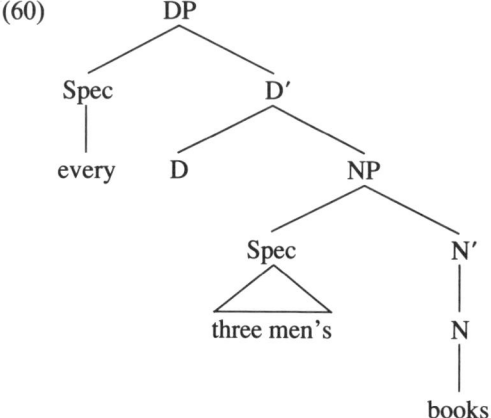

The derivations of (60) are exactly the same as those of (58).

In brief, the contrast between the ambiguity of the English (46a) and the nonambiguity of the Chinese (46b), (57a–d) is due to the existence of Spec-to-Spec movement in English but not in Chinese. As a result, the Spec of D′ position in English is a $\bar{\theta}$-position. In contrast, the lack of such movement in Chinese forces NP-adjunction to apply to quantifier phrases occurring in Spec position. The contrast in the interaction of QPs within nominal expressions therefore is parallel to the contrast in the interaction of QPs in the canonical active sentences in these two languages.

We have so far examined the interaction of QPs with other QPs within nominal expressions. In the next section we show that the structural difference between English and Chinese NPs discussed in this section also affects the interaction of QPs and *wh*-operators.

4.2.3 Endocentric Behavior of QPs/*Wh*-Operators

The facts concerning the interaction of QPs and *wh*-operators within nominal expressions are especially interesting: in English QP/*wh* interaction within nominal expressions results only in unambiguous expressions. For instance, the QP in the bracketed expressions in (61)–(62) can have only a group reading. It cannot be interpreted distributively; that is, it cannot have wide scope with respect to the *wh*-element within the nominal expression.

(61) Who saw [whose pictures of everyone]?　　(QP narrow scope only)

(62) ?Who saw [everyone's pictures of whom]?　　(QP narrow scope only)

On the other hand, QP/*wh* interaction within Chinese nominal expressions may generate ambiguity. As illustrated in (64), the QP may have either narrow or wide scope with respect to the *wh*-operator.

(63) Ni　kanle shenme meigeren de wenzhang?　(QP narrow scope only)
　　 you read　what　 everyone DE article
　　 'What article of everyone did you read?'

(64) Ni　kanle meigeren de shenme　　　　(QP wide & narrow scope)
　　 you read　everyone DE what
　　 wenzhang?
　　 article
　　 'Everyone's articles of what did you read?'

The facts of (61)–(64) are surprising if we contrast them with the behavior of QP/QP interaction in these two languages: although QP/QP interaction within nominal expressions in English usually generates ambiguity (such as *a woman's pictures of everyone*), QP/*wh* interaction in the same structures does not generate ambiguity. On the other hand, although QP/QP interaction within nominal expressions in Chinese does not generate ambiguity (such as *yige nuren de meigeren de zhaopian* 'a woman's pictures of everyone'), QP/*wh* interaction in the same structures can generate ambiguity. In the following sections we provide an account for the interaction of QPs and *wh*-operators within nominal expressions in English and Chinese. We start by considering the English cases.

4.2.3.1 QP/*Wh* Interaction within English Nominal Expressions　First we discuss the nonambiguity of sentences like (61), *Who saw [whose pictures of everyone]?* The S-Structure representation for the bracketed NP in (61) is (65).

(65)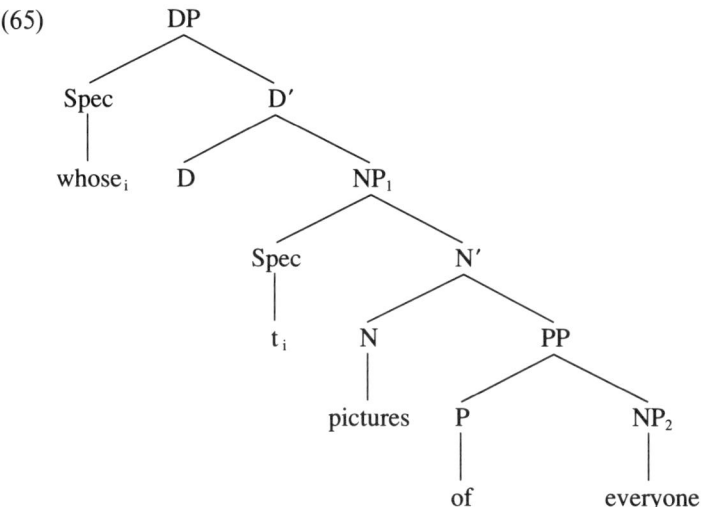

At LF *whose* is raised to Spec of Comp and *everyone* is adjoined to NP_1, generating (66).

(66)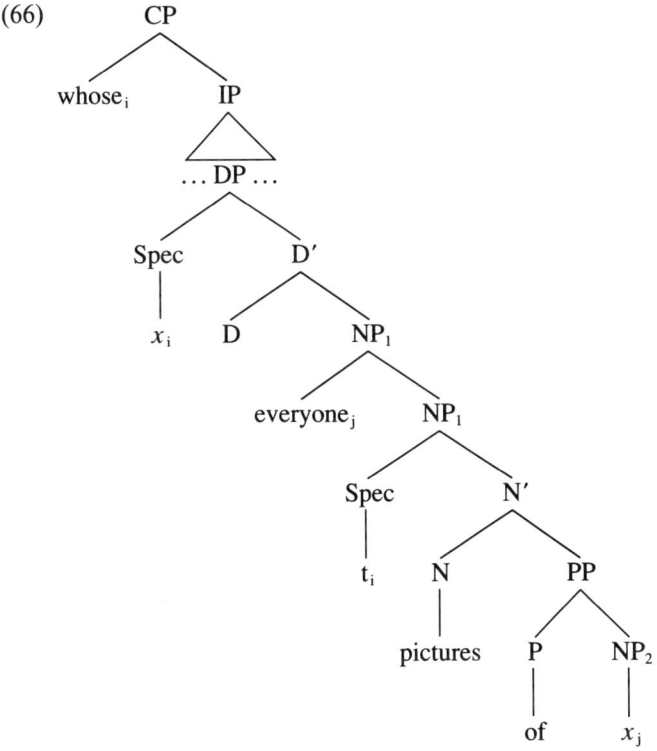

This representation derives only the reading where the *wh*-operator has wide scope because it c-commands the QP. The nonambiguity of (61) thus is accounted for.

Next we consider (62), *Who saw [everyone's pictures of whom]?* The S-Structure representation of (62) is (67).

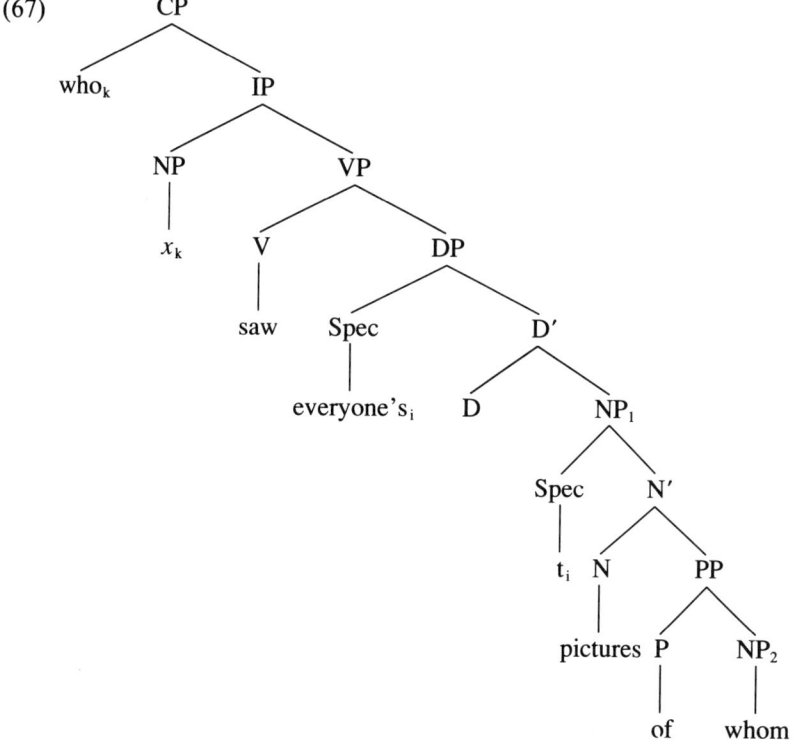

In case *whom* in (67) is raised to (Spec of) Comp and *everyone* adjoins to VP at LF, we derive the representation in (68). Note that the raising of *whom* may leave an intermediate trace adjoined to NP_1. The MBR is satisfied in this representation. The raised *everyone* is not a potential binder for the variable x_j or the intermediate trace t_j generated by *wh*-raising: coindexing *everyone* with either the intermediate trace or the variable x_j would make this variable A-bound by the NP-trace in the Spec of N' position and Principle C would be violated. According to our analysis, (62) should be ambiguous: in the LF representation (68) *whom* c-commands *everyone* and *everyone* c-commands the intermediate trace coindexed with *whom*. However, (62) is not ambiguous.

Nominal Structures and Scope 117

(68)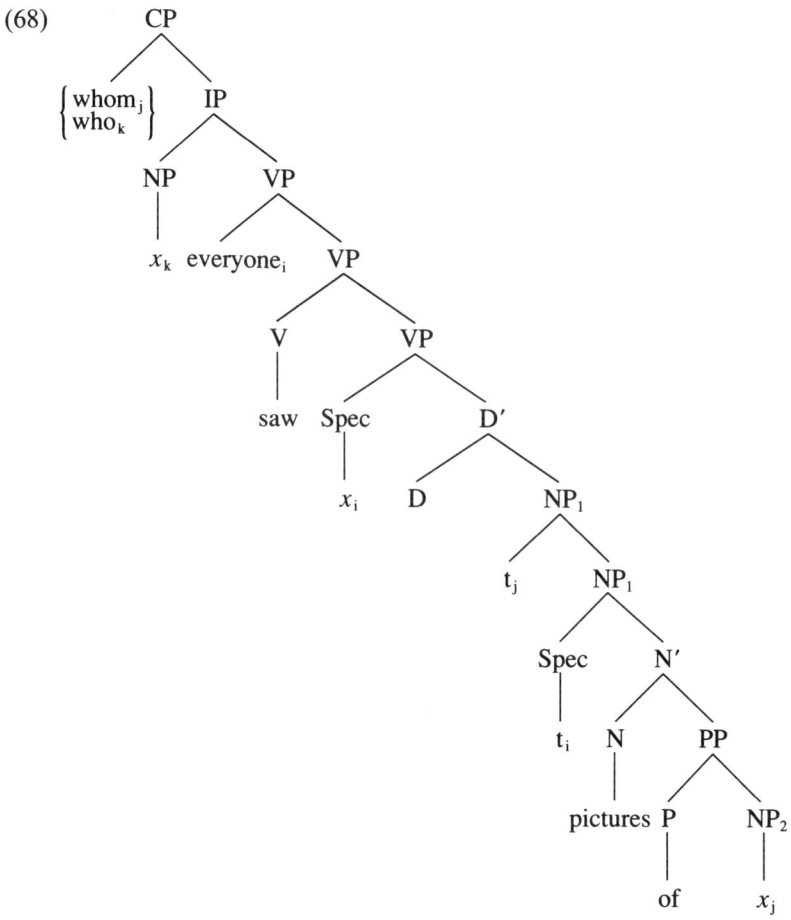

Notice that (62) contains two *wh*-operators. At LF these *wh*-operators undergo Absorption. This Absorption is responsible for the paired reading of these *wh*-operators (see Higginbotham and May 1981). We would like to suggest that Absorption is responsible for the nonambiguity of (62). Informally, as a consequence of Absorption, the *wh*-operators are treated as if they form a single unit (for a formal characterization of Absorption, again see Higginbotham and May 1981). With this in mind, we return to (68). If *everyone* is to have scope over *whom*, it must have scope over *who* because these two operators underwent Absorption. Since *everyone* cannot have scope over *who* in this case, it cannot have scope over *whom*. The gist of this discussion is expressed by the following generalization:

(69) In order for an operator A to have scope over an operator B that has been absorbed into C, A must also have scope over C.

Our approach leads us to expect that the phrase *everyone's pictures of whom* should be ambiguous in case it occurs in a context where *whom* does not undergo Absorption. This expectation cannot be checked in English because of the obligatory nature of syntactic *wh*-movement in this language. (70a–b) cannot be interpreted as direct questions. In other words, the obligatory nature of *wh*-movement in English prevents a *wh*-operator from occurring in situ in a sentence that contains no other *wh*-operator in Spec of Comp:

(70) a. John saw what?
     b. John saw everyone's pictures of whom?

Anticipating the discussion of the facts given in the following section, we note that Chinese provides a direct testing ground for our analysis since syntactic *wh*-movement does not exist in this language. Our analysis leads us to expect the counterpart of the English sentence to be unambiguous, since the two *wh*-operators undergo Absorption at LF. This is the case, as illustrated by the nonambiguity of the Chinese sentence (71).

(71) Shei kanle meigeren de shenme wenzhang? (QP narrow
     who read everyone DE what article   scope only)
     'Who read everyone's articles about what?'

More significantly, it leads us to expect (71) to become ambiguous when the subject is replaced by a non-*wh*-element. This indeed is the case, as illustrated in (72).

(72) Ni kanle meigeren de shenme wenzhang? (QP wide &
     you read everyone DE what article   narrow scope)
     'Everyone's articles about what did you read?'

The contrast between the possibility of a distributive reading for *everyone* in (72) and the impossibility of such a reading in (71) supports the generalization given in (69). We provide a more detailed analysis of the Chinese sentences (71)–(72) in the following sections.

4.2.3.2 QP/*Wh* Interaction within Chinese Nominal Expressions The basic contrast that we need to consider in Chinese is illustrated in the following sentences:

Nominal Structures and Scope   119

(73) a. Ni kanle [shenme meigeren de wenzhang]?   (QP narrow
       you read what everyone DE article   scope only)
       'What articles of everyone did you read?'

    b. Ni kanle [meigeren de shenme wenzhang]?   (QP wide &
       you read everyone DE what article   narrow scope)
       'Everyone's articles about what did you read?'

We first consider (73a). The S-Structure representation for the bracketed nominal expression is (74).

(74)

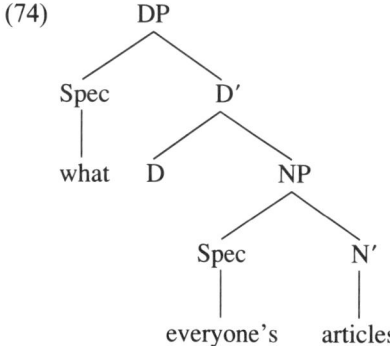

In this derivation the *wh*-element raises to Spec of Comp and the QP adjoins to NP. This QP cannot adjoin to a higher position c-commanding the variable generated by the raising of *what*; if it did, the MBR would be violated. This derives the reading where the *wh*-element has wide scope.

Alternatively, the whole DP may be raised to Spec of Comp since its specifier is a *wh*-element. This option results in the following LF representation, where the QP adjoins to the raised DP:

(75) [$_{CP}$[$_{DP}$ everyone$_j$ [$_{DP}$ what [$_{NP}$ x_j article]$_k$]] [$_{IP}$ ... x_k]]

Were this a possible representation, we would derive the reading where the quantifier has wide scope. (73a) would be ambiguous, although it is not. This derivation can be ruled out, however, if we consider the position where *what* occurs. Note that *what* is in Spec of D' position, which is a θ-position. Let us take the motivation for operator movement (such as *wh*-raising) seriously: operators cannot stay in θ-position. In the case of (75), then, *what* must also undergo raising. It is raised and adjoined to DP. This adjunction of *what* to DP would create an MBR violation, however: the raised *what* would be the first available Ā-binder for the variable bound by *everyone*. (Alternatively, *what* may adjoin to the higher DP, resulting in a violation of the MBR by the trace bound by *what*.)

(76) [$_{CP}$[$_{DP}$ everyone$_j$ [$_{DP}$ what$_i$ [$_{DP}$ x_i [$_{NP}$ x_j article]$_k$]]] [$_{IP}$ ... x_k]]

(76) thus is ill formed: (73a) is unambiguous.[8]

Next we consider (73b). The S-Structure representation of (73b) is (77).

(77)

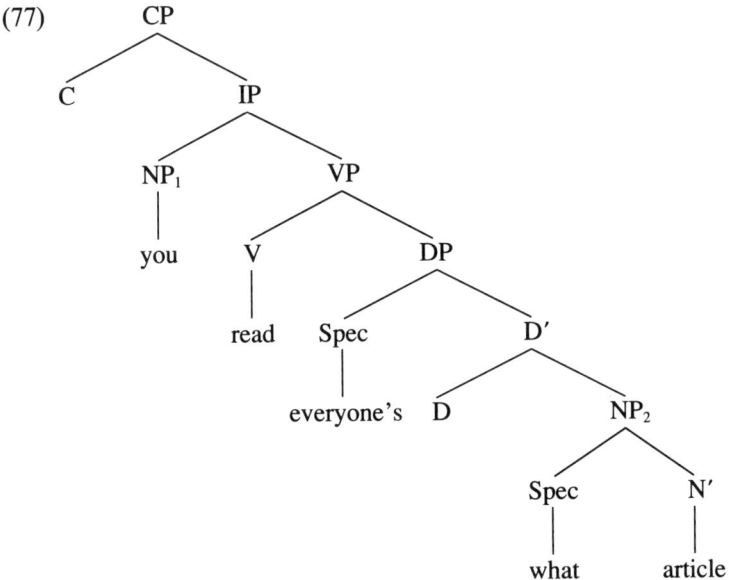

At LF the *wh*-operator is raised to Spec of Comp, as in (78). It can leave an intermediate trace adjoined to NP$_2$. The QP adjoins to VP.

(78) [$_{CP}$ what$_j$ ... [$_{VP}$ everyone$_i$ [$_{VP}$ ... [$_{DP}$ x_i [$_{NP_2}$ t$_j$ [$_{NP_2}$ x_j book]]]]]]

The MBR is not violated in this representation because the raised QP cannot count as a potential Ā-binder for either the intermediate trace or the variable generated by *wh*-raising; if it did, Principle C would be violated by x_j. This representation derives two readings because the raised *wh*-operator c-commands the raised QP, which in turn c-commands the intermediate trace adjoined to NP$_2$.

As indicated in the preceding section, the ambiguity of sentences such as (73b) disappears when Absorption takes place:

(80) Shei kanle meigeren de shenme wenzhang? (QP narrow
     who read everyone DE what   article   scope only)
     'Who read everyone's articles about what?'

The contrast between the ambiguity of (73b) and the nonambiguity of (79) thus confirms the generalization in (69).

4.3 Summary

In this chapter we studied the behavior of operators within nominal expressions and concentrated on their interaction with operators occurring outside and inside the same nominal expressions. This led us to clarify the application of the extraction processes applying at LF. In particular, we showed that

- An NP whose specifier is a quantifier may undergo NP-adjunction.
- Two operators that undergo Absorption are treated as if they form a single unit. Thus, in order for an operator A to have scope over an operator B that has been absorbed into C, A must also have scope over C or an $\bar{A}$-element bound by C.

Chapter 5
Construal, Indices, Domain, and Scope

The two main principles that we assumed in the previous chapters are the Minimal Binding Requirement and the Scope Principle. The MBR regulates the distribution of operators and variables and the Scope Principle regulates the interaction of operators. In this chapter we introduce further important refinements affecting the working of these principles.

Starting with the Scope Principle, we assumed in chapter 1 that the interaction of operators is sensitive to the chain in which the operator occurs. The chain contains the operator, intermediate traces in $\bar{\text{A}}$-position, variables, and NP-traces coindexed with the operator.[1] Concern over the nonsystematic role of NP-traces in determining relative scope led us to completely eliminate these elements in this process. Empirical concerns discussed in section 3.2.1 also forced us to eliminate the role of variables in determining scope relations. We concluded that, in a chain headed by an operator, only the operator and intermediate traces are relevant to this process.

In the cases discussed so far, the operator and the intermediate traces were all in chains generated by movement at S-Structure or LF. In addition to the possibility of being coindexed with an operator through movement rules, an element can be coindexed with an operator through interpretive rules. Examples illustrating this type of coindexation are *tough*-constructions, parasitic gap constructions, and relativized constructions. For instance, in a sentence like (1) the elements coindexed with the relativized QP include the nonovert operator in the Spec of Comp of the relative clause and the intermediate trace generated by the movement of the nonovert operator.

(1) I read $[_{NP}$ an article$_i$ $[_{CP}$ Op$_i$ that $[_{IP}$ everyone $[_{VP}$ t$_i$ $[_{VP}$ wrote x_i]]]]].

The coindexing between *an article* on the one hand and the nonovert operator and its intermediate trace on the other is not due to movement but instead is due to some interpretive mechanism capturing the predication relation between the head of the complex NP and the relative clause. It then is legitimate to wonder whether the nonovert operator and its intermediate trace(s) coindexed with the QP via the interpretive mechanism (Predication rule; see Williams 1980) are relevant for the Scope Principle.

The study of *tough*-constructions and parasitic gap constructions undertaken in section 5.1 will reveal that the Scope Principle is sensitive to the operator and intermediate traces in chains generated by movement but not to the elements coindexed with the operator via interpretive mechanisms. This result provides support for linguistic models that distinguish between two types of indexing mechanisms: the one generated by movement and the one generated by interpretation (see Chomsky 1981, chap. 2).

The study of relativized constructions undertaken in sections 5.2 and 5.3 will provide further support for the relevance of movement chains, but not the elements coindexed with operators via interpretive mechanisms, to the Scope Principle. More importantly, it bears on the working of the MBR and the distinction between variables left by quantified expressions and variables left by *wh*-operators discussed in the previous chapters. Specifically, in sections 5.2 and 5.3 we discuss the interaction of an operator occurring in the head position of the complex NP with operators occurring inside the relative clause. Once again the contrastive study of English and Chinese will uncover systematic differences between the two languages. In chapter 1 we showed that the interaction of quantificational elements—for example, the interaction of quantifiers in active sentences—generates ambiguity in more cases in English than it does in Chinese. Within relativized phrases, however, the interaction of operators generates ambiguity in Chinese, but not in English. For instance, consider the English sentence (1) containing a relative clause (repeated here as (2)).

(2) I read [an article that everyone wrote].

The bracketed English phrase in (2) is not ambiguous: *an article* has scope over *everyone*. The Chinese phrase corresponding to the bracketed phrase in (2) *is* ambiguous, however. In (3) either *everyone* or *an article* may take wide scope.

(3) [meigeren xiede [yipian wenzhang]]
 everyone wrote one article
 'an article that everyone wrote'

It turns out that this surprising state of affairs mirrors other systematic differences between (short-distance) reflexives in these languages. To account for the difference between English and Chinese and for the parallelism between the distribution of reflexives and that of quantifiers, we will be led to assume that variables bound by quantificational elements, but not variables bound by *wh*-operators, obey a locality requirement akin to the one constraining anaphoric reflexives.

5.1 Indices by Interpretive Rules

In a chain generated by movement, the Scope Principle refers to the operator heading the chain and its intermediate traces. Now consider the behavior of operators and intermediate traces that occur in a chain that has not been generated by movement. An instance of such a chain can be found in *tough*-constructions. In (4) the intermediate trace t_i and the nonovert operator Op are coindexed with the *wh*-operator (see Chomsky 1981).

(4) $[_{CP}$ who$_i$ $[_{IP}$ x_{1_i} is tough $[_{CP}$ Op$_i$ $[_{IP}$ to $[_{VP}$ t_i $[_{VP}$ deal with x_{2_i}]]]]]]

Since the nonovert operator and the intermediate trace t_i are coindexed with the *wh*-operator (via the variable x_{1_i}) by an interpretive rule, one may wonder what the status of the nonovert operator and the intermediate trace is with respect to the Scope Principle.

Assuming that the nonovert operators and intermediate traces in question are sensitive to the Scope Principle, the following contrast is not expected:

(5) what$_i$ is tough $[_{CP}$ Op$_i$ $[_{IP}$ to $[_{VP}$ t_i $[_{VP}$ give x_i to everyone]]]]   (unambiguous)

(6) I know $[_{CP}$ what$_i$ $[_{IP}$ he $[_{VP}$ t_i $[_{VP}$ gave x_i to everyone]]]]   (ambiguous)

In the S-Structure representation (5) the *wh*-operator *what* that occurs in the subject position of the *tough* predicate is coindexed with the nonovert operator and the intermediate trace t_i that it binds. The QP *everyone* is generated in the embedded clause. The sentence is unambiguous. On the other hand, in the ambiguous sentence (6), what occurs in the embedded Comp position. If we were to assume that nonovert operators and intermediate traces coindexed with the *wh*-operator via the construal mechanism are relevant for scope interaction, we would expect (5) to display the same behavior as (6). This is not the case, however: whereas (6) is ambiguous, (5) is unambiguous. On the other hand, if we assume that in (5) the nonovert operator and its intermediate trace t_i do not play a role in determining scope relations, we expect this sentence to display the same behavior as a sentence like (7) where no element in the embedded clause is coindexed with the quantifier in the matrix clause. This indeed is the case: both (5) and (7) are unambiguous.

(7) Who wants Mary to give it to everyone? (unambiguous)

The nonambiguity of (5) indicates that the nonovert operator and the intermediate trace that it binds do not play a role in determining relative scope. In other words, nonovert operators and intermediate traces coindexed with the operator because of construal requirements are not relevant to scope interaction.

Parasitic gap constructions provide further evidence for this conclusion (see, among others, Chomsky 1982 and Contreras 1984 for analyses of parasitic gap constructions).[2] (8a) is unambiguous, in contrast to (8b), which is ambiguous. If the parasitic gap is replaced by an NP that is not coindexed with the *wh*-operator, the sentence remains unambiguous, as in (8c).

(8) a. What$_i$ did you file x_i without [Op$_i$ [everyone's [t$_i$ [reading e$_i$]]]]?
    b. What$_i$ did everyone read x_i?
    c. What$_i$ did you file x_i without everyone's reading the book?

The fact that (8a) patterns with (8c) indicates that the nonovert operator and the parasitic gap in (8a) do not play a role in determining scope relations.

This observation is by no means an isolated fact. Nonovert operators (and their intermediate traces) do not play a role with respect to other interpretive mechanisms. As indicated by Barss (1986) and by Stowell and Lasnik (1991), they do not display a weak crossover effect. This is illustrated in the following sentences:[3]

(9) a. ?*Who$_i$ did his$_i$ mother visit x_i?
    b. Who$_i$ did Mary see x_i before his$_i$ mother's visiting e$_i$?

Similarly, nonovert operators do not allow reconstruction effects:[4]

(10) a. Which pictures of himself did John paint x without Mary liking e?
     b. *Which pictures of himself did Mary paint without John liking e?

Thus, nonovert operators (and their intermediate traces) do not seem to be relevant for the interpretive mechanisms discussed. Furthermore, since nonovert operators and their intermediate traces are coindexed with an operator via interpretive mechanisms, the following generalization emerges from the discussion of relative scope in *tough*-constructions and parasitic gap constructions:

(11) Interpretive mechanisms do not feed into the set of elements relevant to determining relative scope.

Direct support for this generalization is provided by the interaction of operators in complex NPs. We first illustrate this by discussing the behavior of complex NPs in English.

5.2 English Complex NPs

The behavior of QP/QP interaction in English is exemplified by sentences like (12a–b).[5]

(12) a. I read [[an article]$_i$ [that [x_i [discussed every woman]]]]. (unambiguous)
  b. I read [[an article]$_i$ [that [every woman [wrote x_i]]]]. (unambiguous)

We first consider (12a). After NP-adjunction applies, the partial LF representation of this sentence is (13a).[6] In this representation the head QP$_1$ of the complex NP is adjoined to the matrix VP and the QP$_2$ in the relative clause is adjoined to the embedded VP. Each variable in this representation is bound by its most local potential antecedent, satisfying the MBR. The nonovert operator is moved from x_2 position to Comp. Although the nonovert operator in Comp of the relative clause is coindexed with QP$_1$ by Predication, this nonovert operator is not relevant to determining the relative scope of QP$_1$. The elements relevant to determining the relative scope of the quantifiers in (13a) are the raised *every woman* and *an article*. This derives only the reading where the head QP$_1$ has wide scope, since the raised QP$_1$ c-commands QP$_2$. The nonambiguity of (12a) is thus accounted for.

The nonambiguity of (12b) is accounted for in exactly the same way. The partial LF representation of (12b) is (13b): the head QP$_1$ adjoins to the matrix VP; QP$_2$ in the subject position of the relative clause adjoins to IP; the nonovert operator (Op$_j$) moves from x_3 position, adjoining to the embedded VP and landing in (Spec of) Comp.

(13) a.
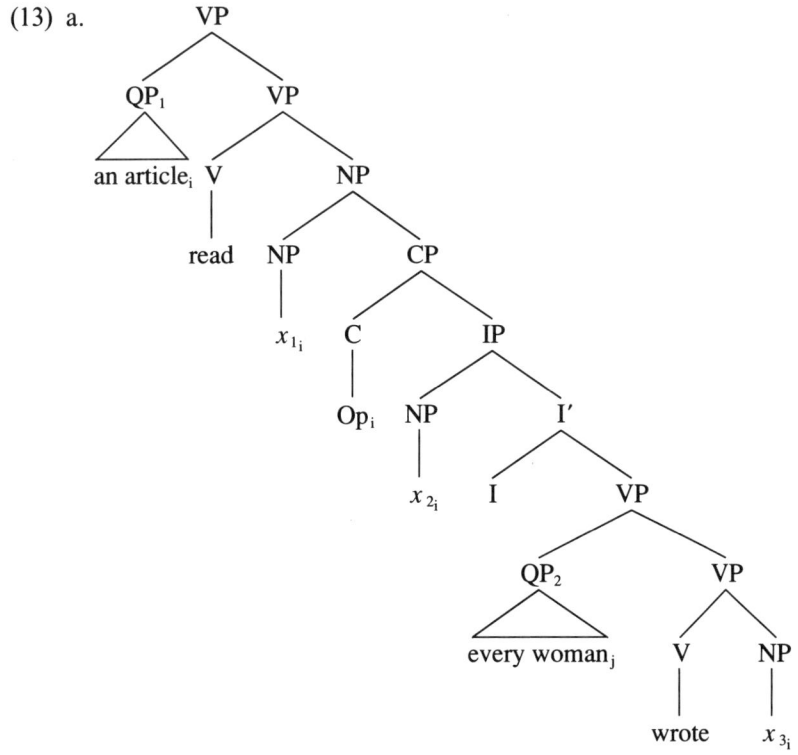

In this representation the elements that are relevant to determining scope relations are the raised *an article* and the raised *every woman*$_i$. Their interaction derives only the reading where QP_1 has wide scope because it c-commands QP_2. (12b) is therefore unambiguous. Note that in (13b), QP_2 c-commands the intermediate trace t_j that is coindexed with QP_1. Were the intermediate traces that are contained in composed chains relevant for scope interaction, (12b) would have the reading where QP_2 has wide scope; that is, it would be ambiguous.

Summarizing, the nonambiguity of the English sentences (12a–b) is straightforwardly accounted for by the MBR and the Scope Principle in case it is assumed that elements coindexed with the QPs via interpretive mechanisms are not relevant to determining relative scope. The same results hold in Chinese, as we will now show.

5.3 Chinese Complex NPs

The relevant cases involving complex NPs in Chinese are (14a–b). (14a) is unambiguous and (14b) is ambiguous.

(13) b.

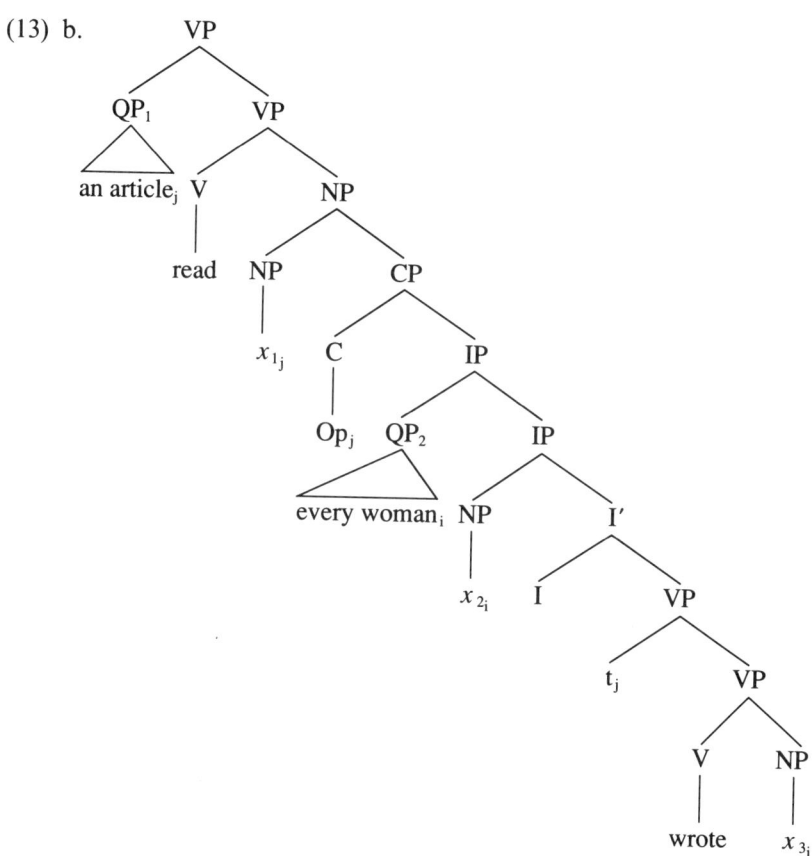

(14) a. Wo kanle [[x xie meige nuren de] [yipian wenzhang]].
    I   read   write every woman DE one   article
    'I read an article that discussed every woman.'

  b. Wo kanle [[meige nuren xie x] de [yipian wenzhang]].
    I   read every woman write   DE one   article
    'I read an article that every woman wrote.'

Whereas (14a), like its English counterpart (12a), is unambiguous, (14b), in contrast to its English counterpart (12b), is ambiguous.

We first consider (14a). The nonambiguity of (14a) is accounted for by the analysis proposed in the previous section. After QPs are raised, the partial LF representation of (14a) is (15a).[7] In (15) *every woman* can only adjoin to VP$_2$ of the relative clause. In this representation *an article* c-commands and has scope over *every woman*.

The ambiguity of (14b), however, is more surprising. The partial S-Structure representation of (14b) is (16).

(15)

(16)

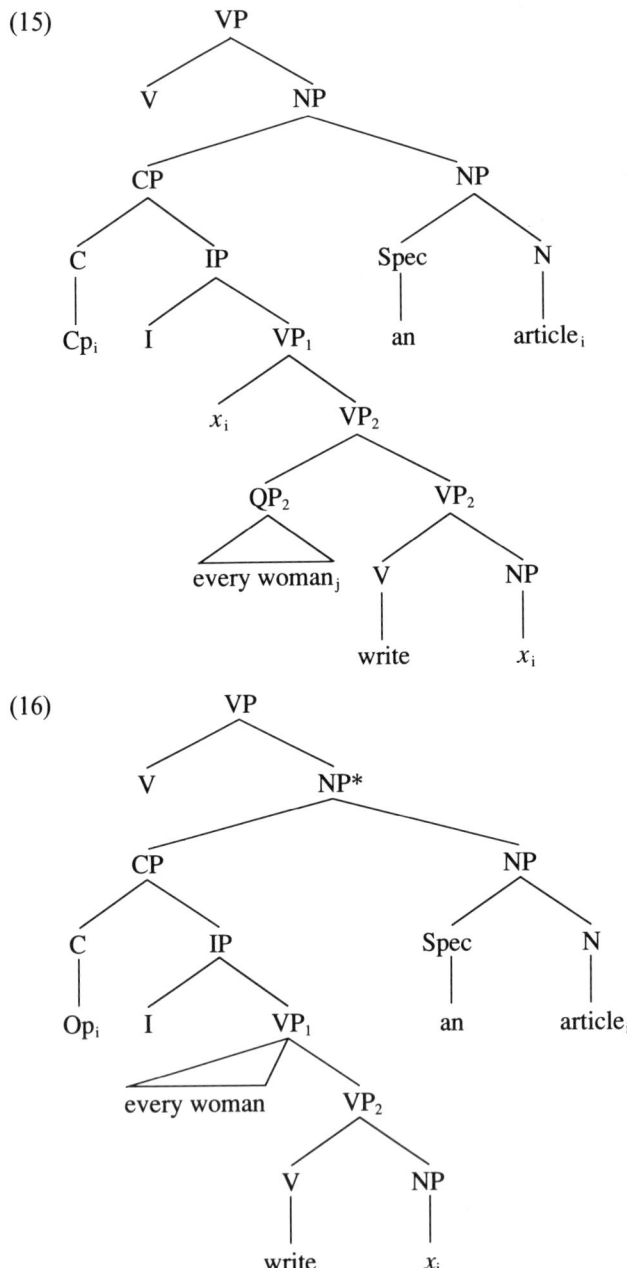

In (17) the subject QP *every woman* adjoins to IP and the relativized QP *an article* adjoins to the matrix VP, since the relative phrase NP* is an argument.

(17)
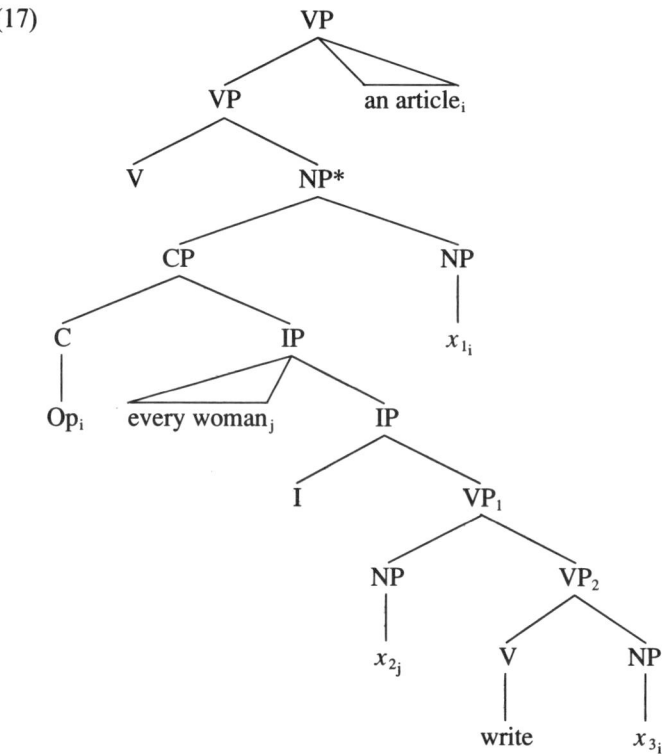

In section 5.2 we showed that the nonovert operator and the intermediate trace within the relative clause are not relevant to determining relative scope. The elements to which the Scope Principle is sensitive are the raised *an article* and *every woman*. The LF representation (17) generates the reading where *an article* has scope over *every woman* because the raised *an article* c-commands the raised *every woman*. In other words, (17) cannot generate the reading where the subject QP of the relative clause has scope over the relativized QP. However, this reading is possible for (14b). The ambiguity of the Chinese sentence (14b) thus suggests that the analysis of this sentence involves more than what has been assumed to this point.

5.3.1 Agr and Domain
We have so far assumed that variables must be bound by the most local potential $\bar{A}$ binder (the MBR). We have also assumed with Aoun and Hornstein (1985) that variables bound by QP-operators are subject to Principle A of the binding theory. Lee (1986) shows that this binding requirement on QP-variables captures some very interesting facts regard-

ing QP scope in Chinese. In particular, it accounts for the contrast between the ambiguity of (18a) and the nonambiguity of (18b). (For a detailed discussion of this locality requirement, see Lee 1986, sec. 1.3.3.)

(18) a. Wo xihuan [[sange ren xie] de shu].
   I like three men write DE book
   i. 'I like books written by a group of three people.'
   ii. 'There are three persons such that I like books of each of them.'
 b. Wo xihuan [[jieshao meige luyoudian] de shu].
   I like introduce every tourist-spot DE book
   'I like books that introduce every tourist spot.'

According to Lee, (18a) is ambiguous: the QP *three men* in the relative clause can have an NP-internal reading or an NP-external reading. In the first case the scope of the QP is restricted to the complex NP. In the second case the scope of the QP extends beyond the complex NP. In contrast, (18b) is not ambiguous: the QP *every tourist spot* in the relative clause can have only an NP-internal reading. In order to account for such a contrast, Lee assumes that traces of QPs must be $\bar{\text{A}}$-bound within their governing category. The governing category is the minimal clause or NP that contains the anaphor (the trace) and a subject. In a sentence containing a complex NP, schematically represented as in (19), the governing category for a QP-variable in the object position (NP_5) is the relative clause. On the other hand, the governing category for a QP-variable in the subject position of a relative clause (NP_4) is the higher clause (the matrix clause in this case) because Chinese lacks Agr(eement), as indicated by Huang (1982) (for further details, see Lee 1986, 165).

Since the governing category for a QP-variable in the object NP_5 position is the relative clause, a QP in NP_5 position can adjoin only to a position within the relative clause. A QP in NP_5 position thus has only an NP-internal interpretation. The governing category for a QP-variable in the subject NP_4 position is the matrix clause; therefore, a QP in NP_4 position can adjoin to a position outside the complex NP and thus has an NP-external reading.

According to the analysis presented so far, the behavior of QP-traces exactly parallels the behavior of standard short-distance anaphors such as the reflexive *taziji* 'himself', as in (20).

(19)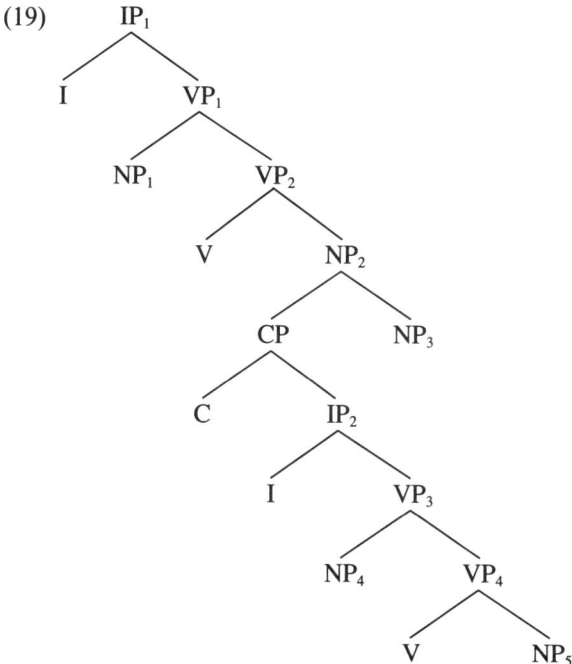

(20) a. Zhangsan$_i$ xihuan [[taziji$_i$ xie x] de shu].
    Zhangsan like   himself write DE book
    'Zhangsan likes the book that (Zhangsan) himself wrote.'

  b. Zhangsan$_i$ xihuan [[x_j da taziji$_{j,*i}$] de ren].
    Zhangsan like   hit himself DE man
    'Zhangsan likes the man that hit himself.'

Given the absence of Agr in Chinese, a reflexive in the subject position of the relative clause (see (20a)) has the matrix clause as governing category, and a reflexive in object position (see (20b)) has the relative clause as governing category. As a result, a reflexive in subject position can be bound by an antecedent in the matrix clause but a reflexive in the object position of the relative clause can be bound only by the antecedent in the relative clause.

In English, on the other hand, Agr defines the domain where an anaphor in the subject position must be bound. This is illustrated by the distribution of lexical anaphors in (21).

(21) a. *John$_i$ expects [that himself$_i$ came]].
  b. John$_i$ expects [that the man$_j$ hit himself$_{j,*i}$].

Coindexing *himself* with *John* is impossible in (21a–b): in (21a) the governing category for *himself* is the embedded clause because the embedded clause contains an Agr marker. In (21b) the governing category for *himself* is the embedded clause.

Similarly, the governing category for a QP-trace in either the subject or the object position of an embedded clause in English is the embedded clause. The embedded QPs in the following sentences cannot have matrix scope:

(22) a. Someone expects [that everyone came]].
    b. Someone expects [that the man hit everyone].

(22a) is to be contrasted with (23), where the QP in the subject position of the embedded infinitive can have matrix scope.

(23) Someone expects everyone to come.

Since an infinitive does not have Agr, the governing category for an anaphor in the subject position of the infinitive is the matrix clause, as indicated by the acceptability of a reflexive in this position (see Aoun and Hornstein 1985, Hornstein 1984 for a detailed discussion of (22a–b) and (23)):

(24) John$_i$ expects himself$_i$ to come.

In brief, a trace generated by the raising of QPs (the process of NP-adjunction of QR) must be $\bar{A}$-bound in a certain domain. NP-adjunction is thus constrained by such a locality condition. The locality condition and the absence of Agr account for the contrast between the Chinese sentences (18a) and (18b). With this established, we now can account for the ambiguity of the Chinese sentence (14b) and the nonambiguity of its English counterpart.

5.3.2 Analysis

Since the QP in the relative clause can only be raised within the relative clause in English, the nonambiguity of the English sentence (12b), repeated here, is accounted for as in section 5.1.

(12) b. I read [[an article]$_i$ that [$_{IP}$ every woman [wrote x_i]]].

We next turn to the corresponding Chinese sentence (14b), repeated here with its LF representation in (25).

(14) b. Wo kanle [[meige nuren xie x] de [yipian wenzhang]].
I read every woman write DE one article
'I read an article that every woman wrote.'

(25)

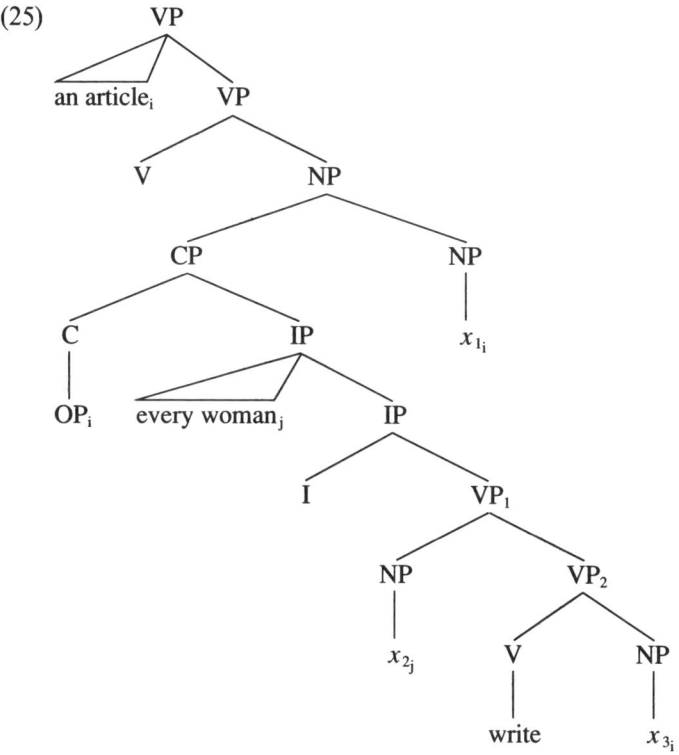

In (25) the elements that enter into scope relations are the raised *every woman* and *an article*. This yields only the reading where *an article* has wide scope, since it c-commands *every woman*. However, (14b) is ambiguous. There must exist another representation where *every woman* c-commands and has scope over *an article*. This representation is indeed available. The domain within which the QP-variable in the subject position of a relative clause in Chinese must be bound is not the relative clause itself but the superordinate clause, since Agr is lacking in this language. Thus, a QP in this subject position can be raised out of this relative clause. It can, for instance, be adjoined to the matrix VP. *An article* in this case need not undergo NP-adjunction, since (as shown in (26)) it is in a $\bar{\theta}$-marked position (the complex NP being the θ-role receiver).[8]

(26)

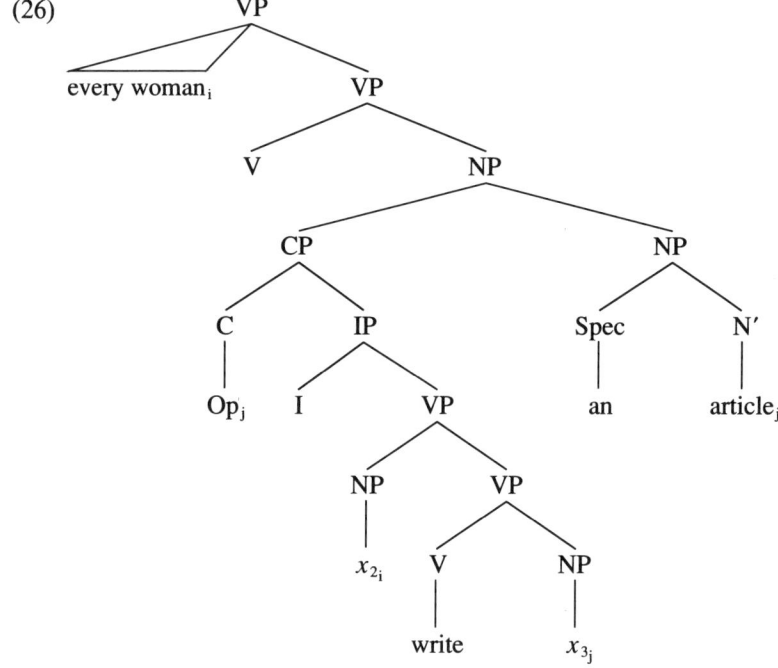

In this representation the raised QP *every woman* c-commands and thus has scope over the QP *an article*.

In brief, in an English relative clause, adjoining a subject QP to a position outside the complex NP is impossible. This is because the domain where QP-variables must be bound is the relative clause itself. The reading where the subject QP in the relative clause has scope over the head QP of the complex NP is thus impossible in the English sentence (12b). In contrast, in a Chinese relative clause, adjoining a subject QP to a position outside the complex NP is possible, since the domain where the QP-variable must be bound extends beyond the relative clause in this language. The contrast between the ambiguity of (14b) in Chinese and the nonambiguity of the corresponding (12b) in English can be derived from the fact that English, but not Chinese, has Agr.

5.3.3 Interaction with *dou*
In the previous section we offered an account for the ambiguity of the Chinese relative clause (14b) and for the nonambiguity of its English counterpart (12b). Surprisingly, the ambiguity of the Chinese sentence (14b) disappears when the quantifier in subject position occurs with the modifier *dou* 'all', as in (27).

(27) Wo kanle [[meige nuren *dou* xie   *x*] de [yipian wenzhang]].
I   read   every woman all write DE one   article
'I read an article that every woman wrote.'

(27) cannot have the interpretation where the subject QP has wide scope. Given that both sentences contain the same QPs in the same position, the contrast between the ambiguity of (14b) and the nonambiguity of (27) is puzzling.

To account for this contrast, we begin with a brief discussion of the function of *dou*. *Dou* 'all' in Chinese is referred to as a totalizing adverb (see Huang 1982), or a distributor, or a universal quantifier (Lee 1986, sec. 1.1). In general, *dou* can cooccur with a *wh*-word, a QP, or a plural NP. The *wh*-word or QP related to *dou* has a universal quantification interpretation.

(28) Shei/Meigeren/Tamen dou laile.
who/everyone/they   all came
'Everyone/They all came.'

Furthermore, *everyone* in subject position requires the presence of *dou* (29a–b) (Lee 1986), although *dou* is not required when the QP is in a relative clause (29c–d).[9]

(29) a. Meigeren *dou* zuole.
         everyone all has done
         'Everyone has done (it).'

     b. ??Meigeren zuole.
         everyone has done
         'Everyone has done (it).'

     c. [meigeren *dou* zuo] de shiqing
          everyone all   do DE thing
         'things that everyone does'

     d. [meigeren zuo] de shiqing
          everyone do   DE thing
         'things that everyone does'

Dou and the NP it is related to must obey certain structural constraints. Various proposals have been made to capture these constraints (see Lee 1986, Chiu 1990, and Li 1992b). In this work, we assume along the lines proposed by Li (1992b) that *dou* must be close enough to the NP related to it at LF (see Heim, Lasnik, and May's (1991) discussion of the distributor (D) in [NP, D]. For the sake of the presentation here, we will simply state that the LF locality requirement is one of government. This requirement captures the facts illustrated in (30)–(31), among others (for more details, see Li 1992b).

(30) a. Wo yiwei   naxie ren ta dou renshi.
       I   thought those men he all   know
       'I thought that those men, he all knows (knows all of them).'

   b. Wo yiwei   shei/meigeren ta dou renshi.
      I   thought who/everyone he all   know
      'I thought that who, he all knows (knows everyone).'

(31) a. Naxie ren wo yiwei   ta dou renshi.
       those men I thought he all   know
       'Those men, I thought that he all knows (all of them).'

   b. *Shei/Meigeren wo yiwei   ta dou renshi.
      who/everyone I   thought he all   know
      'Who, I thought that he all knows (knows everyone).'

In (30a–b) both *those men* and *who/everyone* can be topicalized to the beginning of the embedded clause and be related to *dou*. However, only *those men* can be topicalized to the matrix clause and related to *dou* in (31a–b). This contrast is accounted for by the requirement that *dou* and the NP it is related to must be in a government relation at LF. An important distinction between (31a) and (31b) is that *those men* in the former is not a quantificational expression but *who/everyone* in the latter are. Assume with Huang and Tang (1989) and Katada (1991) that only nonoperators moved to Ā-positions at S-Structure can be reconstructed at LF.[10] *Those men* in (31a) can be reconstructed to the embedded clause and have a structure similar to that of (30a). In contrast, the reconstruction process is not possible with *everyone/who* (also see Liu 1992). (31b) thus cannot have a structure similar to that of (30b). (31a) therefore is acceptable in the same way as (30a). (31b) is not acceptable: the absence of reconstruction makes it impossible for *dou* to govern the element it is related to at LF.

The LF government requirement on the relation between *dou* and its related NP also accounts for the contrast in (32a–b), if we assume with Lee (1986) that traces generated by QR in Chinese are subject to Principle A (see Hornstein 1984, Aoun and Hornstein 1985).

(32) a. [[Meigeren xie de] wenzhang] dou hen you yisi.
      everyone write DE article   all very have interest
      'Articles that everyone wrote are all interesting.'

  b. [[Xie meigeren de] wenzhang] dou hen you yisi.
      write everyone DE article   all very have interest
      'Articles that described everyone are all interesting.'

Unlike *everyone* in (32a), *everyone* in (32b) must have a group reading. This is because *everyone* in (32a), but not (32b), can be raised out of the relative clause to be in a government relation with *dou* and obtain the distributive interpretation. The requirement of Principle A on the traces generated by QR allows the subject of a relative clause in Chinese to be raised out of the relative clause (due to the absence of Agr in this language) but prohibits the object of a relative clause from being extracted from the relative clause (see Lee 1986 for details). Similarly, the QP in (32c) cannot be raised out of the relative clause because of the government requirement between *dou* and the related QP.

(32) c. Wo kanle [[meigeren dou xie] de wenzhang].
      I   read   everyone all write DE article
      'I read articles that everyone wrote.'

With this in mind, let us return to the contrast between the sentences in (14b) and (27). Given the government requirement on the relation between *dou* and the quantifier related to it, a QP cannot be raised to a position outside the government domain of *dou* (see (32c)). With respect to (27), the QP in the subject position of the relative clause cannot be extracted to a position outside the relative clause and c-command the QP in the head position of the complex NP. (27) therefore cannot have the reading where the subject QP has scope over the QP in the head position of the complex NP. In contrast, (14b) does not have *dou*. The subject QP can be raised out of the relative clause and c-command the head QP (Principle A allows the subject of a relative clause in Chinese to be raised out of a relative clause). This derives the reading where the subject QP has wide scope.

In the previous section we argued that the contrast between the ambiguity of (14b) in Chinese and the nonambiguity of the corresponding English sentence (12b) is due to the difference in the domain where QPs can be raised. Our analysis leads us to expect that the ambiguity of the Chinese sentence (14b) would cease to exist in case the subject QP cannot be raised out of the relative clause. We have now shown that this expectation is fulfilled. *Dou* restricts the domain within which a QP it is coindexed with can be raised. The lack of a wide scope reading for the subject QP in (27) thus supports the account provided in the previous section.

In the following section we discuss further cases of quantifier interaction within relative clauses.

5.3.4 Relative Clauses and Spec of NP

In Chinese a relative clause can either precede the Spec of NP, as in (33a), or follow the Spec of NP, as in (34b).

(33) a. [[ta xie   de] naben shu]
        he wrote DE that book

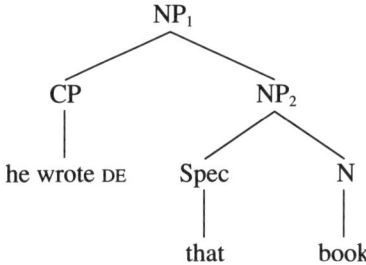

  b. [naben [ta xie   de] shu]
     that he wrote DE book

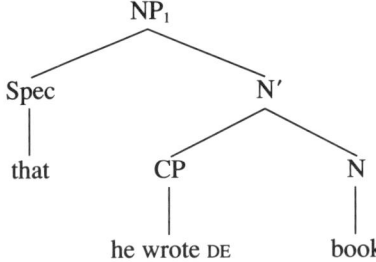

Since the configurations in (33a–b) show different c-command relations between the relative clause and the Spec of NP, we expect some difference between the possible adjunction sites of QPs in the relative clause. More precisely, the MBR would allow a QP in the relative clause of (33a) but not of (33b) to raise outside the complex NP. To see why, consider (34a) and its S-Structure representation (34b).

(34) a. [yipian   [meige nuren xie de [wenzhang]]]
        one + CL   every woman write DE article
        'an article that every woman wrote'

Construal, Indices, Domain, and Scope 141

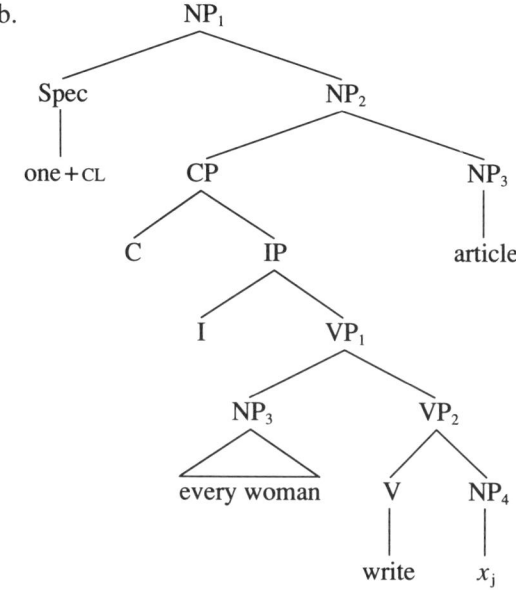

In this structure *one* + CL in Spec position can be raised outside the complex NP, NP_1. On the other hand, adjoining *every woman* to a node outside NP_1 is impossible, since such adjunction would violate the MBR. Since *every woman* cannot raise to a position c-commanding Spec of NP_1 in (34b), this QP cannot have scope over the QP *one* + CL in Spec of NP_1 position. (34a), in contrast to (14b), thus should be unambiguous. This indeed is the case: *one* + CL in (34a) must have wide scope.

For the sake of completeness, we would like to point out that the counterpart of (34a) where the QP in the relative clause occurs in the object position is also unambiguous. This is illustrated in (35a), with its S-Structure representation in (35b). Briefly, the generalization that QP-variables must be bound in the domain of a subject prevents a QP generated in the object position of the relative clause, NP_5 in (35b), from raising to a position outside this relative clause. The QP in the Spec of NP_1 position therefore must have scope over the QP in the object position of the relative clause.

Next we would like to briefly discuss the interaction of QPs and *wh*-operators in complex NP structures. Since a *wh*-element within a relative clause cannot occur without another *wh*-element in the (Spec of) matrix Comp in English,[11] it is hard to simply concentrate on the interaction of a *wh*-element and a QP within a complex NP in this language (see section

(35) a. [yipian [xie   meige nuren   de [wenzhang]]]
       one   write every woman DE article
       'an article that discussed every woman'

b.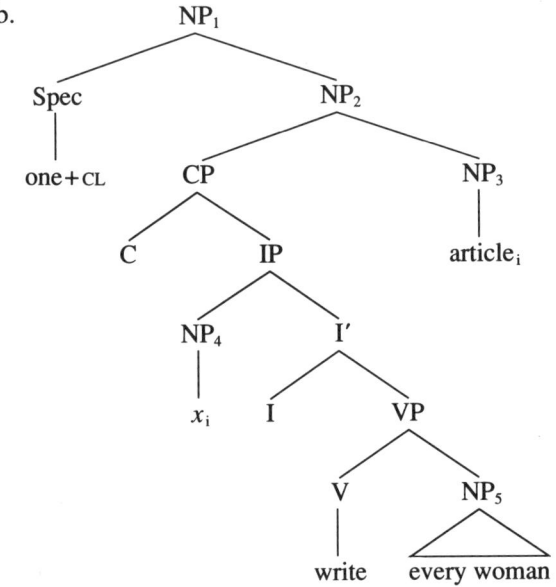

4.2.3.1 for the effect of Absorption on scope). We will therefore focus on the Chinese cases.

5.4 QP/*Wh* Interaction in Chinese Complex NPs

In Chinese a *wh*-word can occur in a relative clause (see Huang 1982):

(36) a. [[*Shei* xie   de] shu]   zui   hao?
        who   write DE book most good
        'The book that who wrote is the best?'

  b. [[Xie *shenme* de] shu] zui   hao?
      write what   DE book most good
      'The book that is about what is the best?'

Moreover, the relativized NP may be a *wh*-element:

(37) a. [[Ta xie   de] shenme shu]   zui   hao?
        he wrote DE what   book most good
        'What book that he wrote is the best?'

b. [[Xie ta de] shenme shu] zui hao?
   write him DE what book most good
   'What book about him is the best?'

Let us now consider the interaction of QPs and *wh*-operators in complex NPs. Four major cases need to be discussed. In the first case the *wh*-element occurs in the relativized NP position and the QP occurs in the object position of the relative clause. This case is represented in (38a) and illustrated in (38b). (38b) is unambiguous; the italicized *wh*-operator must have scope over the QP.

(38) a.

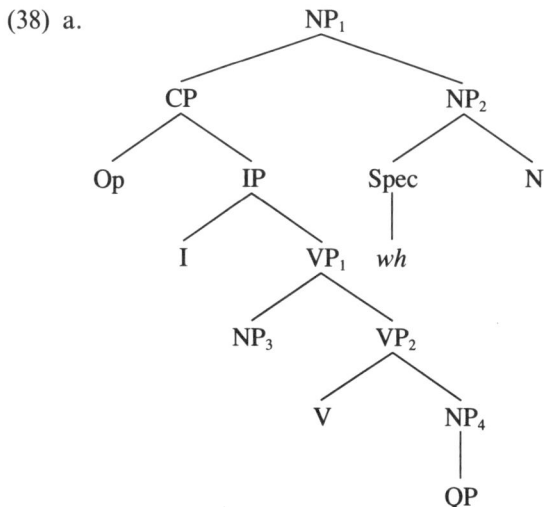

b. Ni yao [[e xie meigeren de] *shenme*   (unambiguous)
   you want   write everyone DE what
   wenzhang]?
   article
   'What article which is about everyone do you want?'

In the second case the QP occurs in the relativized NP position and the *wh*-element occurs in the object position of the relative clause. This case is represented in (39a) and illustrated in (39b), which is also unambiguous. The italicized *wh*-operator has wide scope.

(39) a.
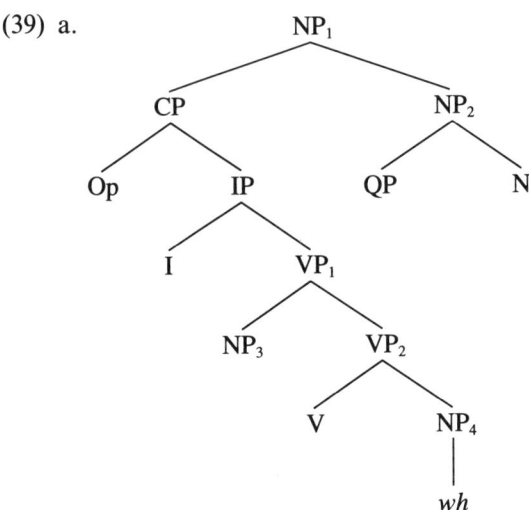

b. Ni yao [[e xie *shenme* de] meipian   (unambiguous)
you want   write what DE every
wenzhang]?
article
'Every article which is about what do you want?'

In the third case the *wh*-element occurs in the relativized NP position and the QP is in the subject position of the relative clause. This case is represented in (40a) and illustrated in (40b). (40b) is ambiguous: either the italicized QP or the italicized *wh*-operator may have wide scope.

(40) a.
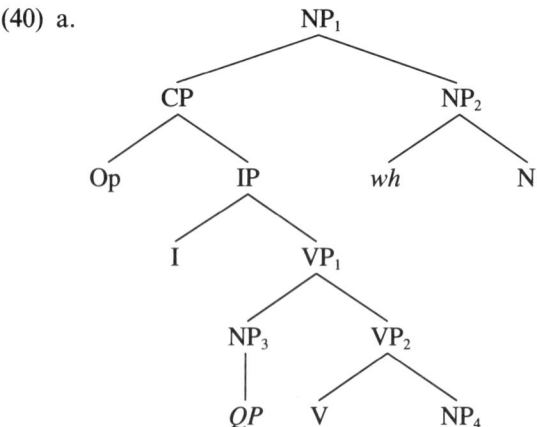

Construal, Indices, Domain, and Scope 145

b. Ni yao [[*meigeren* xie e de] *shenme*   (ambiguous)
   you want   everyone write DE what
   wenzhang]?
   article
   'What article which everyone wrote do you want?'

In the fourth case the QP occurs in the relativized NP position and the *wh*-element occurs in the subject position of the relative clause. This case is represented in (41a) and illustrated in (41b). (41b) is unambiguous. The italicized *wh*-operator has scope over the QP.

(41) a.

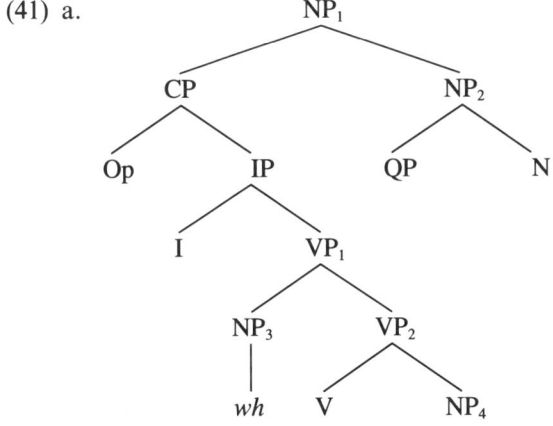

b. Ni yao [[*shei* xie e de] meipian   (unambiguous)
   you want   who write DE every
   wenzhang]?
   article
   'Every article which who wrote do you want?'

We first consider the interaction of operators in (38a). In this case the QP in the object position of the relative clause cannot be raised beyond the relative clause because of the locality condition on QPs (see section 5.3.1). The *wh*-element must move to Spec of Comp. There is no representation where the QP has scope over the *wh*-operator. (38b) is unambiguous: the *wh*-element has scope over the QP *everyone*.

Now consider (39b), where the QP is in the relativized NP position and the *wh*-element occurs in the object position of the relative clause. The S-Structure representation of (39b) is (39a). In (39a) the *wh*-word in the relative clause must move to the matrix Spec of Comp. The quantifier cannot adjoin to a position c-commanding the variable or any intermediate trace bound by the *wh*-operator; if it did the MBR would be violated. It therefore can only adjoin to NP_2, yielding the LF representation in (42).

(42)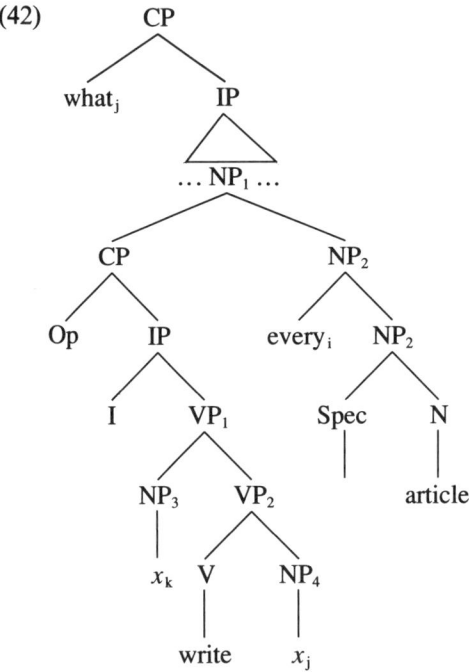

In this representation the raised *wh*-operator c-commands the QP, deriving only the interpretation where the *wh*-operator has wide scope. (39b) is unambiguous.

Next we consider (40a) and (41a), where the operator in the relativized NP position interacts with the operator in the subject position of the relative clause. We first discuss (41a), illustrated in (41b) (repeated here).

(41) b. Ni yao [[*shei* xie e de] meipian wenzhang]?
     you want who write DE every   article
     'Every article which who wrote do you want?'

As in (39b), the *wh*-word in (41b) is raised to Spec of Comp and the QP in the head NP position can only adjoin to the head NP because of the MBR. In the same way that (39b) is unambiguous, (41b) is unambiguous: the *wh*-operator has scope over the quantificational element.

Consider, finally, the case where the QP occurs in the subject position of the relative clause, as in (40b) (repeated here).

(40) b. Ni yao [[*meigeren* xie   e de] *shenme* wenzhang]?
       you want   everyone write DE what   article
       'What article which everyone wrote do you want?'

The operators in (40b) must be raised at LF. The *wh*-operator is raised to the matrix Spec of Comp. The QP cannot adjoin to a position c-commanding the trace generated by *wh*-raising. Our analysis leads us to expect (40b) to be unambiguous. Instead, however, it is ambiguous. The problem, then, is to generate the wide scope reading of the subject QP.

Recall the discussion of pied-piping in section 4.1. There we suggested that Move α at LF may pied-pipe the whole NP whenever the quantificational expression (the operator) occurs in the Spec position of an NP. Since the Spec of the complex NP in (40b) is a *wh*-element, the containing complex NP can undergo *wh*-raising at LF. After *wh*-raising raises the entire complex NP to Spec of Comp, the partial LF representation of (40b) will be (43).

(43) [$_{CP}$[$_{NP}$[$_{CP}$ meigeren xie   e de] shenme wenzhang]$_i$ [$_{IP}$ ni   yao x_i]]
          everyone write DE what   article   you want

After *wh*-raising, NP-adjunction can apply and raise *everyone*. This QP can adjoin to a node outside the relative clause, deriving the reading where the QP has scope over the *wh*-element. The ambiguity of (40b) thus is due to the possibility of pied-piping.

5.5 Summary

We recapitulate here the major points in our account for the complex NP cases in English and Chinese. Some of these cases involve QPs interacting with other QPs, illustrated in (12a–b) and (14a–b), repeated here.

(12) a. I read [[an article]$_i$ [that [x_i [t$_i$ [discussed   (unambiguous)
        every woman]]]]].

    b. I read [[an article]$_i$ that [every woman$_j$ [t$_j$ (unambiguous)
       [wrote x_i]]]].

(14) a. Wo kanle [[x_j xie   meige nuren] de [yipian   (unambiguous)
        I   read   write every woman DE one
        wenzhang]$_i$].
        article
        'I read an article that discussed every woman.'

b. Wo kanle [[meige nuren xie x_i] de [yipian   (ambiguous)
   I   read   every woman write   DE one
   wenzhang]$_i$].
   article
   'I read an article that every woman wrote.'

The account for these sentences can be summarized as follows.

(i) Elements coindexed with QPs or *wh*-elements via construal rules do not play a role in determining relative scope.

(ii) Variables generated by the LF raising of QPs must be bound within their governing category. The domain where a subject QP in the relative clause can be raised is different in English and Chinese. Because of the lack of Agr in Chinese, the subject QP in this language can be raised outside the relative clause. In English, however, the QP in the relative clause cannot be raised outside the relative clause because the clause itself contains Agr and counts as the governing category for this QP. The contrast between the behavior of QPs in complex NPs in English and their behavior in complex NPs in Chinese is thus due to the presence versus absence of Agr.

The proposed analysis accounts not only for the contrast between the English and Chinese sentences in (12) and (14) but also for the interaction of QPs with the adverbial *dou* 'all':

(iii) The relation between *dou* and its related QP must obey a government requirement at LF. This accounts for the contrast between (44a) and (44b), like the one between (14b) and (27).

(44) a. [[meige nuren   xie x] de [yipian wenzhang]]   (ambiguous)
        every woman write   DE one   article
        'an article that every woman wrote'

     b. [[meige nuren   *dou* xie x] de [yipian   (unambiguous)
        every woman all   write   DE one
        wenzhang]]
        article
        'an article that every woman wrote'

(iv) The contrast between sentences like (45a) and (45b) (cf. (14b), (34a)), where the ordering between the relative clause and the Spec of NP differs, is also accounted for by the MBR.

(45) a. [[meige nuren   xie x] de [yipian wenzhang]]   (ambiguous)
        every woman write   DE one   article
        'an article that every woman wrote.'

b. [yipian [meige nuren xie de [wenzhang]]] (unambiguous)
   one every woman write DE article
   'an article that every woman wrote'

The interaction of QPs with *wh*-operators in Chinese relative clauses is as indicated in the (b) sentences of (38)–(41), repeated here, where the element that has wide scope is italicized.

(38) b. Ni yao [[e xie meigeren de] *shenme* (unambiguous)
    you want write everyone DE what
    wenzhang]?
    article
    'What article which is about everyone do you want?'

(39) b. Ni yao [[e xie *shenme* de] meipian (unambiguous)
    you want write what DE every
    wenzhang]?
    article
    'Every article which is about what do you want?'

(40) b. Ni yao [[*meigeren* xie e de] *shenme* (ambiguous)
    you want everyone write DE what
    wenzhang]?
    article
    'What article which everyone wrote do you want?'

(41) b. Ni yao [[*shei* xie e de] meipian (unambiguous)
    you want who write DE every
    wenzhang]?
    article
    'Every article which who wrote do you want?'

The nonambiguity of (38b), (39b), and (41b) and the ambiguity of (40b) are straightforwardly accounted for by the MBR and the Scope Principle and the assumption that an NP whose specifier is quantificational (an operator) may undergo movement at LF.

Chapter 6
QP/*Wh*-Adjunct Interaction

In the previous chapters we have concentrated on the interaction of QPs with *wh*-operators such as *who* and *what*, which bind a variable in an argument position—that is, in a position that receives a grammatical function. In this chapter we will concentrate on the interaction of QPs with *wh*-adjuncts such as *when*, *where*, *how*, and *why*, which bind a variable in a nonargument position—that is, in a position that does not receive a grammatical function.

Wh-adjuncts do not display a uniform behavior in their interaction with QPs. Contrast, for instance, the behavior of *where* and *why* in the following sentences:

(1) a. Where did everyone hit him?   (ambiguous)
    b. Where did he hit everyone?   (unambiguous)
(2) a. Why did everyone hit him?   (unambiguous)
    b. Why did he hit everyone?   (unambiguous)

The behavior of *where* in (1a–b) parallels the familiar behavior of *who* and *what* that was extensively discussed in the previous chapters. The behavior of *why*, however, is puzzling and needs to be accounted for.

In the generative literature dealing with *wh*-interrogatives, a distinction is usually made between *when* and *where* on the one hand and *why* and *how* on the other. For instance, *when* and *where* can stay in situ in English, but *how* and *why* cannot (see Huang 1982):

(3) a. Who slept where?
    b. Who left when?
(4) a. *Who slept how?
    b. *Who left why?

This contrast is accounted for by the ECP (see Huang 1982). What is relevant for the purpose of our presentation is that *wh*-adjuncts are usually divided into two subclasses: the first contains locative and time adjuncts, *where* and *when*, and the second contains manner and reason adjuncts, *how* and *why*.

Given this classification, we expect the interaction of *when* with QPs to be similar to the interaction of *where* with QPs. Similarly, we expect *how*/QP interaction to be similar to *why*/QP interaction. This expectation seems to be fulfilled. The interaction of *when* with QPs is similar to the interaction of *where* with QPs as evidenced by (5a–b) (see (1a–b)).

(5) a. When did everyone hit him?   (ambiguous)
    b. When did he hit everyone?   (unambiguous)

For many speakers, the interaction of *how* with QPs also patterns with the interaction of *why* with QPs, as illustrated in (6) (see (2a–b)).

(6) a. How did everyone hit him?   (unambiguous)
    b. How did he hit everyone?   (unambiguous)

The problem, however, is that speakers' judgments concerning the interaction of *how* and *why* with QPs display much variation. For instance, some speakers find (2a) to be ambiguous, in contrast to (2b), which is not; and they find both (6a) and (6b) to be ambiguous. Others find no difference between *why* and *how*: both (6a) and (2a) are ambiguous, and both (6b) and (2b) are unambiguous.

The behavior of adjuncts in their interaction with QPs is puzzling, given the wide variations of judgments. In this chapter we attempt to provide an analysis of these problems along the lines established in the previous chapters. The discussions in this chapter ought to be construed as speculative rather than conclusive.

As a starting point in section 6.1, we discuss the nature of the distinction between adjuncts and arguments and the role that each of these elements plays in the argument structure of standard sentences. Based on this distinction, we provide an account for the behavior of *when* and *where* in section 6.2 and explore possible accounts for the behavior of *why* and *how* in English in section 6.3 and in Chinese in section 6.4. The discussion of the Chinese cases will lead us to reexamine the MBR and its relation to the binding theory.

6.1 A Typology of Adjuncts

Before discussing the interaction of the various types of adjunct QPs, we need to clarify what their properties are. We start first by distinguishing adjuncts such as *when* and *where* from adjuncts such as *how* and *why*.

Different *wh*-elements may be distinguished with respect to quantification. Essentially, *who* and *what* are operators ranging over (potentially) referential expressions, that is, over individuals. They bind variables that are referential expressions. The answers that generally satisfy questions with *who* or *what* are names for individuals. Furthermore, *who* and *what* have indexicals corresponding to them (*he, she, it*, ...). In this respect, *where* and *when* seem to pattern with *who* and *what*. In other words, *where* and *when* are also operators ranging over individuals, as suggested by the existence of indexicals such as *now, then, here* and *there* (see Aoun, Hornstein, and Sportiche 1981 for relevant discussion concerning these distinctions). In addition, answers to questions with *when* and *where* may be names of individuals (NPs), as in (7) and (8).[1]

(7) When did he come?
    this morning

(8) Where did he come from?
    some place outside of this world

Syntactically, *when* and *where*, like *who* and *what*, may occur in positions that generally take NPs, such as the object of a preposition (see Huang 1982, 536):[2]

(9) a. From where did he come?
    b. Since when have you been here?

(10) a. To whom did he speak?
     b. About what did he talk to you?

In various languages the counterparts of the English words *when* and *where* are true NPs. In Chinese, for instance, *when* is expressed as *shenme shihou* 'what time' and *where* as *shenme difang* 'what place', both NPs. *When* and *where* are thus like *who* and *what* in that they can be NPs themselves and can occur in typical NP positions. Furthermore, like *who* and *what*, they quantify over individuals. Since the gaps that *who* and *what* bind are treated as referential expressions, the gaps bound by *where* and *when* are also treated as referential expressions (see Aoun 1985, AHLW 1987): these gaps are subject to Principle C of the binding theory.[3] With Rizzi (1990) and Cinque (1990), it also is possible to assume that these elements are assigned "referential θ-roles."

In contrast, *why* and *how* quantify not over individuals but over propositions or predicates. Unlike *when* and *where*, *how* and *why* do not have corresponding indexicals. They are not NPs and therefore do not occur in the typical NP positions, as in (11)–(12) (Huang 1982, 536).

(11) *For why did he come?

(12) *By how did he come?

In contrast to the answers to questions with *where* and *when*, the answers to questions with *how* and *why* cannot be referential expressions. It thus is natural to assume that the gaps that *how* and *why* bind are not referential expressions (see Aoun 1985, AHLW 1987). Therefore, these gaps will not be subject to Principle C. With Rizzi (1990) and Cinque (1990), it is possible to assume that these elements are not assigned referential θ-roles.

In brief, *why* and *how* differ from *when*, *where*, *who*, and *what*. Categorially, the former cannot be treated as NPs but the latter can. With respect to quantification, the former quantify over propositions or predicates but the latter quantify over individuals. The gaps bound by *who/what/when/where* are treated as referential expressions, whereas the gaps bound by *how/why* are not referential expressions. In brief, we are distinguishing two types of *wh*-operators. One type binds gaps that are referential expressions and the other binds gaps that are not referential. The former consists of *who*, *what*, *where*, and *when*; the latter consists of *why* and *how*. Since *where*, *when*, *how*, and *why* have traditionally been referred to as adjuncts, in contrast to *who* and *what*, we will refer to *where* and *when* as *referential adjuncts* and to *how* and *why* as *nonreferential adjuncts*.[4]

A direct consequence of this classification is that arguments and referential adjuncts will display a parallel behavior with respect to various syntactic processes. This indeed seems to be the case. We noted earlier that referential adjuncts such as *when* and *where* can stay in situ in English but the nonreferential adjuncts such as *why* and *how* cannot (see (3)–(4)). In this respect, *when* and *where* behave like *who* and *what*, which can also stay in situ. (For an analysis of these facts, see Huang 1982.)

(13) a. Who saw what?
   b. What was given to whom?

Another piece of evidence for the fact that arguments and referential adjuncts display parallel behavior is provided by Chinese. Chinese lacks syntactic *wh*-movement. In this language, too, it is possible to justify the separation of nonreferential adjuncts from arguments and referential adjuncts. Indeed, the latter but not the former can have a wide scope reading in *wh*-island contexts such as the following:

(14) a. Ni xiang-zhidao shei maile   shenme?
       you wondered   who bought what

   b. Ni xiang-zhidao shei zai nar   shuijiao?
      you wondered   who at where slept
      'You wondered who slept where?'

   c. Ni xiang-zhidao shei shenme shihou likai?
      you wondered   who what   time   left
      'You wondered who left when?'

(15) a. Ni xiang-zhidao shei zenme likai?
       you wondered   who how   left

   b. Ni xiang-zhidao shei weishenme likai?
      you wondered   who why   left

In (14) the argument *what* and the referential adjuncts *where* and *when* can have a wide scope interpretation over the subject *who*. The behavior of these elements contrasts with the behavior of nonreferential adjuncts, which cannot have wide scope with respect to the subject *who* in (15); in other words, the scope of nonreferential adjuncts is restricted to the embedded clause. For the purpose of our discussion, it is important to note that arguments and referential adjuncts seem to form a natural class as opposed to nonreferential adjuncts (detailed analyses of these facts may be found in Huang 1982, Lasnik and Saito 1984, 1992, Aoun 1986, Chomsky 1986a, AHLW 1987, Cinque 1990, Rizzi 1990).[5]

Summarizing, we have indicated that *wh*-elements may be distinguished with respect to the type of variable they bind: arguments (*who*, *what*) and referential adjuncts (*where*, *when*) bind a gap that is a referential expression, and nonreferential adjuncts (*how*, *why*) bind a gap that is not a referential expression. Since only referential expressions are subject to Principle C, the distinction between the types of variables bound by *who/what/where/when* and *how/why* has implications for the interaction between QPs and *wh*-operators. We first discuss the interaction of QPs with *when* and *where* in section 6.2 and then the interaction of QPs with *how* and *why* in section 6.3.

6.2 Referential Adjuncts and QPs

The interaction of *wh*-operators such as *who* and *what* with QPs was discussed in chapters 2–5. The main contrast illustrating this interaction was the one given here in (16a–b).

(16) a. What did everyone see? (ambiguous)
     b. Who saw everything? (unambiguous)

Since *when* and *where* pattern with *who* and *what* (binding a variable that is treated as an R-expression), we expect *when* and *where* to behave exactly like *who* and *what*. This indeed is the case, as illustrated in (5a–b), repeated here as (17a–b), and in (18a–b).

(17) a. Where did everyone hit him? (ambiguous)
     b. Where did he hit everyone? (unambiguous)

(18) a. When did everyone hit him? (ambiguous)
     b. When did he hit everyone? (unambiguous)

(17a) and (18a), where the QP is in subject position, are ambiguous. On the other hand, (17b) and (18b), where the QP is in object position, are unambiguous. Since the variables bound by *where* and *when* and the variables bound by *who* and *what* are of the same type, the similarity between (16) on the one hand and (17)–(18) on the other hand is expected.

For the sake of completeness, we point out that in Chinese the interaction of *when* and *where* with QPs is exactly the same as the interaction of *who* and *what* with QPs:

(19) a. Meigeren dou maile   shenme? (ambiguous)
       everyone all   bought what

     b. Shei maile   meige dongxi? (unambiguous)
       who bought every thing

(20) a. Meigeren dou zai shenme shihou/difang maile (ambiguous)
       everyone all   at   what   time/place   bought
       dongxi?
       things
       'When/Where did everyone buy things?'

     b. Ta zai shenme shihou/difang maile   meige (unambiguous)
       he at   what   time/place   bought every
       dongxi?
       thing
       'When/Where did he buy everything?'

As expected, then, the interaction between QPs and *where*/*when* in both English and Chinese is similar to the interaction between QPs and *who*/*what*. Next we turn to the interaction of QPs with *how* and *why*.

6.3 Nonreferential Adjunct/QP Interaction in English

Consider the following paradigm involving QPs and nonreferential adjuncts such as *how* and *why*:

(21) a. Why did everyone hit him?   (unambiguous)
     b. Why did he hit everyone?   (unambiguous)
(22) a. How did everyone hit him?   (unambiguous)
     b. How did he hit everyone?   (unambiguous)

Examples like these raise two questions: the first concerns their well-formedness with respect to the MBR and the second the working of the Scope Principle in such sentences.

6.3.1 Adjuncts and the MBR

Let us first address the well-formedness of these sentences with respect to the MBR.[6] Bearing in mind that *how* and *why* do not quantify over individuals and that the variable they bind is therefore not treated as an R-expression and not subject to Principle C, consider (21) and (22). The LF representation of these sentences need not violate the MBR. For instance, consider the LF representation (23) of (21b). In (23) *why* is in Spec of Comp and *everyone* is adjoined to VP.

(23) $[_{CP}$ why$_i$ $[_{IP}$ he $[_{VP}$ everyone$_j$ $[_{VP}$ hit $x_j]]$ $x_i]]$

The MBR would not allow the adjunction of *everyone* to a position c-commanding the traces bound by *why*. For the LF representation of (22b), since the object QP cannot adjoin to a position c-commanding the variable bound by the *wh*-operator, (24) is the only well-formed representation (but see section 6.4.1).

(24) $[_{CP}$ how$_i$ $[_{IP}$ he $[_{VP}$ everyone$_j$ $[_{VP}$ hit $x_j]]$ $x_i]]$

Possible LF representations for (21a) and (22a) are (25a) and (25b), respectively. In these LF representations, the *wh*-operator moves to Spec of Comp and the subject QP adjoins to IP.

(25) a. $[_{CP}$ why$_j$ $[_{IP}$ everyone$_i$ $[_{IP}$ x_i [hit him $x_j]]]]$
     b. $[_{CP}$ how$_j$ $[_{IP}$ everyone$_i$ $[_{IP}$ x_i [hit him $x_j]]]]$

In (25a–b) the raised QP is the first available $\bar{A}$-binder for the variable bound by *how*/*why*; hence, a violation of the MBR occurs.

Other LF representations are available, however. Recall that an NP in a $\bar{\theta}$-position need not undergo NP-adjunction. If NP-adjunction does not apply to *everyone* in (21a) and (22a), we derive the following well-formed LF representations for these sentences:

(26) a. [$_{CP}$ why$_j$ [$_{IP}$ everyone [hit him] x_j]]
     b. [$_{CP}$ how$_j$ [$_{IP}$ everyone [hit him] x_j]]

For the sake of completeness, we should mention that the LF representations of (27a–b) need not violate the MBR.

(27) a. Why$_i$ did everyone say [$_{CP}$ t$_i$ [$_{IP}$ John betrayed him x_i]]?
     b. How$_i$ did everyone say [$_{CP}$ t$_i$ [$_{IP}$ John betrayed him x_i]]?
     c. Why$_i$ did Bill [$_{VP}$[$_{V'}$ say to everyone] [$_{CP}$ t$_i$ [$_{IP}$ John betrayed him x_i]]]?
     d. How$_i$ did Bill [$_{VP}$ [$_{V'}$ say to everyone] [$_{CP}$ t$_i$ [$_{IP}$ John betrayed him x_i]]]?

In (27a–b), as in (26a–b), NP-adjunction need not apply to *everyone*, which is in a $\bar{\theta}$-position. As for (27c–d), to the extent that they are acceptable they need not involve a violation of the MBR either since the QP *everyone* has the option of adjoining to V'. The LF representations of (27a–d) thus can be (28a–d).[7]

(28) a. why$_i$ did everyone say [$_{CP}$ t$_i$ [$_{IP}$ John betrayed him x_i]]
     b. how$_i$ did everyone say [$_{CP}$ t$_i$ [$_{IP}$ John betrayed him x_i]]
     c. why$_i$ did Bill [$_{VP}$[$_{V'}$ everyone$_j$ [$_{V'}$ say to x_j]] [$_{CP}$ t$_i$ [$_{IP}$ John betrayed him x_i]]]
     d. how$_i$ did Bill [$_{VP}$[$_{V'}$ everyone$_j$ [$_{V'}$ say to x_j]] [$_{CP}$ t$_i$ [$_{IP}$ John betrayed him x_i]]]

In brief, in the LF representations of sentences involving a nonreferential adjunct and a QP, the QP cannot come to c-command any gap bound by the nonreferential adjunct because of the MBR. This being the case, it comes as no surprise that these sentences are not ambiguous: since the *wh*-adjunct will always asymmetrically c-command the QP, it will have scope over the QP. This accounts for the nonambiguity of the sentences in (21), (22), and (27).

6.3.2 Variation concerning Nonreferential Adjuncts

So far the discussion of nonreferential adjuncts (*why/how*) and QPs has focused on the speakers for whom these nonreferential adjuncts necessarily have scope over the cooccurring QP. As indicated previously, however, there are also speakers for whom the interaction of nonreferential adjuncts and QPs can generate ambiguity, as illustrated in (29)–(30).

(29) a. Why did everyone hit him? (ambiguous)
   b. Why did he hit everyone? (unambiguous)

(30) a. How did everyone hit him? (ambiguous)
   b. How did he hit everyone? (ambiguous)

Finally, there are speakers who share the judgments in (29a–b) and (30a) but not (30b). The analysis explored so far has relied on the assumption that the gap left by a *wh*-adjunct such as *why* and *how* is not referential and is not subject to Principle C. As a result, no quantifier can intervene and c-command the gap left by a nonreferential adjunct (the MBR). If this analysis is on the right track, we cannot account for the ambiguity of (29a) and (30a–b) by assuming that the QP *everyone* c-commands the trace bound by the adjunct, as in (31) and (32a–b).

(31) $[_{CP}$ why$_j$ $[_{IP}$ everyone$_i$ $[_{IP}$ x_i [hit him x_j]]]]

(32) a. $[_{CP}$ how$_j$ $[_{IP}$ everyone$_i$ $[_{IP}$ x_i [hit him x_j]]]]
   b. $[_{CP}$ how$_j$ $[_{IP}$ everyone$_i$ $[_{IP}$ he [hit x_i x_j]]]]

There are empirical reasons supporting this conclusion. They clearly indicate that the ambiguity of (29a) and (30a–b) does not involve the trace left by the movement of the adjuncts. The relevant speakers distinguish between the ambiguous sentences (29a), (30a–b) and the nonambiguous sentences (33a–b).[8]

(33) a. Why$_i$ did everyone say $[_{CP}$ t$_i$ $[_{IP}$ John betrayed him x_i]]?
   b. How$_i$ did everyone say $[_{CP}$ t$_i$ $[_{IP}$ John betrayed him x_i]]?

For these speakers, the *wh*-adjunct originating in the embedded clause has scope over the QP in (33a–b). Were we to assume that traces bound by adjuncts contribute to the ambiguity of (29a), (30a–b), we would expect (33a–b) to be ambiguous.[9]

Thus, the following conclusions emerge from the discussion of the ambiguous sentences involving a nonreferential adjunct and a QP for the relevant speakers:

(34) a. The ambiguity in question does not involve any trace bound by the nonreferential adjunct.
   b. The contexts where this ambiguity arises are rather limited. Essentially, for an ambiguity to arise, the nonreferential adjunct and the QP must have been (base-)generated within the same clause (see the contrast between (29)–(30), (33)).
   c. Sentences involving *why* and a QP display scope ambiguity only when the QP is in subject position ((29a) vs. (29b)). On the other

hand, sentences involving *how* and a QP display scope ambiguity when the QP is in subject or object position (see (30a–b)).

6.3.3 Modification

Let us first consider a possible account for the facts reported in (29)–(30), according to which *how* and *why* differ in their interaction with an object QP. We would like to suggest that the difference in the ambiguity of such sentences involving *how* and *why* may be linked to the modification function of these words. *Modification* refers to the semantic relation between an adverb and an IP or a VP or between an adjective and a noun (see Jackendoff 1972, Zubizarreta 1987). Usually, the adverb is adjoined to the node it modifies. The semantic relation of Modification is realized in the syntactic configuration defined in (35) (see Zubizarreta 1987, 23).

(35) A modifies B in the context
 [c ... A ... B ...]
 iff C immediately dominates A and B, C is a projection of B, and B is not a head.

Generally, *why* is taken to modify a proposition and *how*, a predicate. Syntactically, then, we may assume that *why* is adjoined to IP (or a projection of Infl) and *how* to VP (or a projection of V), as in (36).

(36)

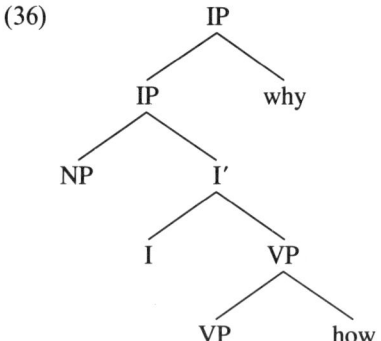

There is syntactic evidence that the non-*wh* adverbial corresponding to *why* occurs in a higher position than the non-*wh* adverbial corresponding to *how*, as illustrated by the ordering between these two types of elements in (37).

(37) a. He did it carefully because of its importance.
 b. *He did it because of its importance carefully.

The adverbial corresponding to *how* can be part of a VP, but the one corresponding to *why* cannot:

(38) a. He said he would type it carefully; and type it carefully he did.
b. *He said he would type it because it was important, and type it because it was important he did.

With this structural difference between *why* and *how*, we may attempt to capture the facts in (29)–(30) in the following way. Suppose an argument may have scope over an adjunct if it is coindexed with this adjunct. In (36) the subject can be coindexed with the head Infl, via Spec-head agreement. *Why* is coindexed with IP (or a projection of Infl) via modification relations; it thus is coindexed with the head Infl and the subject, as illustrated in (39).

(39)

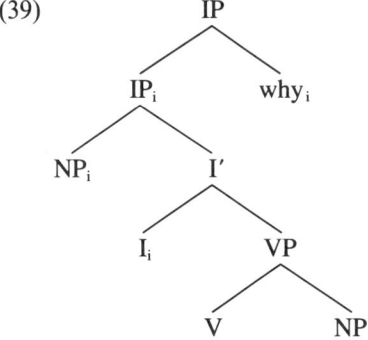

On the other hand, *why* is not coindexed with the object NP. A subject-object asymmetry thus arises.

Before considering the cases with *how*, we should state the assumption that is needed: a V (and the projections of V) carries the index of its arguments. That is, the lexicosemantic structure of a simple transitive verb such as *hit* is as in (40), where y = internal argument variable and x = external argument variable (see Williams 1980, 1987, Zubizarreta 1987, and Stowell 1989, 1991, among others, for detailed discussion of representations such as (40)).

(40) hit y; x

In a sentence such as (41), the index of *Mary* will assign a value to the external argument variable of *hit*, and *John* will assign a value to its internal argument variable (also cf. Higginbotham's (1983) and Williams's (1989) studies of argument saturation and θ-role assignment).

(41) Mary hit John.

With this in mind, let us return to the cases with *how*. *How* modifies a VP and thus is coindexed with it. Since VP, like V, carries the index of all the arguments, *how* is coindexed with these arguments (i.e., the subject and object NP), as in (42).

(42)
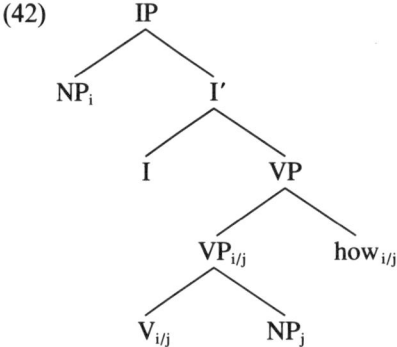

In brief, through Modification and Spec/head agreement, *why* ends up coindexed with the subject, and *how* ends up coindexed with the subject and object. If we take the possibility of coindexation to allow scope ambiguity, the subject-object asymmetry in (29) and the lack of such an asymmetry in (30) may be captured.

Finally, we need to determine why some speakers find (30b) unambiguous, even though they find (29a) and (30a) ambiguous and (29b) unambiguous. We will entertain several possibilities here, though none of them definitely resolves the issues.

First, there have been studies showing that *how* behaves more like *who* and *what* in various ways, such as obligatoriness with respect to movement (see, for instance, Rizzi 1990 for the proposal that *how*, like *who* and *what*, can stay in situ more readily than *why* in some languages) and the possibility of violating islands (see Tang's (1990) and Lin's (1991) studies of Chinese *wh*-words, contra Tsai's (1991) study showing that *how*, but not *why*, in Chinese can always violate island constraints). The similarity between *how* and *who/what* may explain why there is a subject-object asymmetry.

Another possibility is to assume that *how* is adjoined to a higher projection, such as the projection of small clause containing an internal subject and a VP (see Koopman and Sportiche 1991) or the projection of Predicate Phrase (see Bowers 1988, 1989), which contains a subject in the Spec of Predicate Phrase and a Predicate head taking a VP complement. *How* will then be coindexed with the Spec of the projection that it modifies (the subject), but not the object, just like *why*.

These options are essentially speculative, however, and we will not venture further to search for supporting or opposing arguments. Instead, we would like to return to the proposal according to which Modification accounts for the facts noted in (29)–(30), (see (34c)). This line of research may be promising, because it also sheds light on how to account for the limited contexts within which an ambiguity arises (see (34b)). (33a–b), repeated here, are not ambiguous because the adjuncts—or rather, the variable they bind—modify the embedded proposition or the embedded predicate. As a result, they do not end up coindexed with the arguments of the matrix clause.

(33) a. Why$_i$ did everyone say [$_{CP}$ t$_i$ [$_{IP}$ John betrayed him x_i]]?
 b. How$_i$ did everyone say [$_{CP}$ t$_i$ [$_{IP}$ John betrayed him x_i]]?

Recapitulating, the interaction of nonreferential adjuncts and quantificational elements is problematic because of the wide variation among speakers. Essentially, for some speakers (speakers A), this interaction does not generate any ambiguity (see (21)–(22)), and for others (speakers B), it generates an ambiguity in some rather limited contexts as indicated (see (29–30) and (34a–c)). This ambiguity does not involve any gap bound by the nonreferential adjunct. We showed that the nonambiguity of this interaction (speakers A) is not surprising. Since the gap left by adjuncts such as *why* and *how* is not referential, it is not subject to Principle C. Consequently, no quantifier can c-command any gap bound by these adjuncts; otherwise, the MBR would be violated. In other words, a quantifier will never be in a position to intervene between a gap coindexed with a nonreferential adjunct and this adjunct. This is why the interaction of *why* and *how* with QPs for speakers A does not generate any ambiguity. This analysis also explains why no gap could be involved in the ambiguous interaction of nonreferential adjuncts and QPs for speakers B. For these speakers, we suggested that the rather limited ambiguity generated by the interaction of nonreferential adjuncts and quantifiers is to be understood via the notion of modification. The interaction of *why* and *how* with QPs generates ambiguity only when these adjuncts, qua modifiers, end up coindexed with the quantifier. One may wonder in this respect how it is possible to characterize the difference between these speakers—or, to phrase the question slightly differently, why it is that some speakers do not use the Modification strategy in constructions involving nonreferential adjuncts and QPs. Clearly, it is not possible to claim that these speakers do not use the Modification strategy at all, since they make use of it in their interpretation of adverbs. Rather, we would surmise that the difference between the two sets of speakers may be understood as follows.

The working of Modification involves distinct requirements and operations:

(43) a. It operates in a specific structural context defined in (35).
  b. The modifier has access to the arguments of the element it modifies.

Usually, these operations involve a modifier that is overtly realized (an adverb, for instance) and the element that it modifies. It is possible to speculate that for speakers A, operation (43b) involves the modifier but not the gap (if any) coindexed with it. That is, the modifier itself must be in a context of modification in order for operation (43b) to take place. For example, in sentences such as (29)–(30), repeated here, the adjuncts *why* and *how* are in the Spec of Comp.

(29) a. Why did everyone hit him?
  b. Why did he hit everyone?

(30) a. How did everyone hit him?
  b. How did he hit everyone?

In other words, the adjuncts per se are not in the Modification context characterized in (35). Rather, the gap they are coindexed with is in such a context. Since we are assuming that for speakers A, operation (43b) is restricted to overt modifiers, it will not apply in (29)–(30). In these sentences, the overt modifier does not have access to the argument(s) of the element it modifies. These sentences are therefore not ambiguous. On the other hand, for speakers B, operation (43b) does not require the modifier itself to be in a context of Modification. It can take place when the gap left by the adjunct is in a Modification context. This is the case in (29)–(30).[10,11]

6.4 Nonreferential Adjunct/QP Interaction in Chinese

Having discussed the interaction of nonreferential adjuncts and QPs in English, we now turn to the interaction of these elements in Chinese. The interaction of nonreferential adjuncts and QPs in Chinese is very similar to the interaction of these elements in English. The interaction of QPs and *how* is shown in (29) and (44), and the interaction of QPs and *why* is shown in (30) and (45).

(29) a. How did everyone hit him? (ambiguous)

    b. How did he hit everyone? (ambiguous)

(44) a. Meigeren dou zenme da ta? (ambiguous)
      everyone all how hit him
      'How did everyone hit him?'

    b. Ta zenme da meigeren? (ambiguous)[12]
      he how hit everyone
      'How did he hit everyone?'

(30) a. Why did everyone hit him? (ambiguous)

    b. Why did he hit everyone? (unambiguous)

(45) a. Meigeren dou weishenme da ta? (ambiguous)
      everyone all why hit him
      'Why did everyone hit him?'

    b. Ta weishenme da meigeren? (unambiguous)
      he why hit everyone
      'Why did he hit everyone?'

Why in Chinese may occur before or after the subject. The interaction of *why* and a subject QP yields different interpretations when *why* occurs before the subject. The interpretation of (46) minimally contrasts with the interpretation of (45a).

(46) Weishenme meigeren dou da ta? (unambiguous)
     why everyone all hit him
     'Why did everyone hit him?'

The above paradigm raises the following questions: (i) How are the Chinese sentences well formed with respect to the MBR? (ii) How are the interpretations of these sentences derived?

6.4.1 The MBR

The well-formedness of these sentences (with respect to the MBR in particular) concerns us because, unlike subjects in English, subjects in Chinese occur in θ-positions. Recall that when a QP is in a θ-position, NP-adjunction must apply. This ought to derive the following LF representations for (44a) and (45a), representations that violate the MBR:

(47) a. $[_{CP}$ weishenme$_i$ $[_{IP}$ meigeren$_j$ $[_{IP}$ x_j dou$_j$ x_i $[_{VP}$ da ta]]]]
      why everyone all hit him

b. [$_{CP}$ zenme$_i$ [$_{IP}$ meigeren$_j$ [$_{IP}$ x_j dou$_j$ x_i [$_{VP}$ da ta]]]]
   how   everyone   all   hit him

One may suggest that, since *everyone* must be coindexed with *dou* (see the discussion in chapter 5), *dou* somehow plays a role in the well-formedness of LF representations like (47a–b). This is not possible, however, because the following sentence, which does not contain *dou*, is still acceptable:

(48) Ta gen meigeren zenme jieshi?
     he with everyone how explain
     'How did he explain to everyone?'

After the QP in (48) is raised, the LF representation would violate the MBR:

(49) [$_{CP}$ zenme$_i$ [$_{IP}$ ta [$_{VP}$ meigeren$_j$ [$_{VP}$[gen x_j] x_i jieshi]]]]
     how   he   everyone   with   explain

In this representation the first available binder for the variable coindexed with *how* is the raised *everyone*.

The acceptability of (48) and other sentences such as (44a), (45a) raises the issue of how the MBR is satisfied. A direct approach to this problem is to simply deny the relevance of the MBR in these cases—that is, to claim that *wh*-adjuncts and QPs do not interact with respect to the MBR. This in fact is the proposal made by Rizzi (1990). Rizzi distinguishes *wh*-adjuncts that are moved from Spec to Spec position and QPs that are adjoined to some projections. Specifier positions are different from adjoined positions. In terms of Rizzi's Relativized Minimality, QPs and *wh*-adjuncts do not serve as potential antecedents for each other's traces. Recast in our terms, *wh*-adjuncts and QPs will not be potential binders for each other's traces. They therefore will not interact with respect to the MBR.

However, this proposal is not consistent with the analysis discussed in the previous chapters. Recall that the contrast between sentences like (50a) and (50b) is attributed to their different LF representations. In particular, (50b) cannot have an LF representation like (51) because the raised QP will be the first potential antecedent for the variable generated by the movement of *who*.

(50) a. What did everyone buy?   (ambiguous)
     b. Who bought everything?   (unambiguous)

(51) *[$_{CP}$ who$_i$ [$_{IP}$ everything$_j$ [$_{IP}$ x_i [$_{VP}$ bought x_j]]]]

The claim that (51) violates the MBR indicates that an adjoined QP should be considered as a potential binder for the variable generated by *wh*-movement. Rizzi's account thus cannot be adopted directly.

We may search for other explanations for the noninteraction between QPs and *wh*-adjuncts with respect to the MBR. That is, we need to explain why QPs like *everyone* have a blocking effect on the extraction of *who* and *what* but not of *why* and *how*. Such an explanation may be available if we assume that a variable seeking its potential binder needs to consider the contents of the potential binder. QPs like *everyone* and *wh*-arguments like *who/what* share the property that they are operators binding a variable in an argument position. *Wh*-adjuncts such as *how* and *why*, on the other hand, bind a variable in an adjunct position. To put it differently, QPs and *wh*-arguments are participants of an event expressed in a proposition, whereas *wh*-adjuncts are modifiers of predicates or propositions. By refining the MBR along the lines of content-sensitivity, we may claim that the interaction of QPs and *wh*-adjuncts vacuously satisfies the MBR, since a raised QP is not a potential binder for the variable left by the raising of a *wh*-adjunct and vice versa. On the other hand, a QP will be a potential binder for the variable generated by the raising of a *wh*-argument. The contrast between (49) and (50) thus can be captured.

There is evidence suggesting that this distinction might be correct. For instance, a reason adverbial, which is generally in an adjoined position, seems to block the extraction of *why* (52a–b) but not the extraction of *who* (53).

(52) a. He said because of John that Harry killed Mary because of Bill.
   b.* Why did he say because of John that Harry killed Mary?

(53) Who did he say because of John that Harry killed?

Again, if the MBR requires a variable to look for a binder with the proper content, the contrast between (52b) and (53) is captured.

This proposal is not without its problems, however. It is not clear that *wh*-adjuncts can be clearly distinguished from QPs and *wh*-arguments with respect to the MBR. QPs and *wh*-arguments do not always behave alike, in contrast to *wh*-adjuncts. Consider the blocking effects of negation. Following Ross (1983), Travis (1984), and Kayne (1986, n. 17), Rizzi (1990) notes that negation interferes with extraction of adverbial elements but does not affect the extractability of arguments:

(54) a. It is for this reason that I believe that John was fired.
   b. It is for this reason that I don't believe that John was fired.

(54a) is ambiguous; the clefted adverbial can be construed with the main clause or with the embedded clause. (54b) is not ambiguous; the negation on the main verb blocks the lower construal. The argument-adjunct asymmetry is also illustrated by the following examples:

(55) a. What do you believe he weighed (last week)?
 b. What do you not believe he weighed (last week)?

(55a) allows both "Potatoes" and "200 pounds" as possible answers. (55b) allows only the first answer.

Given the earlier discussions, we expect negation not to interfere with the extraction of QPs, since QPs should pattern like arguments rather than adjuncts. This is not true, however. Negation does have an effect on the raising of QPs, as illustrated by the contrast between the ambiguity of (56a) and the lack of ambiguity of (56b).

(56) a. Someone loves everyone.
 b. Someone does not love everyone.

Someone in (56a) can have wide or narrow scope with respect to *everyone*. (56b), in contrast, allows only the reading where *someone* takes scope over *everyone*. This contrast can be accounted for if we assume that negation is a potential binder for the variable generated by QR: *everyone* needs to be raised to a position c-commanding the subject in order to take wide scope. This raising process will be ruled out by the MBR in (56b), because of the intervening negation. The contrast between (56a) and (56b) thus indicates that negation interferes with extraction of QPs.

We now face a dilemma. The facts indicate that QPs interfere with extraction of *wh*-arguments but not *wh*-adjuncts. Negation interferes with extraction of *wh*-adjuncts and QPs but not *wh*-arguments. If QPs interact with negation and negation interacts with *wh*-adjuncts, it is not clear why QPs do not interact with *wh*-adjuncts. If negation interacts with QPs and QPs interact with *wh*-arguments, it is not clear why negation does not interact with *wh*-arguments. The analysis discussed so far does not provide an answer. In what follows, we attempt to refine our analysis to accommodate these seemingly puzzling facts.

Let us first reconsider the types of elements in question. The generalizations are that negation interferes with extraction of QPs and *wh*-adjuncts but not of *wh*-arguments and that QPs interfere with extraction of *wh*-arguments and other QPs but not of *wh*-adjuncts. To understand why elements are grouped in such a way, we need to examine the characteristics of these elements to uncover their distinguishing properties. First, it is possible to make a distinction between QPs and *wh*-arguments on the one hand and *wh*-adjuncts on the other (the distinction necessary for the blocking effect of QPs), as suggested earlier. The former set includes elements that can be called "argument"-type operators: they bind a variable in an argument position. In contrast, the latter set includes only elements that are "adjunct"-type operators: they bind a variable in an adjunct position (see Aoun 1986, AHLW 1987, Rizzi 1990, Cinque 1990). The two sets of operators thus may be distinguished in terms of their content.

Next we consider the possible differences between *wh*-arguments on the one hand and *wh*-adjuncts and QPs on the other, the type of distinction required by the blocking effect of negation. As noted repeatedly in the literature, the extraction of *wh*-adjuncts and the raising of QPs are fairly restricted: these elements can only be extracted locally.[13] The apparent long-distance movement of *wh*-adjuncts must be achieved through successive-cyclic movement. In contrast, the movement of *wh*-arguments is generally unbounded. Successive-cyclic movement is not required. Various proposals have been put forward to account for the discrepancy between extraction of *wh*-arguments and extraction of *wh*-adjuncts (see Huang 1982, Lasnik and Saito 1984, 1992, Chomsky 1986a, Aoun 1986, AHLW 1987, Rizzi 1990, among others) or for the limited extraction of QPs (see Aoun and Hornstein 1985). The essence of these proposals is that variables bound by QPs and *wh*-adjuncts need to have an antecedent in a local domain, whereas variables bound by *wh*-arguments do not. The relevance of a local domain thus distinguishes these two sets of operators.

Briefly summarizing the discussion so far, the interaction of QPs, *wh*-elements, and negation led us to recognize the existence of the following generalizations:

(57) a. QPs interfere with extraction of *wh*-arguments and other QPs but not *wh*-adjuncts.

b. Negation interferes with extraction of *wh*-adjuncts and QPs but not *wh*-arguments.

We would like to suggest that these generalizations may be accounted for if a distinction is made between the domain, if any, in which a variable must be bound and the fact that it must have an antecedent. In other words, adopting the essence of the various proposals discussed in the previous paragraphs, we are assuming that some variables have a local domain in which they must find a binder and others do not have such a domain: variables bound by QPs or *wh*-adjuncts such as *why* and *how* need to have a binder and variables bound by *wh*-arguments need not. However, all variables should ultimately have a c-commanding antecedent. To see this distinction, consider (58). (The following discussion is based on Aoun 1986, 84–86.)

(58) Why$_i$ do you think [t$_i$ [John left x$_i$]]?

Here the domain in which the variable x_i left by the extraction of *why* must have a binder is the embedded clause. In this embedded clause, the binder of this variable is the empty category in the Spec of Comp t_i.. Moreover, assuming that every variable must ultimately be linked to an operator (see Chomsky 1982, Koopman and Sportiche 1982, and May 1985), the variable x_i in (58) is linked to the operator *why*, which serves as an antecedent for this variable.

A similar situation exists for anaphors. Consider (59).

(59) John$_i$ seems [t$_i$ to like himself$_i$].

In this sentence the reflexive has to be bound in the embedded clause; the binder is the trace t_i left by the extraction of the name *John*. Ultimately, this reflexive gets its actual reference from the name *John*, which serves as an antecedent for this variable.

A more striking example involves reciprocals. As discussed by Higginbotham (1980), Lebeaux (1983), Chomsky (1986b), and Heim, Lasnik, and May (HLM) (1991), (60a) is ambiguous. The ambiguity is described paraphrastically in (60b–c) (see HLM 1991, 84–85).

(60) a. John and Mary think they like each other.
 b. "John and Mary think they (John and Mary) like each other."
 c. "John think that he likes Mary and Mary thinks that she likes John."

Assuming with the above-mentioned authors that the ambiguity of (60a) is a matter of the scope of the reciprocal, (60b) is a paraphrase of the narrow reading and (60c) a paraphrase of the broad reading. According to HLM, the difference between the two readings is represented by (61a–b) ((67a–b) in HLM 1991, 85).

(61) a. [John and Mary$_1$ D] think [that [they$_1$ each$_2$] like [e$_2$ other]$_3$]
 b. [John and Mary$_1$ each$_2$] think [that they$_2$ like [e$_2$ other]$_3$]

In (61a) "...the pronoun picks up the reference of the NP *John and Mary*; in turn, this reference comes under the scope of a distributor, namely, that introduced by the extracted *each* attached to the pronoun" (HLM 1991, 85). In (61b) "...the pronoun is bound by the index of *each*, attached now to the matrix subject, and in turn it binds the trace of *each*, bringing this structure as well into compliance with Principle A [of the binding theory]" (p. 85). HLM further note that "to say that *each* can have broad scope is, on our view, tantamount to claiming that reciprocal expressions can have 'long-distance' antecedents. But, as is well known and as we have maintained, reciprocals are subject to Principle A of the binding theory, which requires that they have local antecedents" (pp. 96–97). This is precisely the point that we are stressing: a distinction should be recognized between the local binder an anaphor must have and the appropriate antecedent to which the anaphor must ultimately be linked.[14]

The discussion of (58)–(61) suggests that there are two requirements at work for anaphors and for variables: the requirement concerning the domain, if any, in which these elements must have a binder, and the requirement that they must have an appropriate antecedent. For anaphors, these two requirements are made to follow from the binding theory proposed by Chomsky (1981, chap. 3). The clearest case illustrating this involves sentences like (62).

(62) *[$_i$ For each other to win] Agr$_i$ would be difficult.

In such a sentence there is no governing category for the reciprocal because this anaphor has no accessible SUBJECT. As a result the binding theory is not relevant:

(63) a. An anaphor must be A-bound in its governing category.
   b. B is a governing category for A iff B is the minimal clause containing A, a governor of A, and a SUBJECT accessible to A.

Nothing rules out (62) unless the extension of the definition of governing category given in (63c) is incorporated (see Chomsky 1981, 220).

(63) c. A root sentence is a governing category for a governed anaphor that lacks an accessible subject.

According to the extension of the definition of governing category in (63c), the governing category for the reciprocal in (62), which lacks an accessible SUBJECT, is the root clause. In this clause, the binding theory is violated since the anaphor has no c-commanding binder.

The extension given in (63c) virtually amounts to saying that a governed anaphor should have a binder. In other words, the fact that an anaphor requires an antecedent is made to follow from the binding theory via the extension in (63c). In Aoun 1986, however, it is indicated that the extension of the definition of governing category can be dispensed with. The binding theory as formulated in (63a–c) is seen as conflating two requirements: the requirement concerning the domain in which an anaphor must have a binder, and the requirement that an anaphor must have an appropriate antecedent. It is argued there that these two requirements ought to be distinguished: binding theory should only characterize the domain, if any, in which an anaphor must have a binder. This theory does not specify that an anaphor ought to have an antecedent. This being the case, the extension of the definition of governing category can be dropped. For a sentence such as (62), the binding theory would be irrelevant: the anaphor does not have a governing category. However, as a general property, anaphors should have a c-commanding antecedent. This rules out (62). The requirement that anaphors should have a c-commanding antecedent may be made to follow from the fact that these elements do not have inherent reference. As in Chomsky 1981, it is possible to assume that these elements are potentially referential and that they pick their actual reference by virtue of being coindexed with an antecedent. This is why they need an antecedent.

In brief, instead of the binding theory formulated in (63a–c), we assume that anaphors are subject to two requirements: the requirement that they must have an antecedent (the antecedent requirement), and the requirement that specifies the domain, if any, in which they must have a binder (the locality requirement). A similar distinction between an antecedent requirement and a locality requirement may be at work for variables. Specifically, the antecedent requirement for variables requires these elements to seek the first available appropriate antecedent; this, essentially, is the MBR (see (64a)). The locality requirement specifies the domain in which variables subject to it have a binder (see (64b)).[15]

(64) a. *The Antecedent Requirement (The MBR)*
A variable must be bound by the most local potential antecedent.

b. *The Locality Requirement*
A variable, if it is subject to the Locality Requirement, must be bound by an $\bar{A}$-binder α within the minimal maximal category containing α and the variable.

A contains B iff B is dominated by all segments of A (see Chomsky's (1986a, 9) definition of exclusion and the relevant discussions in May 1985).[16]

The variables subject to the Locality Requirement are those bound by a nonargument *wh* or by a QP (and intermediate traces coindexed with adjuncts). In terms of the Generalized Binding approach (see Aoun 1985, 1986, AHLW 1987), these are variables that have an accessible SUBJECT. In terms of the Relativized Minimality approach (see Rizzi 1990), they will be the non-theta-marked variables. This last approach would have to be extended to include variables left by QR.

With this, let us return to (57a–b), repeated here.

(57) a. QPs interfere with extraction of *wh*-arguments and other QPs but not *wh*-adjuncts.
b. Negation interferes with extraction of *wh*-adjuncts and QPs but not *wh*-arguments.

We would like to suggest that (57a–b) can be captured by the Antecedent Requirement in (64a) and the Locality Requirement in (64b). (57a) will mainly be accounted for by the Antecedent Requirement and (57b) by the Locality Requirement. In order to illustrate how these requirements account for all the relevant cases, we discuss the paradigmatic examples in the following subsections.

6.4.1.1 QPs and Wh-Arguments The canonical sentences illustrating the interaction of QPs and *wh*-arguments are (65a) and (65b).

(65) a. What did everyone buy?
b. Who bought everything?

(65a–b) have the well-formed LF representations in (66a–b), respectively. (65b) cannot have the LF representation in (67).

(66) a. $[_{CP}$ what$_j$ $[_{IP}$ everyone$_i$ $[_{IP}$ x_i $[_{VP}$ buy x_j]]]]
b. $[_{CP}$ who$_i$ $[_{IP}$ x_i $[_{VP}$ everything$_j$ $[_{VP}$ bought x_j]]]]

(67) *$[_{CP}$ who$_i$ $[_{IP}$ everything$_j$ $[_{IP}$ x_i $[_{VP}$ bought x_j]]]]

Since the Locality Requirement is irrelevant for the variables generated by the movement of *wh*-arguments, we only need to consider the application of the Antecedent Requirement, which is the MBR. Since the representations in (66)–(67) have been accounted for by the MBR in earlier chapters, we will not repeat the account here.[17]

6.4.1.2 QPs and *Wh*-Adjuncts The representative sentences illustrating the interaction of QPs and *wh*-adjuncts are (68) and (69).

(68) a. Why did everyone hit him?
b. Why did he hit everyone?

(69) a. How did everyone hit him?
    b. How did he hit everyone?

The Antecedent Requirement will be vacuously satisfied in these cases because QPs and *wh*-adjuncts are different types of elements: they do not count as potential antecedents for each other's variables. We will therefore concentrate on the Locality Requirement. First, the LF representation of (68a) is (70a).

(70) a. [$_{CP}$ why$_j$ [$_{IP}$ everyone$_i$ [$_{IP}$ x_i hit him x_j]]]

The minimal maximal category within which the variable x_j must be bound is CP, since IP does not contain an $\bar{A}$-binder (the raised *everyone* is not contained in IP). This variable is bound by an $\bar{A}$-binder contained in CP (the raised *why*) and satisfies the Locality Requirement. So does the variable x_i. The minimal maximal category containing an $\bar{A}$-binder and this variable is also CP, again because not all segments of IP dominate the raised *everyone*.

This account thus allows not only (70b) to be a well-formed LF representation for (68b), but also (70c).[18]

(70) b. [$_{CP}$ why$_i$ [$_{IP}$ he [$_{VP}$ everyone$_j$ [$_{VP}$ hit x_j]] x_i]]
    c. [$_{CP}$ why$_i$ [$_{IP}$ everyone$_j$ [$_{IP}$ he [$_{VP}$ hit x_j]] x_i]]

The acceptability of (69a–b) can be accounted for along the same lines. Similarly, the problematic Chinese cases that prompted our reconsideration of the MBR are accounted for. To illustrate, (48), repeated here as (71a), now is well formed because it can have the well-formed LF representation in (71b). The LF representation (49), repeated here as (71c), is still ill formed because it fails to meet the Locality Requirement.

(71) a. Ta gen meigeren zenme jieshi?
    he with everyone how explain
    'How did he explain to everyone?'

  b. [$_{CP}$ zenme$_i$ [$_{IP}$ ta [$_{VP}$ t$_i$ [$_{VP}$ meigeren$_j$ [$_{VP}$[gen x_j] x_i jieshi]]]]]
     how he everyone with explain

  c. [$_{CP}$ zenme$_i$ [$_{IP}$ ta [$_{VP}$ meigeren$_j$ [$_{VP}$[gen x_j] x_i jieshi]]]]
     how he everyone with explain

In (71c) the minimal maximal category for the variable x_i is IP, which contains an $\bar{A}$-binder (the raised QP) and the variable. This variable is not bound in this domain. (71c) therefore is ruled out by the Locality Requirement. In (71b) the minimal maximal category where the variable x_i must

QP-*Wh*-Adjunct Interaction 175

be bound is still IP. This IP also contains an $\bar{\text{A}}$-binder (the intermediate trace bound by *how* or the raised QP) and the variable. In this case, however, unlike (71c), the variable x_i has an $\bar{\text{A}}$-binder contained in this domain, the intermediate trace bound by *how*. Similarly, the variable x_j is properly bound within its minimal maximal category IP, which contains an $\bar{\text{A}}$-binder and this variable. (71c) therefore is well formed and (71a) is acceptable.

6.4.1.3 QPs and Negation Before turning to the interaction of QPs with negation, we need to clarify our assumption concerning the structure of sentences involving negation. We will assume with Pollock (1989), Chomsky (1991) that negation heads its own phrase, the Negation Phrase (NegP). Moreover, we assume with Ouhalla (1990) that a negation operator occupies the Spec of Neg position.

The blocking effect on the raising of QPs by negation is illustrated by the nonambiguity of sentences like (72).

(72) Someone does not love everyone. (unambiguous)

As mentioned earlier, the lack of ambiguity in (72) indicates that *everyone* is not raised to a position higher than the subject QP; it is blocked by negation. The blocking effect of negation is accounted for by the Locality Requirement. (72) has the S-Structure representation in (73). (The IP has been split into Tense Phrase (TP), Agreement Phrase, Aspect Phrase, and so on; this does not affect the discussions below whether the highest node is marked as IP or TP.)

(73)
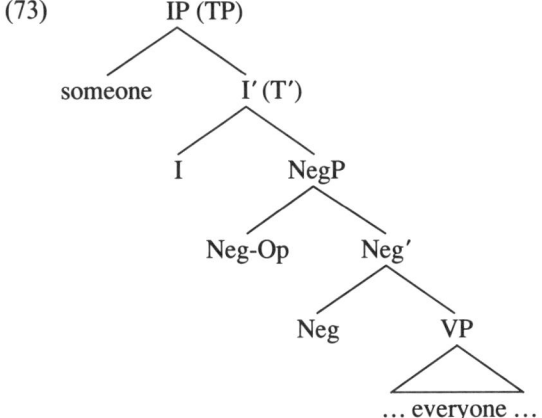

As illustrated in (74a), the object QP can adjoin to VP. If it is adjoined to VP, the minimal maximal category containing the variable and the raised *everyone* adjoined to VP will be the NegP. Within this domain, the object variable is properly bound.

(74) a.
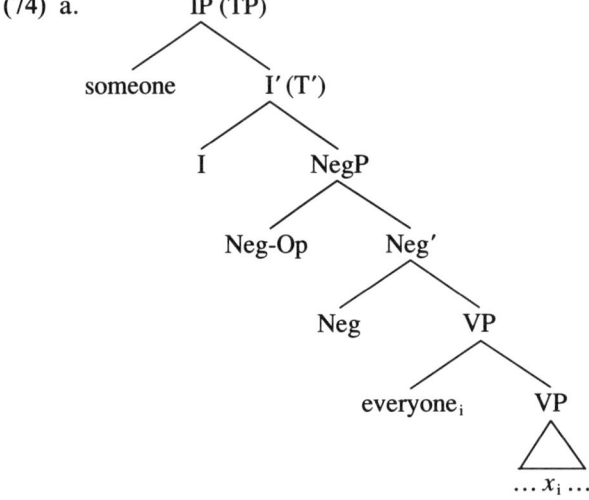

Alternatively, the object QP may adjoin to the NegP, as in (74b).

(74) b.
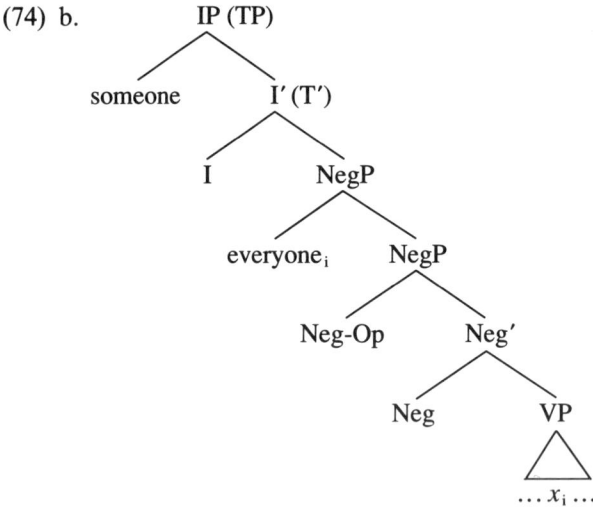

In this representation the minimal maximal category within which the object variable must be bound is the NegP, which contains the variable x_i and an $\bar{A}$-operator, the Neg operator.[19] The object variable is not bound by this Neg operator. (74b) therefore violates the Locality Requirement.[20]

QP-*Wh*-Adjunct Interaction 177

This account of the ill-formedness of (74b) suggests that negation in a sentence will always interfere with extraction of those elements subject to the Locality Requirement. An element E adjoined to the NegP or any higher projection, crossing the Neg operator, will always result in a violation of the Locality Requirement: the Neg operator will make the NegP immediately dominating it the *minimal* maximal projection containing an $\bar{A}$-binder to which the trace coindexed with the raised E must be bound. This explains why extraction of elements subject to the Locality Requirement cannot cross negation.

6.4.1.4 Negation and *Wh*-Adjuncts Just like QPs, *wh*-adjuncts such as *why* and *how* cannot move across negation. A representative case, (55b), repeated here with the LF representation in (75), will be ill formed (*what* being interpreted as an adjunct, i.e., the answer being "200 pounds").[21]

(55) b. What do you not believe he weighed (last week)?

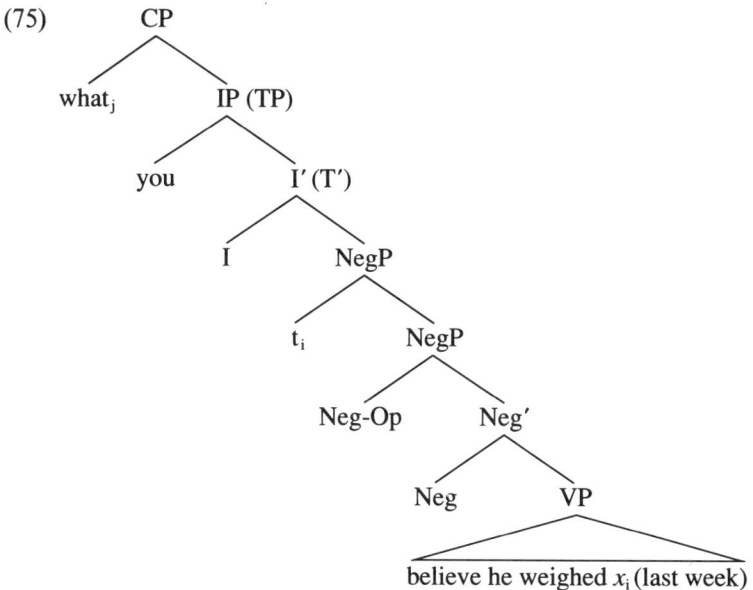

6.4.1.5 Negation and *Wh*-Arguments Since *wh*-arguments are not subject to the Locality Requirement, negation does not interfere with extraction of *wh*-arguments.

The introduction of the Locality Requirement and the Antecedent Requirement (the MBR) thus captures the interaction between *wh*-arguments, *wh*-adjuncts, QPs, and negation with respect to their interference with extraction. This discussion also clarifies the relation of the MBR to the locality effects (the Locality Requirement). In the previous chapters we focused on establishing the MBR and on illustrating its applications. The MBR only requires a variable to be bound by an antecedent that is most local to it. It does not specify the domain, if any, within which a variable must be bound. This is dealt with by the Locality Requirement. Next we turn to the scope interaction of QPs and *wh*-adjuncts.

6.4.2 Scope

We have shown that LF representation (70c) for sentence (68b), repeated here, satisfies the Locality requirement.

(68) b. Why did he hit everyone?

(70) c. [$_{CP}$ why$_i$ [$_{IP}$ everyone$_j$ [$_{IP}$ he [$_{VP}$ hit x_j]] x_i]]

The possibility of an LF representation like (70c) raises the question of how the relative scope between QPs and *wh*-adjuncts should be determined. According to the Scope Principle, (70c) would be ambiguous: the raised QP is c-commanded by the moved *wh*-element and in turn c-commands the variable generated by *wh*-movement. Under the assumption that the variable bound by an adjunct is in an $\bar{\text{A}}$-position, it should play a role when the Scope Principle applies. Similarly, the intermediate trace bound by *why* adjoined to IP, illustrated in (76), should also play a role in determining the relative scope.

(76) [$_{CP}$ why$_i$ [$_{IP}$ everyone$_j$ [$_{IP}$ t$_i$ [$_{IP}$ he [$_{VP}$ hit x_j]] x_i]]]

Nevertheless, (68b) is unambiguous. Such an ambiguity arises if the adjunct has access to the index of the QP. In (68b), for instance, *why* modifies the proposition. The object QP is contained in the proposition. As stated earlier, *why* does not have access to the index of the object QP. (68b) therefore is unambiguous. With this, we turn to the determination of relative scope between QPs and *wh*-adjuncts in Chinese.

We start with the canonical sentences involving the interaction of nonreferential adjuncts and QPs, (44a–b) and (45a–b), repeated here.

(44) a. Meigeren dou zenme da ta? (ambiguous)
everyone all how hit him
'How did everyone hit him?'

b. Ta zenme da meigeren? (ambiguous)
he how hit everyone
'How did he hit everyone?'

(45) a. Meigeren dou weishenme da ta? (ambiguous)
　　　 everyone all　why　　　 hit him
　　　 'Why did everyone hit him?'

　　b. Ta weishenme da meigeren? (ambiguous)
　　　 he why　　　 hit everyone
　　　 'Why did he hit everyone?'

We first discuss the cases involving the interaction of *how* with QPs (section 6.4.2.1) and then those involving the interaction of *why* with QPs (section 6.4.2.2).

6.4.2.1 *How* and QPs As discussed in section 6.3.3, the modification relation is the main factor determining the relative scope between *wh*-adjuncts and QPs. Thus, the Chinese sentences (44a–b) are ambiguous for the same reason as the English sentences (29a–b).

There is empirical evidence from constructions involving the interaction of *how* and QPs in Chinese showing that indeed it is the modification relation that determines the relative scope of these elements, rather than the chain of operators and traces in $\bar{\text{A}}$-positions considered by the Scope Principle. If the chain were to be considered, we would expect sentences of the following form in Chinese always to be ambiguous:

(77) QP...*how/why*

As long as (77) is acceptable, the *wh*-adjunct can leave a trace (and an intermediate trace) in a position c-commanded by the QP. In this case (77) can have the well-formed LF representation in (78), which ought to yield ambiguity.

(78) $[_{\text{CP}}$ how/why$_i$...QP$_j$...x_j...(t$_i$)...$x_i]$

This expectation is not fulfilled, however. The sentences in (79) have the form in (77) but are not ambiguous.

(79) a. Ta dui meigeren shuo ni　 zenme jieshi　 zheijian shi?
　　　 he to　everyone say　you how　 explain this　　 matter
　　　 'How did he say to everyone you explained this matter?'

　　b. Meigeren dou yiwei ta zenme jieshi　 zheijian shi?
　　　 everyone all　think he how　 explain this　　 matter
　　　 'How does everyone think he explained this matter?'

　　c. Ta hui wei meigeren de mianzi zenme jiejue zhege wenti　 ne?
　　　 he will for everyone DE face　 how　 solve this　problem Q
　　　 'How will he solve this problem for the sake of everyone's face?'

The LF representations of (79a–c) can be (80a–c).

(80) a. [$_{CP}$ zenme$_j$ [$_{IP}$ ta [$_{VP}$ meigeren$_i$ [$_{VP}$ dui x_i ([$_{VP}$ t$_j$)
　　　　　how　　　he　　everyone　　to
　　　[$_{VP}$ x_j [$_{VP}$ shuo [$_{CP}$ ni　x_j jieshi　zheijian shi]]]]]]]]
　　　　　say　　　you　explain this　matter

　b. [$_{CP}$ zenme$_j$ [$_{IP}$ meigeren$_i$ dou$_i$ [$_{VP}$ t$_j$
　　　　how　　　　everyone　all
　　　[$_{VP}$ yiwei [$_{CP}$ ta x_j jieshi　zheijian shi]]]]]
　　　　think　　he　explain this　matter

　c. [$_{CP}$ zenme$_j$ [$_{IP}$ ta hui [$_{VP}$ meigeren$_i$ [$_{VP}$ wei x_i mianzi ([$_{VP}$ t$_j$)
　　　　how　　　he will　everyone　for　face
　　　[$_{VP}$ x_j jiejue zhege wenti]]]]]]
　　　　solve this　problem

The nonambiguity of (79a–c) indicates that the variable (and intermediate traces) bound by adjunct *wh*-elements in (77) cannot play a role in determining relative scope.

In brief, various empirical considerations suggests that variables and intermediate traces bound by *how* cannot play a role in determining scope interaction with QPs. The ambiguity of (44a–b) will thus be attributed to Modification, just like the ambiguity of the corresponding English cases (29a–b), *How did everyone hit him?* and *How did he hit everyone?* This account leads us to expect that the ambiguity will be lost in cases where *how* does not have access to the argument NPs in the matrix clause. This is the case, as illustrated by the nonambiguity of (79a–c).

6.4.2.2 *Why* and QPs We now proceed to account for the interaction of *why* with QPs in Chinese. The canonical cases are illustrated in (45a–b), repeated here.

(45) a. Meigeren dou weishenme da ta?　　　　　(ambiguous)
　　　everyone all why　　hit him
　　　'Why did everyone hit him?'

　b. Ta weishenme da meigeren?　　　　　　(unambiguous)
　　　he why　　　hit everyone
　　　'Why did he hit everyone?'

The nonambiguity of (45b) is expected: the LF representation of this sentence is (81). The QP is contained in the proposition modified by *why*. *Why*, modifying a proposition, does not have access to an object NP.

(81) [$_{CP}$ weishenme$_i$ [$_{IP}$ ta x_i [$_{VP}$ meigeren$_j$ [$_{VP}$ də x_j]]]]
    why   he   everyone   hit

The ambiguity of (45a) is also expected if the analysis of the corresponding English sentence (29a) *Why did everyone hit him?* applies straightforwardly to this sentence: *why* modifies an IP and hence ends up coindexed with the subject through Infl. Furthermore, just like the English sentence (33a), where the QP is in the matrix clause and the *wh*-operator originated in the embedded clause, the Chinese sentences (82a–b) are unambiguous.

(33) a. Why$_i$ did everyone say [John betrayed him x_i]?

(82) a. Ta dui meigeren shuo ni weishenme jieshi zheijian shi?
       he to everyone say you why explain this matter
       'Why did he say to everyone you explained this matter?'

   b. Meigeren dou yiwei ta weisheme jieshi zheijian shi?
       everyone all think he why explain this matter
       'Why does everyone think he explained this matter?'

Despite the fact that the above analysis accounts for the interpretation of (44a–b), it does not straightforwardly account for the nonambiguity of (46), repeated here.

(46) Weishenme meigeren dou da ta?   (unambiguous)
     why   everyone all hit him
     'Why did everyone hit him?'

We would expect (46) to be ambiguous, just like (45a), if *why* were coindexed with the subject through Infl. The nonambiguity of (46) may be accounted for if we assume with Rizzi (1990) and Lin (1991) that *why* can be base-generated in Spec of Comp. Suppose that *why* is always base-generated in Spec of Comp when it precedes the subject. Then it will not be sister to IP, and therefore, it will not be coindexed with Spec of IP. The lack of ambiguity thus is expected.

If *why* can be base-generated in Spec of Comp, the ambiguity of (45a) may be attributed to the ambiguity of the position where *why* can be base-generated. Alternatively, its ambiguity can be understood in light of the following considerations involving the interaction of adverbs with other adverbs. *Dou* 'all', which is an adverb, interacts with other adverbs and yields different scope relations depending on the linear order of these elements (see Huang 1982, Ernst 1991):

(83) a. Tamen dou you laile.
　　　　they　all　again came
　　　　'For all of them, they came again.'
　　b. Tamen you dou laile.
　　　　they　again all came
　　　　'It is again the case that they all came.'

In (83a) *dou* has scope over *you* 'again'; in (83b) *you* has scope over *dou*. The contrast between (83a) and (83b) is expected if we assume with Huang (1982) that Chinese essentially has binary branching structures. That is, (83a–b) have the structures in (84a–b), where the higher adverb has scope over the lower adverb.

(84)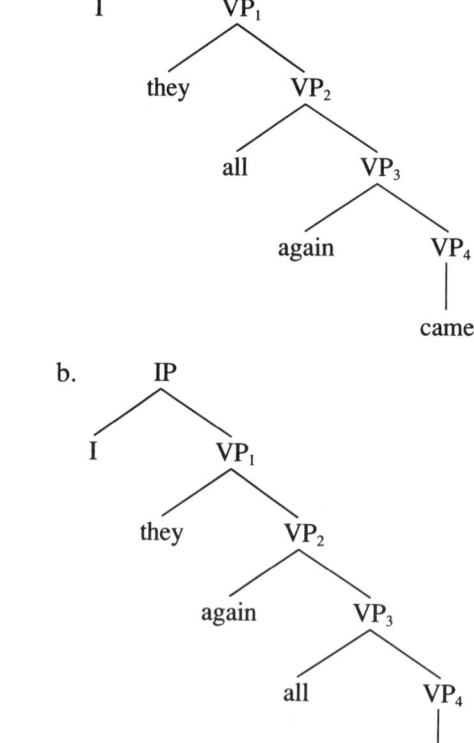

In brief, *dou* is just like a regular adverb that takes scope over the following adverb (the adverb having wide scope is italicized):

(85) a. Ta *mei* changchang lai.
　　　　he not often　　　come
　　　　'He did not come often.'

　　b. Ta *changchang* mei lai.
　　　　he often　　　not come
　　　　'He often did not come.'

(86) a. Ta *changchang* zai xuexiao kan shu.
　　　　he often　　　at school read book
　　　　'He often reads at school.'

　　b. Ta *zai xuexiao* changchang kan shu.
　　　　he at school often　　　read book
　　　　'At school, he often reads.'

(87) further illustrates the interaction between *dou* and other adverbial elements:

(87) a. Tamen *dou* bu lai.
　　　　they all not come
　　　　'All of them will not come.'

　　b. Tamen *bu* dou lai.
　　　　they not all come
　　　　'Not all of them will come.'

All of the above examples show that *dou* is a scope-bearing element and that it has scope over the adverb to its right.

A final clarification concerning the determination of the relative scope of adverbs is in order. In a sentence like (88), although the matrix adverb does c-command the embedded adverb, it does not have scope over it.

(88) Ta changchang shuo ni mei lai.
　　　he often　　　say you not come
　　　'He often says that you did not come.'

The scopal interaction of adverbs seems to occur only when these elements are generated within the same clause. Consider (89a–b), for instance.

(89) a. Ta changchang shuo ni lai guo.
　　　　he often　　　say you come ASP
　　　　'He often says that you have been here.'

b. Ta mei shuo ni lai guo.
   he not say you come ASP
   'He did not say that you have been here.'

Changchang 'often' in (89a) and the negation marker in (89b) modify only *shuo* 'say' and do not modify any element in the embedded clause.

This restriction concerning the interaction of adverbs can once again be understood in light of the notion of modification discussed in section 6.3.3. There we assumed that Modification is realized in the syntactic configuration defined in (35), repeated here.

(35) A modifies B in the context
   $[_C \ldots A \ldots B \ldots]$
   iff C immediately dominates A and B, C is a projection of B, and B is not a head.

In a configuration like (84a), *again* modifies VP_4 and *all* modifies VP_3. In this configuration *all* has scope over *again*. On the other hand, in (84b) *all* modifies VP_4 and *again* modifies VP_3. In this configuration *again* has scope over *all*. It is now clear that the restriction concerning the clause-boundedness of adverbial scope can be accounted for if we assume that the scope of an adverb is restricted to the elements immediately dominated by the phrase it modifies. An adverb A has scope over another adverb B when B is immediately dominated by a phrase that A modifies.[22]

Returning to (45a), we would like to suggest that the wide scope reading of the QP is due to the interaction of the two adverbs *dou* and *why*. (45a) is structurally represented in (90).

(90)

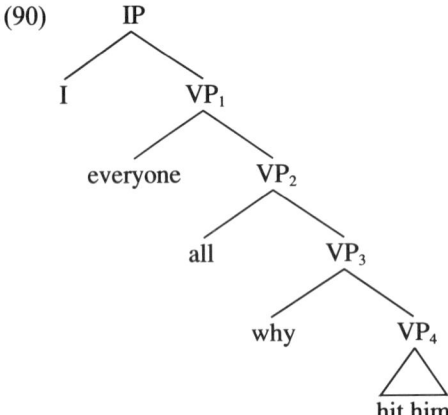

In (90) *dou* 'all' modifies VP_3[23] and thus has scope over *why*, which is immediately dominated by VP_3.[24]

Support for the account just outlined may be provided by the following contrast:

(91) a. Ta weishenme meitian dou lai kan ni? (unambiguous)
    he why every day all come see you
    'Why did he come to see you every day?'

  b. Ta meitian dou weishenme lai kan ni? (ambiguous)
    he every day all why come see you
    'Why did he come to see you every day?'

(91a) has the structural representation shown in (92).

(92)

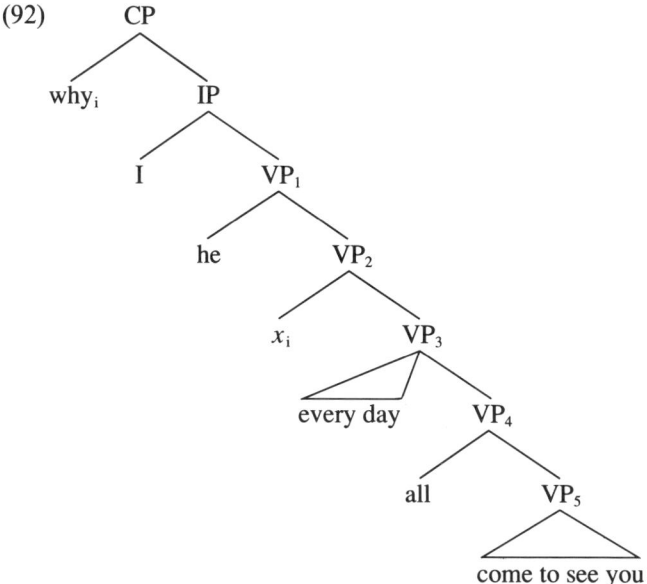

(92) generates only the reading where the *wh*-operator has wide scope.

Sentence (91b) has the structural representation shown in (93). In (93) the raised *wh*-element c-commands and has scope over the quantifier and *dou*. Furthermore, the adverb *dou* modifies VP_4 and has scope over the variable bound by *why*, which is immediately dominated by VP_4. This accounts for the ambiguity of (91b).

We have accounted for the generalization that the scope of an adverb is restricted to the minimal clause in which it occurs by assuming that the scope of an adverb is restricted to the elements immediately dominated by the phrase it modifies. This account leads us to expect (91b) to be unam-

(93)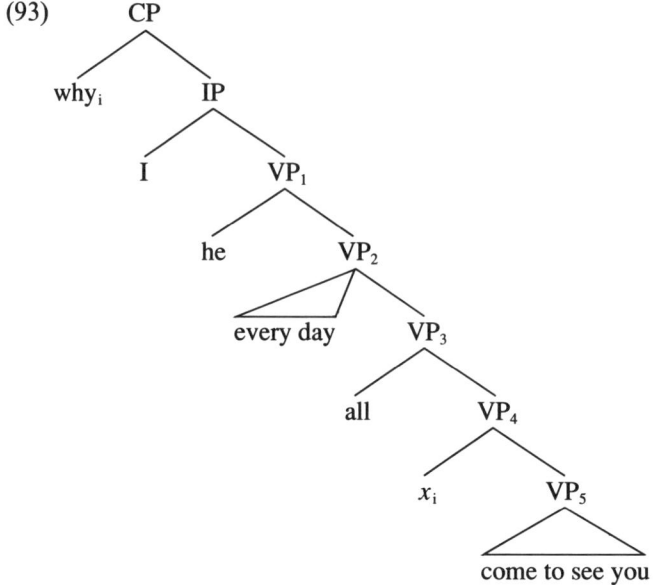

biguous when the adverb *dou* is not generated in the same clause as the adverb *why*. This expectation is fulfilled, as illustrated by the nonambiguity of (94).[25]

(94) Ta meitian dou shuo ni weishenme lai?
    he every day all say you why come
    'Why did he say every day you came?'

6.5 Summary

In this chapter we discussed the interaction of QPs and adjunct *wh*-elements. We argued that an adequate account for the well-formedness of the LF representations of sentences containing traces generated by QR and *wh*-movement needs to incorporate both a locality requirement and an antecedent requirement (the MBR). The former, stated in (64a), defines the domain where an empty category must be bound, and the latter, stated in (64b), defines the type of antecedent that an element is bound to. Both requirements contain a notion of minimality (minimal domain and minimal binder).

(64) a. *The Antecedent Requirement (The MBR)*
    A variable must be bound by the most local potential antecedent.

b. *The Locality Requirement*
A variable, if it is subject to the Locality Requirement, must be bound by an $\bar{\text{A}}$-binder α within the minimal maximal category containing α and the variable.

A contains B iff B is dominated by all segments of A (see Chomsky's (1986a, 9) definition of exclusion and the relevant discussions in May 1985).

As for the determination of the relative scope of QPs and nonreferential *wh*-elements, it is to be accounted for via the notion of modification.

Chapter 7
A Case Study: Japanese

In the previous chapters we have shown how the interaction of operators in a wide range of structures in English and Chinese is accounted for by the MBR and the Scope Principle.

In this chapter we will show how the analysis developed for English and Chinese can be readily extended to other languages. We illustrate this with data from Japanese, a language that differs significantly from both English and Chinese with respect to the interaction of operators.

We will first discuss the interaction of QPs with other QPs (section 7.1) and then discuss the interaction of QPs with *wh*-operators (section 7.2).

7.1 QP/QP Interaction

Hoji (1985) indicates that a Japanese sentence of the form (1) is unambiguous if (1) is base-generated but is ambiguous if QP_1 is a fronted QP derived by scrambling.

(1) $QP_1 \ldots QP_2$

For instance, the structures in (2) are unambiguous but the structures in (3) are ambiguous. (It suffices to say here that -*ga* is a subject marker, -*o* a direct object marker, and -*ni* an indirect object marker.)

(2) a. QP-*ga*...QP-*o* (unambiguous)
   Dareka-ga   daremo-o   semeta.
   someone-NOM everyone-ACC criticized
   'Someone criticized everyone.'

   b. QP-*ni*...QP-*o* (unambiguous)
   John-ga   daremo-ni   [Bill ka Mary]-o   syookaisita (koto).
   John-NOM everyone-DAT Bill or Mary ACC introduced
   'John introduced Bill or Mary to everyone.'

(3) a. QP-*o*...QP-*ga* (ambiguous)
Dareka-o daremo-ga semeta.
someone-ACC everyone-NOM criticized
'Someone, everyone criticized.'

b. QP-*o*...QP-*ni* (ambiguous)
John-ga [bara ya wain]-o [Susan ka Mary]-ni okutta.
John-NOM rose and wine ACC Susan or Mary DAT sent
'John sent roses or wine to Susan and Mary.'

The contrast between (2) and (3) is meant to illustrate the following generalization: when scrambling occurs, ambiguity arises; otherwise, there is no ambiguity. The analysis put forward in the previous chapters seems to provide a straightforward account for the contrast between the structures in (2) and the structures in (3).

We expect the structures in (2) to be unambiguous, if we assume that subjects in Japanese, in contrast to subjects in English, are not raised from the Spec of VP position to the Spec of I' position. This is a plausible assumption. Kitagawa (1986) argues that an important difference between the constituent structures of English and Japanese is that English raises its subject NP from Spec of VP position to Spec of I' position. Japanese, on the other hand, does not raise its subject NP (cf. Kitagawa's proposal of raising Infl from V and relabeling VP as IP). The lack of subject raising in Japanese can also be deduced from Kuroda's (1988) analysis of scrambling. Kuroda suggests that scrambling in Japanese is an instance of NP-movement to Spec of I' position, and that a subject NP in Japanese is generated in Spec of VP position, not Spec of I' position. Moreover, it has been independently argued that a subject NP in Japanese cannot undergo scrambling (see Saito 1985). If a subject NP cannot undergo scrambling and if scrambling is movement to Spec of I' position, it follows that a subject NP cannot move to Spec of I' position, that is, subject raising does not exist in Japanese.[1]

The lack of subject raising in Japanese indicates that the basic constituent structures of Japanese sentences containing a -*ga*, -*ni*, and -*o* phrase is either (4a) or (4b), but not (4c). In (4a) the subject NP is base-generated in Spec of I' position, and in (4b) it is base-generated in Spec of VP position. In the nonavailable representation, (4c), the subject is base-generated in Spec of VP position and subsequently moved to Spec of I' position. (The dative -*ni* phrase c-commands the direct object -*o* phrase in these structures, as argued for in Hoji 1985, Saito 1985.)

A Case Study: Japanese 191

(4)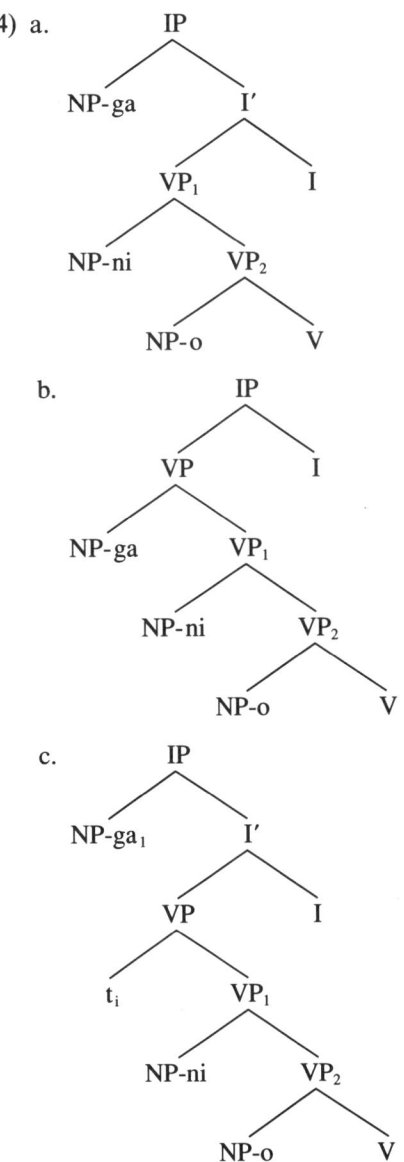

For expository reasons, we will adopt structure (4b), since we will assume with Kuroda (1988) that scrambling in Japanese is movement to Spec of I' position (see (5b)).

Assuming (4b) to be the basic constituent structure for sentences of the form (2), we can straightforwardly derive the nonambiguity found in (2). We first consider (2a), repeated here with labeled structures.

(2) a. [$_{IP}$[$_{VP_1}$ QP-ga ... [$_{VP_2}$ QP-o V]]]

At LF NP-adjunction adjoins QP-*ga* to VP$_1$ and QP-*o* to VP$_2$. QP-*o* cannot adjoin to a node higher than VP$_1$ because of the MBR. Therefore, a sentence with the form in (2a) has only the reading where QP-*ga* has scope over QP-*o*. The nonambiguity of (2b), whose S-Structure representation is (4b), is accounted for along the same lines: QP-*ni* adjoins to VP$_1$ (or a higher node), and QP-*o* can only adjoin to VP$_2$. QP-*ni* therefore c-commands and has scope over QP-*o* but not vice versa.

Before we account for the ambiguity of the sentences in (3), we discuss the structures of sentences involving scrambling. Hoji (1985) and Saito (1985) claim that scrambling is an instance of A-to-$\bar{\text{A}}$ movement, specifically, adjunction of an NP to IP:

(5) a. [$_{IP}$ NP$_i$ [$_{IP}$ ... x_i ...]]

On the other hand, as mentioned previously, Kuroda (1988) argues that scrambling is an instance of A-to-A movement, that is, NP-movement. It moves an NP to Spec of I′ position (structure (4b)):

(5) b. [$_{IP}$ NP$_i$ [$_{I'}$ I [$_{VP}$ ... t$_i$ ...]]]

These two proposals make very different claims: in (5a) the trace generated by scrambling is a variable, and in (5b) the trace generated by scrambling is an NP-trace. There is empirical evidence, however, suggesting that the trace generated by scrambling does not behave like a variable. The evidence concerns weak crossover effects in scrambled constructions. A sentence like (6) displays a standard weak crossover effect: the pronoun cannot be construed as a bound variable (see Saito and Hoji 1983).

(6) *[e$_i$ hitome   e$_j$ mita] hito$_i$-ga   subete-no hito$_j$-o
    one-glance   looked person-NOM every-GEN person-ACC
    sukini natta.
    fell-in-love
    'The person$_i$ that e$_i$ saw e$_j$ fell in love with everyone$_j$.'

On the other hand, the weak crossover effects disappear when the quantificational phrase is scrambled. In (7) the pronoun can be construed as a variable bound by the QP.

(7) Subete-no hito$_j$-o,   [e$_i$ hitome   e$_j$ mita]   hito$_i$-ga
    every-GEN person-ACC   one-glance looked person-NOM
    sukini natta.
    fell-in-love
    'Everyone$_j$, the person$_i$ that e$_i$ saw e$_j$ fell in love with.'

A Case Study: Japanese

The absence of weak crossover effects in scrambled sentences was discussed by Yoshimura (1989) and the references cited there for Japanese and by Suh (1990) for Korean.

The contrast between (6) and (7) can be straightforwardly accounted for if we assume with Kuroda (1988) that traces generated by scrambling are NP-traces rather than variables. With this in mind, we proceed to account for the ambiguity of the sentences in (3).

We first consider (3a). The S-Structure representation of (3a) is (8), t_j being a trace generated by scrambling.

(8)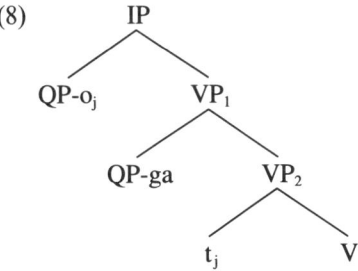

At LF NP-adjunction adjoins QP-*o* to IP and QP-*ga* to VP_1, as illustrated in (9).

(9)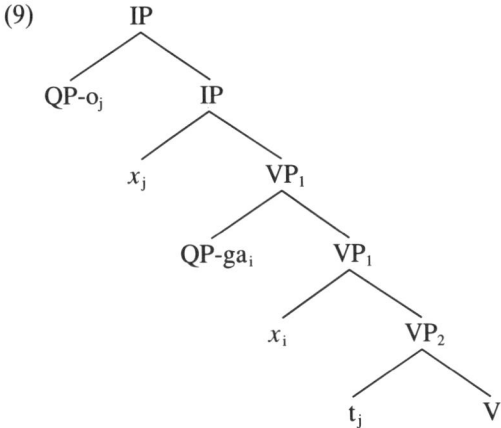

This representation satisfies the MBR: both variables are properly bound, and the NP-trace generated by scrambling is not subject to the MBR. In this representation QP-*o* c-commands and has scope over QP-*ga*. Since (3a) is ambiguous, there should be another derivation that would derive the reading where QP-*ga* has wide scope. Such a derivation is available: since QP-*o* assumes its S-Structure position via NP-movement, it is in a

$\bar{\theta}$-position. NP-adjunction thus need not apply to NP-*o*. As shown in (10), QP-*ga* can then adjoin to IP without violating the MBR.

(10)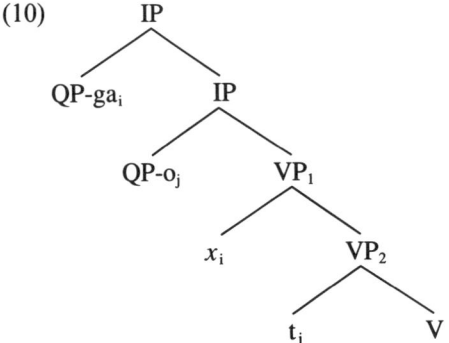

This representation derives the reading where QP-*ga* has scope over QP-*o*. (3a) therefore is ambiguous. The ambiguity of (3b) can be accounted for in exactly the same manner.

In brief, the ambiguity of (3) follows straightforwardly from our analysis if we assume with Kuroda (1988) that scrambling is an instance of NP-movement.

So far we have discussed the interaction of QPs in Japanese. We now discuss the interaction of QPs with *wh*-operators in this language.

7.2 QP/*Wh* Interaction

In Japanese, just as in English or Chinese, a sentence with the form in (11a), such as (11b), is unambiguous.

(11) a. *wh-ga*...QP-*o* (unambiguous)

    b. Dare-ga daremo-o syootaisimasita ka?
       who-NOM everyone-ACC invited Q
       'Who invited everyone?'

Our analysis of QP/*wh* interaction in English and Chinese applies straightforwardly to Japanese. However, the interaction of QPs and *wh*-elements is not exactly the same in Japanese as in English and Chinese. According to Hoji (1985), in Japanese, unlike English or Chinese, it is not possible to have a sentence with the form in (12a).

(12) a. * QP-*ga*...*wh-o*

b. ??Daremo-ga   nani-o   kaimasita ka?
   everyone-NOM what-ACC bought   Q
   'What did everyone buy?'

c. *[John ka Bill]-ga   nani-o   nomimasita ka?
   John or Bill NOM what-ACC drank   Q
   'What did John or Bill drink?'

However, such sentences become acceptable if the *wh*-element is scrambled, as in (13). (13) is unambiguous: only the *wh*-element has wide scope.

(13) *wh-o*...QP-*ga*   (unambiguous)
      Nani-o   daremo-ga   kaimasita ka?
      what-ACC everyone-NOM bought   Q
      'What did everyone buy?'

In fact, when a sentence contains a QP and a *wh*-word, the *wh*-word always has wide scope regardless of whether or not it is c-commanded by the QP. This is further illustrated by (14), where the *wh*-operator must have wide scope.

(14) QP-*o*...*wh-ga*   (unambiguous)
      Daremo-o   dare-ga   syootaisimasita ka?
      everyone-ACC who-NOM invited   Q
      'Everyone, who invited?'

In brief, the relevant facts in Japanese that need to be accounted for are as follows: (i) a *wh*-word must always have wide scope with respect to a QP, even when the QP c-commands the *wh*-word at S-Structure; (ii) structure (12) is unacceptable. Table 7.1 summarizes the relevant facts.

To account for these facts, it is relevant to discuss the role of the question marker and *wh*-words in Japanese. In this language a question marker such as *ka* must occur at the end of a clause when this clause is a question.[2] Thus, the absence of *ka* in (15) is not acceptable.

Table 7.1
QP/*wh* interaction in Japanese

	Structure	Status
(11)	*wh-ga*...QP-*o*	unambiguous
(12)	QP-*ga*...*wh-o*	unacceptable
(13)	*wh-o*...QP-*ga*	unambiguous
(14)	QP-*o*...*wh-ga*	unambiguous

(15) Boku-wa [dare-ga kuru *(ka)] sirimasen.
 I-TOP who-NOM come Q know-not
 'I don't know who is coming.'

Since *ka* obligatorily occurs in the Comp of the interrogative clause, the selectional restriction requirements are satisfied without resorting to the existence of an LF *wh*-movement, as suggested by Kim (1991). We thus assume with Kim that *wh*-words in this language do not undergo *wh*-movement at LF. Further, adopting the insight of Kim (1991) and Nishigauchi (1990, chap. 2), we assume that *wh*-words will undergo raising at LF to a position governed by the question marker.[3] More precisely, we assume with Kim that the raising process *wh*-words undergo is a quantifier-raising process: *wh*-words are just like QPs in this language.

With this, we turn to the cases in (11)–(14). First, consider (11). The government requirement between the question marker *ka* and the *wh*-word would force the *wh*-element to be adjoined to IP, deriving the partial representation shown in (16). (Recall that the subject is base-generated in Spec of VP position.)

(11) *wh-ga*...QP-*o* (unambiguous)

(16) [$_{CP}$ ka [$_{IP}$ wh-ga$_i$ [$_{IP}$[$_{VP_1}$ x_i [$_{VP_2}$ QP-o V]]]]][4]

In this representation QP-*o* is adjoined to VP$_2$. The MBR would not allow it to be adjoined to VP$_1$ or any other higher node. The LF representation of (11) is thus (17).

(17) [$_{CP}$ ka [$_{IP}$ wh-ga$_i$ [$_{IP}$[$_{VP_1}$ x_i [$_{VP_2}$ QP-o$_j$ [$_{VP_2}$ x_j V]]]]]]

This representation yields only one reading, the one where the *wh*-element (and *ka*) has scope over the object QP.[5]

The same analysis applies to structure (13). The LF representation for (13) is (18), after *wh-o* is adjoined to IP (to be governed by C) and the subject QP-*ga* is adjoined to VP$_1$.

(13) *wh-o*...QP-*ga* (unambiguous)

(18) [$_{CP}$ ka [$_{IP}$ wh-o$_j$ [$_{IP}$ x_j [$_{VP_1}$ QP-ga$_i$ [$_{VP_1}$ x_i [$_{VP_2}$ t$_j$ V]]]]]]

The proposal that *wh*-elements undergo QR at LF, together with the MBR, also accounts for the unacceptability of (12). Note that (12) may have the representations in (19a–b), after QR applies.

(12) QP-*ga*...*wh-o* (unacceptable)

A Case Study: Japanese

(19) a. [$_{CP}$ ka [$_{IP}$ wh-o$_j$ [$_{IP}$[$_{VP_1}$ QP-ga$_i$ [$_{VP_1}$ x_i [$_{VP_2}$ x_j V]]]]]]
b. [$_{CP}$ ka [$_{IP}$[$_{VP_1}$ QP-ga$_i$ [$_{VP_1}$ x_i [$_{VP_2}$ wh-o$_j$ [$_{VP_2}$ x_j V]]]]]]

In (19a) the object QP (the *wh*-element) is adjoined to IP and the subject QP to VP$_1$. This representation is not well formed, however, since the raised subject QP-*ga* is the first potential $\bar{A}$-binder for the variables in both subject and object positions, a violation of the MBR. In contrast, (19b), where the subject QP-*ga* is adjoined to VP$_1$ and the object QP (*wh-o*) is adjoined to VP$_2$, is well formed with respect to the MBR. However, *wh-o* in this case is too far away from the question marker *ka* and fails to be governed by it. (19b) thus cannot be a well-formed representation for (12). Since neither (19a) nor (19b) is acceptable, (12) does not have a well-formed LF representation; it therefore is not acceptable.

This analysis predicts that a QP generally cannot c-command a *wh*-element and be c-commanded by the question marker at S-Structure *[*ka...*QP...*wh*]: the MBR would not allow the *wh*-element to move over the QP to be governed by the question marker. On the other hand, if somehow the *wh*-element c-commanded by the QP could be raised over the QP to take the position governed by *ka* without violating the MBR, the form would be possible. This is indeed the case with (14). (14), just like (12), may have the two LF representations, (20a–b).

(14) QP-*o*...*wh-ga* (unambiguous)

(20) a. [$_{CP}$ ka [$_{IP}$ wh-ga$_i$ [$_{IP}$ QP-o$_j$ [$_{IP}$ x_j [$_{VP_1}$ x_i [$_{VP_2}$ t$_j$ V]]]]]]
b. [$_{CP}$ [ka$_i$ [$_{IP}$ QP-o$_j$ [$_{IP}$ x_j [$_{VP_1}$ wh-ga$_i$ [$_{VP_1}$ x_i [$_{VP_2}$ t$_j$ V]]]]]]

(20a–b) are ill formed for the same reasons (19a–b) are ill formed. (14), however, has a third possible representation. The QP in this case is a scrambled QP, which is in a $\bar{\theta}$-position. NP-adjunction thus need not apply to QP-*o*. We thus can have the representation in (20c), where QP-*o* does not undergo NP-adjunction and *wh-ga* is adjoined to IP.

(20) c. [$_{CP}$ ka [$_{IP}$ wh-ga$_i$ [$_{IP}$ QP-o$_j$ [$_{VP_1}$ x_i [$_{VP_2}$ t$_j$ V]]]]]

This representation respects the MBR. Moreover, *wh-ga* is close enough to the question marker: it is governed by this question marker. (20c) thus is well formed, deriving the reading where the *wh*-element takes wide scope because both *ka* and the raised *wh*-element c-command QP-*o*.

In brief, following Hoji (1985), the interaction of QPs and *wh*-operators is always unambiguous in Japanese and sentences of the form in (12) are not acceptable. We have provided an account for these facts by assuming with Kim (1991) that *wh*-elements in this language are to be assimilated to

QPs. They do not undergo *wh*-raising at LF. Instead, they undergo QR. As proposed by Nishigauchi (1990), they are raised to a position governed by the question marker *ka*. The QR status of *wh*-elements and the government requirement between the question marker and the *wh*-element together account for the unacceptability of (12) and the acceptability of (11), (13), and (14). The scope interaction of these well-formed sentences parallels the interaction of QPs with other QPs (2)–(3). The difference is to be traced back to the government requirement between the question marker and the *wh*-element, which prohibits a QP from being raised to a position intervening between the question marker and the *wh*-element. This prevents a QP from taking scope over a *wh*-element in this language.

7.3 Conclusion

In this chapter we illustrated how the account of operator interaction elaborated for English and Chinese can be extended to Japanese. The interaction of operators in this language differs significantly from the interaction of operators in English and Chinese. Based on the insights of Hoji (1985), Kuroda (1988), Kim (1991), and Nishigauchi (1990), we provided an account for the interaction of operators in Japanese in terms of the MBR and the Scope Principle. These two principles capture the core of operator interaction in this language in the same way they capture the core of operator interaction in English and Chinese. As for the differences between Japanese on the one hand and English and Chinese on the other, we demonstrated that they should be traced back to the operation of scrambling and to the specific role played by the question marker and the *wh*-element (which must undergo QR to a position governed by the question marker),[6] rather than to an intrinsically different set of interpretive principles in this language.

Notes

Introduction

1. The scope of α is the set of nodes that α c-commands. A more precise characterization will be given in subsequent chapters.

2. In May 1985 the option of Chomsky-adjoining a quantifier to a VP is incorporated. This option generates a third possible representation, namely, (i).

(i) [$_{IP}$ some man$_i$ [$_{IP}$ x_i [$_{VP}$ every woman$_j$ [$_{VP}$ loves y_j]]]]

In (i) *some man* c-commands and has scope over *every woman*. (i), like (3a), generates the interpretation (2a). As a matter of fact, in May's (1985) system, a representation like (3a) is ambiguous. According to his system, the two quantifiers in (3a) govern each other and thus, each has scope over the other (see chapter 2). Therefore, LF in May's system is not a pure level of disambiguation: two representations may generate the same interpretation, and one representation may generate two interpretations. Relevant considerations concerning this point can be found in chapter 3.

3. Several papers illustrate the application of other major grammatical principles at LF, including Subjacency (Pesetsky 1987, Fiengo et al. 1988) and binding theory (Aoun and Hornstein 1986).

4. The contrast between (5b) and (7a) is discussed by Huang (1988a).

5. See Katada 1991 for the types of anaphors and their raising or nonraising properties in Japanese and some Romance and Germanic languages.

6. The use of such examples and the absence of Chinese examples corresponding to the English (16b) are discussed in chapter 1.

Chapter 1

1. In this work *Chinese* refers to Mandarin Chinese.

2. This definition will be revised in chapter 3.

3. Chinese does not have an expression like *someone*. The expressions that are closest to *someone* are bare NPs or *mogeren* 'a certain person' or *you (yi)ge ren* 'there is a person'. In fact, Chinese generally does not allow an indefinite NP in subject position unless a modal occurs in the sentence, the subject is in a condi-

tional clause, the subject is preceded by *you* 'have, exist' (see Hudson 1986 and Lee 1986 for accounts of such phenomena), or the clause containing such a subject is an *if*-clause:

(i) a. *Yige ren laile.
       one man came
    b. Yige ren hui lai.
       one man will come
    c. *You* yige ren laile.
       have one man came
       'There existed one man that came.'
    d. Yaoshi yige ren lai...
       if   one man came

4. For ease of presentation, we simplify Huang's analysis in this introduction.

5. There are complications for the passive construction in Chinese. The types of verbs and verb phrases that can appear in the passive in Chinese are highly constrained (see Wang 1970 and others). For instance, *xihuan* 'like' (see (1a)) cannot occur in the passive construction. This is why a different verb is used in (4a). Moreover, when the numeral NP is preceded by *you* 'have, exist', this QP must have wide scope with respect to another QP in the sentence, even in a passive sentence:

(i) You yige xiansuo bei meige nuren   zhaodaole.
    have one clue   by every woman found
    'There was a a clue found by every woman.'

The lack of ambiguity in (i) need not be a counterexample to our claim in the text, however. Note that *you* is a verb itself. The expression *you NP* can only occur in subject position:

(ii) *Ta sha   you yige ren.
      he killed have one man
      'He killed someone.'

It is possible to analyze (i) as a complex sentence containing two clauses. That is, the structure of (i) may be (iii).

(iii) [$_{CP}$ e you yige xiansuo] [$_{CP}$ e bei meige nuren   zhaodaole]
             have one clue   by every woman found

6. *De*, a so-called function word, has many uses. It can occur in the structure [$_{NP}$ XP *de* N] or in the structure [$_{VP}$ V *de* clause/Adj Phrase]. Its grammatical status has been the subject of debate in many works on Chinese. Since it has no significant bearing on our discussion in this book, we will gloss all instances of *de* as DE.

7. We assume with May (1977, 1985) that IP is a possible adjunction site for quantifier raising (QR). This assumption is necessary in any framework that assumes that QPs, including subject QPs, are subject to QR. In fact, although Chomsky (1986a) disallows adjunction to IP, he nonetheless allows adjunction of QPs to IP: he states (p. 5) that "although the rule of quantifier raising QR may

involve adjunction to IP, this option is barred for operators of the *wh*-phrase type."

8. We adopt definition (i) of *c-command* (see Reinhart 1983, 23).

(i) Node A c(onstituent)-commands node B iff the branching node α_1 most immediately dominating A either dominates B or is immediately dominated by a node α_2 that dominates B, and α_2 is of the same category type as α_1.

For reasons that will become clear in later discussions, we do not adopt May's (1985) or Chomsky's (1986a) definition of c-command, which incorporates the notion of exclusion.

9. Huang (1982) distinguishes QPs such as *sange* [Q + Classifier] from Quantificational NPs or expressions such as *sange ren* 'three men'. In this work we will use the term *QP* to stand for both of these phrases. Furthermore, the terms *quantificational phrase* and *quantifier phrase* will be used interchangeably when no confusion arises.

10. Recall that verbs in passive constructions in Chinese are much more limited than those in English (see note 5). The verb in (16a–b) can be *arrest*, as in (4), without affecting the scope interpretation; the passive sentences in English are ambiguous:

(i) a. Some/A woman was arrested by everyone.
    b. Everyone was arrested by some/a woman.

11. Hoji (1985) assumes the IP formulated in (i) to account for the interaction of QPs in Japanese.

(i) At LF *$QP_i\ QP_j\ t_j\ t_i$, where each member c-commands the member to its right.

Condition (i) accounts for the nonambiguity of basic Japanese active sentences with the structure shown in (ii), where -*ga* is a nominative marker and -*o* an accusative marker.

(ii) QP-ga QP-o V

As for the ambiguity of sentences like (iii), where the object QP has been scrambled, Hoji assumes that they have the two LF representations shown in (iva) and (ivb).

(iii) [QP-o_j [QP-ga t_j V]]

(iv) a. [$_{IP}$ QP-o_j [$_{IP}$ QP-ga_i [$_{IP}$ t'_j [$_{IP}$ t_i [$_{VP}$ t_j V]]]]]
     b. [$_{IP}$ QP-ga_i [$_{IP}$ QP-o_j [$_{IP}$ (t'_j) [$_{IP}$ t_i [$_{VP}$ t_j V]]]]]

In order for representation (iva) to be well formed, Hoji assumes that the variable t_j in object position does not count when (i) is checked. In order to account for the well-formedness of (ivb), he assumes that the variable in the scrambled position is deleted. Despite the differences between Hoji's account and ours, they ultimately share one common insight: movement can induce ambiguities. See chapter 7 for the discussion of QPs in Japanese.

12. An element E qualifies as an $\bar{A}$-binder for *x* in case it c-commands *x* and is in an $\bar{A}$-position. *Locality* may be defined as in Chomsky 1981, 59:

(i) A locally binds B if A and B are coindexed, A c-commands B, and there is no C coindexed with A that is c-commanded by A and c-commands B.

(See Epstein 1986 for discussion of various definitions of locality conditions.)

13. For the sake of simplicity, we will in most cases represent Chinese forms by English glosses in italics. However, Chinese forms will still be used together with the English glosses when necessary.

14. We are assuming that the small clause has a predicate node. See Larson 1988, 1990 and section 1.5.3 for discussion of double object and dative constructions.

15. It has been widely assumed and has been argued for in the Chinese literature that passivization involves movement (see, among others, Wang 1970, Tang 1979, Teng 1977, Huang 1982, Shi 1987, Li 1990).

16. The definition of the Scope Principle given here is different from the definition given in May 1985. We discuss the interaction of QPs and *wh*-words and compare May's scope Principle with ours in chapter 2.

17. Although the D-Structure subject is sister of VP in (30b), we refer to this subject as the Spec of VP.

18. Wible (1990) suggests that the subject is sister to V', rather than sister to VP. See Huang 1990, Kitagawa 1986, Kuroda 1988, Koopman and Sportiche 1991, Speas 1986, Zagona 1988 for discussion of the position of the subject.

19. For some speakers of English, sentences such as (34a) are unacceptable. These speakers require the quantifier to c-command the bound pronoun at S-Structure (see Reinhart 1983). The unacceptability of the Chinese sentence (34b) may not be due to a c-command requirement at S-Structure, however. That is to say, it is not possible to assume that a bound pronoun in Chinese must be c-commanded by the quantifier at S-Structure. The acceptability of (i) rules out this possibility (see Aoun and Hornstein 1986 for further details).

(i) Meigeren$_i$ de pengyou dou dui wo shuo Lisi renwei ta$_i$ zui ben.
everyone DE friend all to me said Lisi thought he most stupid
'Everyone's friend told me that Lisi thought that he is the most stupid.'

20. More precisely, the IP nodes in (35b) should be replaced by VP, given the assumption that a subject in Chinese is base-generated as Spec of VP. The use of IP does not make any difference here, however.

21. The incorporation is further restricted to cases where the verb is a native stem. This rules out (i), which contains the nonnative stem verb *donate*.

(i) *John donated the church 500 dollars.

22. Since the publication of Thompson 1973, it has been recognized that a verb and an object (inner object) can combine to take another object (outer object) in Mandarin Chinese. Huang (1988b) discusses V and V' objects in detail.

Chapter 2

1. It does not matter here, however, if topicalization is movement to Spec of CP (Shi 1992) or adjunction to CP (Tang 1990).

2. In order to account for such a subject-object asymmetry, Torrego (1984) and Jaeggli (1985) indicate that the V is preposed when the Comp is filled by an argument *wh*-word. They also argue that, as a consequence of V-preposing, the V no longer properly governs its object in (24a–b): when V is preposed, the trace of V will not properly govern an empty category in the object position. Torrego (1984) suggests that after the V is preposed, it properly governs the subject position, thus allowing the subject to be moved (also see Rizzi 1982, Jaeggli 1982, 1985). Jaeggli (1985) entertains the possibility that the subject can be extracted from postverbal position, which is properly governed by Infl (government being directional). It does not matter in our discussion here whether the subject is extracted from preverbal or postverbal position. What matters is that the subject remains in a higher position than the object. The PCC thus predicts that the object must be moved to a position higher than the subject so that the paths generated will not overlap.

3. Again, the subject may be postverbal. See note 2.

4. *Zhiding* 'assign' must be combined with *give* 'give, to' in order to take double objects. See Tang 1979 for the claim that *gei* and the V form a lexical unit.

5. To account for the nonambiguity of (37), we assume that PP is not a possible adjunction site. Consider the partial schematic representation for (37) given in (i).

(i) ... [$_{VP}$[P QP$_1$ [$_{V'}$ V QP$_2$]]] ...

A well-formed LF representation for (i) would be one where QP$_1$ adjoins to VP or a higher node. The MBR forces QP$_2$ to adjoin to the small VP-V'-. This derives the only reading available for (37), namely, the one where QP$_1$ has wide scope. The claim that PPs are not possible adjunction sites may be accounted for if PPs are treated as arguments, as suggested by Koopman and Sportiche (1991) and Larson (1985).

6. The notion of "chain" in this work thus does not correspond exactly to the notions of "A-chains" or "$\bar{\text{A}}$-chains" derived via movement (A-chain headed by an A-element and ended with an NP-trace; $\bar{\text{A}}$-chain headed by an $\bar{\text{A}}$-element and ended with a variable). See chapter 5 for further discussion of movement and chains.

7. In order to have minimal pairs, we use *everyone* in the *by*-phrase. The subject is *a woman*. Because of the Specificity constraint on subjects in a canonical Chinese sentence, *if* is added. See note 3 of chapter 1.

8. (66b) is not quite acceptable. The unacceptability of this sentence is due to some constraint on overt movement (for example, the Lexical Integrity Hypothesis, see Stowell 1981, chap. 5). To the extent that it can be interpreted, it has only the reading where the *wh*-operator has wide scope. The corresponding Chinese sentence is quite acceptable and has the interpretation indicated (see Li 1990).

Chapter 3

1. For a discussion of rigid and relativized interpretations of the MBR, see Rizzi 1990.

2. *Government* is defined in terms of Aoun and Sportiche's (1983) minimal maxi-

mal projection, without incorporating the notion of segments proposed by May (1985) and Chomsky (1986a).

3. These two processes are essentially equivalent to Heim's (1982) NP-prefixing and quantifier-construal.

4. Implicit in the relevant literature on LF is the assumption that relative scope is determined with respect to operators in $\bar{\text{A}}$-positions. This assumption should not come as a surprise given the considerations outlined in section 3.3, where LF is viewed as the locus of $\bar{\text{A}}$-relations and where only $\bar{\text{A}}$-elements are considered relevant to determining relative scope.

5. A representation such as (25) lends itself to a straightforward logical translation. It also is useful to point out that the government requirement between the raised Q and its restriction is parallel to the government requirement between a nominal element and its modifier (see Zubizarreta 1987, Sportiche 1988), between an anaphor and its antecedent (see Chomsky 1986b), or between the LF raised affix and the element to which it attaches (see Pesetsky 1985, Lebeaux 1984).

6. Since Q-adjunction does not play any direct role in the derivation of relative scope, for the sake of simplicity, it will not be represented in the subsequent discussions.

7. Chomsky (1986a) proposes that adjunction should be subject to a categorial constraint: An XP category adjoins to an XP category; an X^0 category adjoins to an X^0 category. If Chomsky's assumption is to be retained, the existence of a process of Q-adjunction will have to be reconsidered.

As illustrated, the process of Q-adjunction does not play a major role in the analysis of quantifier scope. With respect to the MBR, the optionality of NP-adjunction is sufficient to derive the well-formed representations without referring to the Q-operator generated by Q-adjunction. With respect to the Scope Principle, the Q-operator does not play a role either: the scope of a quantifier is the c-command domain of the NP (in $\bar{\theta}$-position) containing the raised quantifier (the higher NP_1 in (i)).

(i)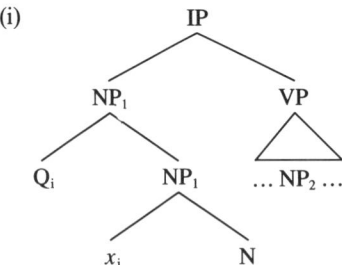

The c-command (scope) domain of the quantifier is VP in (i). On the other hand, if Q-adjunction does not apply, the c-command domain of NP_1 (which contains the nonraised Q) is still the VP, as illustrated in (ii). Empirically, then, Q-adjunction can be dispensed with. In fact, if we assume that the rule of QR is governed by θ-theory (θ-Criterion), it is no longer clear why QR must apply. Quantificational phrases, like other operators, are not referential expressions. These elements cannot remain in a θ-position at LF; if they did, the θ-Criterion (ii)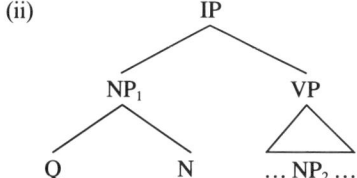

would be violated. On the other hand, nothing either forces or prevents the application of QR when the quantificational phrase occurs in a $\bar{\theta}$-position. (iii) summarizes the application of QR.

(iii) QR is governed by the θ-Criterion.
   a. A QP in a θ-position must undergo QR.
   b. A QP in a $\bar{\theta}$-position need not undergo QR.

We will leave it open in this work whether Q-adjunction must apply. Suffice it to say that the (non)application of Q-adjunction does not have empirical effects on the analysis. For further discussion, see chapters 4 and 5.

8. The assumption that operators and intermediate traces play a role in determining scope relations runs counter both to Haïk's (1984) claim that only variables play a role in determining scope relations and to May's (1985) claim that only operators play a role in determining scope relations.

9. Since the minimal NP in $\bar{\theta}$-position immediately dominating an operator plays a role in determining scope (section 3.1.3), a more accurate reformulation of the Scope Principle will be as follows:

(i) *The Scope Principle*
An operator A may have scope over an operator B iff A or the minimal $\bar{\theta}$-phrase immediately dominating the operator and its restriction c-commands B or a $\bar{\text{A}}$-element coindexed with B.

Chapter 4

1. As mentioned in note 6 of chapter 3, for the sake of simplicity, the process of Q-adjunction is not represented because it does not play a direct role in determining relative scope.

2. This assumption will be reconsidered in section 4.3.

3. The possibility of raising the whole NP containing the QP is in the spirit of May 1977, where the following condition on analyzability is assumed:

(i) *Condition on Analyzability*
If a rule α mentions Spec, then α applies to the minimal [+N]-phrase dominating Spec, which is not immediately dominated by another [+N]-phrase. (p. 14)

4. In the Chinese sentence (3b) the whole subject NP is in a θ-position. It thus must undergo NP-adjunction in case it is treated as quantificational. In other words, there will be no derivation corresponding to (10). This accounts for the nonambiguity of (3b).

5. A reviewer points out that (i) is ambiguous.

(i) Whose book did everyone buy?

The ambiguity of this sentence follows from our account: *whose book* is treated like *what* in (ii) (see the discussion of generalization (22) in section 4.1.2).

(ii) What did everyone buy?

6. Tang (1990) suggests that a DP structure in Chinese contains a head D that selects a Classifier Phrase (CLP), as in (i).

(i)
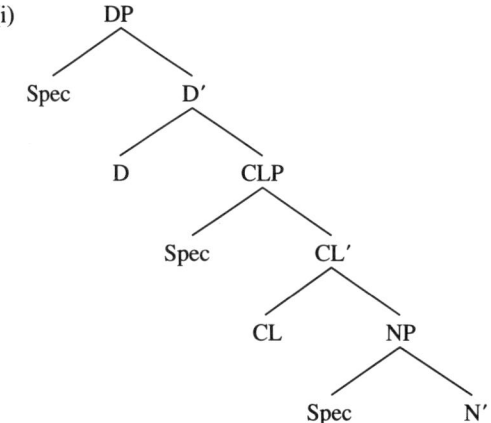

This structure can be adopted as well, as long as we maintain the claim that there is no Spec-to-Spec movement within DP.

7. Huang (1982, 196–97) suggests that expressions involving inversely linked quantification in English are basically ambiguous. Some interpretations are harder to get because of pragmatic effects.

8. The same analysis applies to the English counterpart of (73a), (61). (61) therefore is not ambiguous. Of course, the nonambiguity of (61) can also be captured by the Absorption process that accounted for the nonambiguity of (62).

Chapter 5

1. As pointed out by a reviewer, the "chain" here in fact involves two chains, one an A-chain (variable, NP-trace) and the other an $\bar{\text{A}}$-chain (operator, intermediate trace, variable).

2. Cleft constructions display the same behavior as parasitic gap constructions or *tough*-constructions (cf. (i) and (ii)), although it is not quite acceptable to cleft a QP (iii).

(i)   What is it that everyone likes?   (unambiguous)
(ii) What does everyone like?   (ambiguous)
(iii) ??It is everyone that someone likes.

3. Although relative structures involve nonovert operators, Stowell and Lasnik (1991) assume with Safir (1984, 1986) that restrictive relative clauses, in contrast to appositive relative clauses, exhibit weak crossover effects. See Chomsky 1982 for the claim that weak crossover effects are absent in relative clauses generally.

4. As pointed out by a reviewer, the following *tough*-construction seems to allow the reflexive to be coindexed with *John*:

(i) Pictures of himself$_i$ are difficult for John$_i$ to talk about.

Note that the structure of (i) can be (ii) (see Chomsky 1981, 204-6).

(ii) [pictures of himself are difficult for John [PRO to talk about]

The correctness of this possibility may be supported by the contrast between the following sentences:

(iii) Pictures of himself$_i$ are difficult for John$_i$ for Mary to talk about.

(iv) *Pictures of herself$_i$ are difficult for John for Mary$_i$ to talk about.

5. The same facts obtain if the relative pronoun is *which*:

(i) I read three articles which discussed every woman.   (unambiguous)

(ii) I read three articles which every woman wrote.   (unambiguous)

6. To simplify the discussion in this chapter, we assume the following structure in (i) for complex NPs, instead of the more complex DP structures.

(i)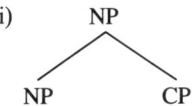

This simplification of the representations does not make any difference empirically. Furthermore, for simplicity of illustration, operators (including *wh*-operators) will be represented under the C(omp) node instead of the Spec of Comp.

7. As with the English cases, the Chinese nominal expressions are represented in the traditional NP structure rather than the DP structure discussed in chapter 4. Again, the choice of DP or NP structures does not affect the analysis of the cases discussed in this chapter.

8. Alternatively, since numerals such as *one* (and other quantifiers such as *mei* 'every') always cooccur with a classifier and the numeral-plus-classifier expressions behave like typical NPs in their distribution, these expressions may be treated like NPs and undergo NP-adjunction.

9. *Wh*-words in all positions would require licensers to be interpreted as universal quantifiers (see Li 1992a). With respect to QPs related to *dou*, it is not clear why there is such a distinction between relative clauses and nonrelative clauses. Note that embedded clauses generally require *dou*:

(i) Wo zhidao meigeren *dou* zuole.
    I   know   everyone all did
    'I know that everyone has done (it).'

(ii) ??Wo zhidao *meigeren* zuole.
     I   know   everyone   did
     'I know everyone has done (it).'

10. Huang and Tang (1989) claim that Chinese *ziji*, but not *taziji*, can be reconstructed, since the former but not the latter is an operator:

(i) a. Zhangsan$_i$ yiwei ziji$_{i/*j}$ Lisi$_j$ hen xihuan.
Zhangsan think self Lisi very like
'Zhangsan thought self, Lisi likes very much.'
b. Zhangsan$_i$ yiwei taziji$_{i/j}$ Lisi$_j$ hen xihuan.
Zhangsan think himself Lisi very like
'Zhangsan thought himself, Lisi likes very much.'

Similar facts in Japanese are discussed by Katada (1991).

11. In English, at best, a *wh*-element can occur in the relative clause only when it can stay in situ:

(i) Who likes the man that saw whom?

Chapter 6

1. A reviewer points out that the possibility of the answer in (ii) to the *how* question in (i) would pose a problem for the distinction we are trying to make here.

(i) How did you do it?

(ii) This way.

Note, however, that (i) cannot be answered by (iii).

(iii) This manner.

This points to the manner/means distinction for *how*: a manner *how* is less like *who* or *what* than a means *how*. See AHLW 1987 and note 5.

2. A reviewer points out that the test for NP-hood may be invalidated by the acceptability of sentences like (i).

(i) He came from [under the table].

It is true that (i) exhibits an apparent case of a PP being the object of a P. Such examples are very limited, however. Safir (1983) calls the bracketed PP in (i) an "honorary NP"; that is, such NPs are like NPs. Li (1990) also argues that the pattern in (i) is possible only with words like *under* and *behind* that have a semantic function of denoting location. Note that sentences like (ii) are not possible. The preposition *at* must not occur.

(ii) *He came from [at the table].

(iii) He came from the table.

3. Principle C in the Government-Binding framework (Chomsky 1981, for instance) applies to R-expressions. R-expressions "include noun phrases with heads that are in some intuitive sense 'potentially referential' (e.g., *John, wood, sincerity, book*' etc.) and variables" (Chomsky 1981, 102).

4. The terms *argument, referential adjunct*, and *nonreferential adjunct* refer to the gaps bound by the operators and not to the operators themselves. For ease of presentation, however, we will sometimes refer to *who* and *what* as *wh-arguments*, to *when* and *where* as *referential adjuncts*, and to *how* and *why* as *nonreferential adjuncts*.

5. In his analysis of Chinese *wh*-elements, Tsai (1991) suggests that with respect to

zenme 'how', one must distinguish between "means *how*" and "manner *how*" and that with respect to *weishenme* 'why', one must distinguish between "purpose *why*" (for what) and "reason *why*." Means *how* and purpose *why*, but not manner *how* and reason *why*, behave like referential expressions such as *what* and *who* with respect to extraction from islands.

6. We will return to the application of the MBR and its relation to the binding theory in section 6.4.1.

7. For a revised analysis of these structures, see section 6.4.1.

8. To the extent that (ia–b) are acceptable for these speakers, these sentences are not ambiguous.

(i) a. Why$_i$ did Bill [$_{VP}$[$_{V'}$ say to everyone] [$_{CP}$ t$_i$ [$_{IP}$ John betrayed him x_i]]]?
   b. How$_i$ did Bill [$_{VP}$[$_{V'}$ say to everyone] [$_{CP}$ t$_i$ [$_{IP}$ John betrayed him x_i]]]?

9. For the sake of completeness, we should mention that (i) is ambiguous.

(i) What$_i$ did everyone say [$_{CP}$ t$_i$ [$_{IP}$ Mary bought x_i]]?

The ambiguity of (i) is expected: the *wh*-operator c-commands the QP, which in turn c-commands the intermediate trace left by the *wh*-operator.

10. We are also drawing a distinction between modifiers and arguments, and we are claiming that only true modifiers have access to the arguments of the elements they modify. This being the case, we do not expect the mechanism of modification to be relevant for *wh*-arguments such as *who* and *what* or referential adjuncts such as *where* and *when*. In fact, referential adjuncts such as *when* and *where* have been treated as true arguments (see Sportiche 1985, Huang 1982, according to which *when* and *where* are arguments of P).

11. Modification determines the scope interaction between arguments and adjuncts. The Scope Principle will be relevant for the interaction between arguments, as in the cases discussed in previous chapters. Ernst (1991) argues that the Scope Principle is also relevant to the scope interaction of adjuncts with other adjuncts.

12. The ambiguity of (44b) is clearer when a focus marker *shi* occurs:

(i) Ta shi zenme zhaogu meigeren de?   (ambiguous)
    he be how   care   everyone DE
    'HOW (focused) did he take care of everyone?'

(i) still contrasts with the unambiguous (ii), where the focus marker also occurs.

(ii) Ta shi weishenme zhaogu meigeren de?   (unambiguous)
     he be why   care   everyone DE
    'WHY (focused) did he take care of everyone?'

It is not clear to us why the occurrence of a focus marker highlights the ambiguity of (44b). The important point, however, is that there is a contrast between the ambiguity of (44b), (i) on the one hand and (45b), (ii) on the other.

13. For an analysis of QP extraction, see Aoun and Hornstein 1985.

14. Of course, the local binder may happen to be an appropriate antecedent, as in (i).

(i) John likes himself.

15. The notion of minimality is relevant for both the Antecedent Requirement and the Locality Requirement. The Antecedent Requirement defines the minimal binder (an antecedent at a minimal distance); the Locality Requirement defines the minimal domain within which a variable must be bound.

16. This definition of *contain* should not be confused with Chomsky's (1992, 15) definition.

17. The Chinese counterparts in this case and the following cases will meet the Antecedent Requirement and the Locality Requirement in the same way. For the sake of simplicity, they will not be repeated unless necessary.

18. (70c) was not a licit representation in our account earlier in the chapter (see section 6.3.1). This representation raises the question of how the relative scope is determined. We will come back to this question in section 6.4.2.

19. The raised *everyone* is not contained in the Neg projection.

20. If the object QP is adjoined first to VP and then to NegP, it will be the intermediate trace adjoined to VP that violates the Locality Requirement. Lasnik and Saito (1984, 1992) and AHLW (1987) show that intermediate traces coindexed with adjuncts are subject to locality requirements.

21. The fact that *wh*-adjuncts need to move through the lower Spec of Comp can be accounted for under the assumption that the Spec of Comp is a potential $\bar{\text{A}}$-binder position. If *wh*-adjuncts do not move through Spec of Comp, the Locality Requirement will be violated. The formulation of the Locality Requirement thus needs to be modified so as to include an $\bar{\text{A}}$-position (which could contain an $\bar{\text{A}}$-binder) or an actual $\bar{\text{A}}$-binder (which could be in an adjoined position): variables subject to the Locality Requirement must be bound within the minimal maximal category containing an $\bar{\text{A}}$-binder or an $\bar{\text{A}}$-position and the variable.

Another possibility is to assume that movement of *wh*-adjuncts such as *why* and *how* must proceed through the most proximate (Spec of) Comp in order to coindex the Comp and thus provide a lexical governor for the trace left by the *wh*-movement (see Rizzi 1990).

22. This descriptive statement can be generalized as follows: An adverb A has scope over another adverb B when B is immediately dominated by a phrase C that A modifies or a "subprojection" of C. This generalization would allow the adverb A to have scope over B in configuration (i), for instance.

(i)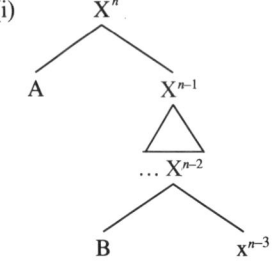

For the purpose of our discussion, the formulation given in the text suffices.

Notes to Pages 185–186

In section 6.3.3 we indicated that a modifier has access to the argument-variables borne by the head of the phrase it modifies. In the previous paragraphs we indicated that the scope of an adverb is restricted to the elements immediately dominated by the phrase it modifies. These two generalizations may be technically brought together as follows.

Consider representation (ii).

(ii)
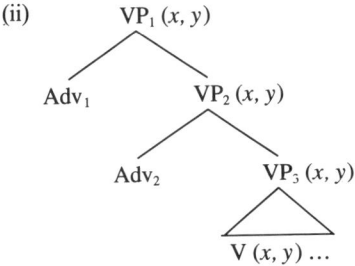

In (ii) the verb V is generated with its argument-variables x, y. The features of this head will be projected onto its various projections, VP_3, VP_2, VP_1, as illustrated in (ii). We can now assume that the scope of a modifier is restricted to the phrase it modifies and the elements immediately dominated by that phrase. In (ii) Adv_2 has scope over $VP_3(x,y)$ and Adv_1 has scope over Adv_2, $VP_2(x,y)$.

We said in section 6.3.3 that the interaction of a nonreferential adjunct and a QP generates ambiguity only when this adjunct as a modifier has access to the argument-variable coindexed with this QP. A representation such as (ii) gives us a means of formally encoding this statement. In (ii) the argument-variables x and y have scope over the adverbs (Adv_1, Adv_2).

23. Even though the main function of *dou* is to license the occurrence of the QP *meigeren* 'everyone', it is plausible to claim that *dou* also modifies the following VP: the structural relation between *dou* and the following VP is a typical modification structure, and (as illustrated in (ii)) *dou* must occur before a VP. The Chinese sentence (iia) corresponding to the English sentence (i) is not acceptable, even though the constraint according to which *dou* must occur to the left of its licensee *tamen* 'them' is obeyed.

(i)   I saw them all.
(ii) a. *Wo kandao tamen dou.
        I   saw   them all
     b. Tamen wo dou kandao.
        they   I all saw
        'They, I all saw.'

24. Since *why* will end up in Spec of Comp and c-commands *dou*, it must have wide scope as well.

25. For the sake of completeness, we should mention that the English sentence (i) corresponding to (89a–b) ought to be unambiguous according to our account. The reason is that English does not have an element corresponding to *dou*.

(i) Why did he come to see you every day?   (unambiguous)

Chapter 7

1. In Kuroda's (1988) analysis, the existence of a double subject structure does not necessarily indicate the absence of subject raising (see section 1.4), even though Japanese also has double subject structures. This is because, according to Kuroda, Case theory does not exert its full effects in Japanese. In particular, an overt argument NP need not be assigned abstract Case. In this instance, the NP in Japanese may be licensed by a morphological case such as -*ga* or -*o*. Japanese thus contrasts with Chinese, where morphological case does not exist. In brief, for Kuroda, an argument NP licensed by a morphological case is not assigned a structural Case. In this analysis, the existence of double subject constructions in Japanese cannot be taken to signal the lack of subject raising. The reason is that a subject generated in the Spec of VP has the option of not receiving structural Case. It thus will be possible to raise this subject to the Spec of I' position without violating the Case uniqueness requirement on chains. If this account were to be adopted, the existence of double subject structures would indicate the lack of subject raising only in languages without the mechanism of morphological case licensing.

2. *Ka* may be deleted when the clause is a matrix clause. See, among others, the relevant discussion by Nishigauchi (1990).

3. Nishigauchi (1990) assumes that *wh*-words also undergo *wh*-raising, to account for the observed Subjacency effects. A QR analysis, however, can also capture the Subjacency effects; see Kim's (1991) arguments for a QR analysis based on the parallelism between QPs and *wh*-words. These subjacency effects may also be accounted for if it is assumed that a question operator in Japanese is base-generated with the *wh*-element and subsequently undergoes syntactic movement to the appropriate COMP.

4. *Ka* in Japanese, a head-final language, should occur at the end of the clause. For the sake of clearly representing the hierarchical order linearly, we will place *ka* in clause-initial position.

5. Kim (1991) suggests that the question marker and the *wh*-element must have the same scope. This is captured by the government requirement on the relation between the question marker and the related *wh*-element.

6. The most important difference between Japanese and Chinese lies in the status of the *wh*-elements: in Japanese, but not in Chinese, they are treated as QPs and undergo QR. Alternatively, the distinction between Japanese and Chinese may be captured by base-generating a question operator with the *wh*-element in Japanese (see note 3) but not in Chinese, as discussed in an earlier draft of this work. The choice of either approach does not have significant difference in this work. However, see Aoun and Li 1993 and Li 1992a for further discussions on this issue.

References

Abney, S. (1987). "The English Noun Phrase in Its Sentential Aspect." Doctoral dissertation, MIT, Cambridge, Massachusetts.

Aoun, J. (1985). *A Grammar of Anaphora*. MIT Press, Cambridge, Massachusetts.

Aoun, J. (1986). *Generalized Binding*. Foris, Dordrecht.

Aoun, J., and N. Hornstein (1985). "Quantifier Types." *Linguistic Inquiry* 16, 623–36.

Aoun, J., and N. Hornstein (1986). "Bound and Referential Pronouns." to appear in J. Huang and R. May eds., *Logical Structure and Linguistic Structure*, Kluwer, Dordrecht.

Aoun, J., N. Hornstein, D. Lightfoot, and A. Weinberg (1987). "Two Types of Locality." *Linguistic Inquiry*, 18, 537–78.

Aoun, J., N. Hornstein, and D. Sportiche (1981). "Aspects of Wide Scope Quantification." *Journal of Linguistic Research* 1, 67–95.

Aoun, J., and Y.-H. A. Li (1989). "Constituency and Scope." *Linguistic Inquiry* 20, 141–72.

Aoun, J., and Y.-H. A. Li (1990). "Minimal Disjointness." *Linguistics* 28, 189–204.

Aoun, J., and Y.-H. A. Li (1991). "The Interaction of Operators." In R. Freidin, ed., *Principles and Parameters in Comparative Grammar*, 163–81. MIT Press, Cambridge, Massachusetts.

Aoun, J., and Y.-H. A. Li (1993). "*Wh*-in-Situ: Syntax of LF." *Linguistic Inquiry* 24.2.

Aoun, J., and D. Sportiche (1983). "On the Formal Theory of Government." *The Linguistic Review* 2, 211–36.

Barss, A. (1984). "Chain Binding." Ms., MIT, Cambridge, Massachusetts.

Barss, A. (1986). "Chains and Anaphoric Dependence: On Reconstruction and Its Implications." Doctoral dissertation, MIT, Cambridge, Massachusetts.

Barss, A., and H. Lasnik (1986). "A Note on Anaphora and Double Objects." *Linguistic Inquiry* 17, 347–54.

Bowers, J. (1987). "Extended X-bar Theory, the ECP and the Left Branch Condition." In *Proceedings of West Coast Conference on Formal Linguistics*, vol. 6, 47–62. Stanford Linguistics Association, Stanford University, Stanford, California.

Bowers, J. (1988). "A Structural Theory of Predication." Ms., Cornell University, Ithaca, New York.

Bowers, J. (1989). "The Syntax and Semantics of Predication." Ms., Cornell University, Ithaca, New York.

Chiu, B. (1990). "NP-*Dou* as a Case of Quantifier Floating." Paper presented at the Second Northeast Conference on Chinese Linguistics, University of Pennsylvania, Philadelphia.

Chomsky, N. (1970). "Remarks on Nominalization." In R. Jacobs and P. S. Rosenbaum, eds., *Readings in English Transformational Grammar*, 184–221. Ginn, Waltham, Massachusetts.

Chomsky, N. (1973). "Conditions on Transformations." In S. R. Anderson and P. Kiparsky, eds., *A Festschrift for Morris Halle*, 232–86. Holt, Rinehart and Winston, New York. [Reprinted in Chomsky 1977.]

Chomsky, N. (1976). "Conditions on Rules of Grammar." *Linguistic Analysis* 2, 303–51. [Reprinted in Chomsky 1977.]

Chomsky, N. (1977). *Essays on Form and Interpretation*. Elsevier North-Holland, New York.

Chomsky, N. (1981). *Lectures on Government and Binding*. Foris, Dordrecht.

Chomsky, N. (1982). *Some Concepts and Consequences of the Theory of Government and Binding*. MIT Press, Cambridge, Massachusetts.

Chomsky, N. (1986a). *Barriers*. MIT Press, Cambridge, Massachusetts.

Chomsky, N. (1986b). *Knowledge of Language*. Praeger, New York.

Chomsky, N. (1991). "Some Notes on Economy of Derivation and Representation." In R. Freidin, ed., *Principles and Parameters in Comparative Grammar*, 417–54. MIT Press, Cambridge, Massachusetts.

Chomsky, N. (1992). "A Minimalist Program for Linguistic Theory." In *MIT Occasional Papers in Linguistics* 1. Department of Linguistics and Philosophy, MIT, Cambridge, Massachusetts.

Chomsky, N., and H. Lasnik (1977). "Filters and Control." *Linguistic Inquiry* 8, 425–504.

Cinque, G. (1990). *Types of $\bar{A}$-Dependencies*. MIT Press, Cambridge, Massachusetts.

Clark, R. (1992). "Scope Assignment and Modification." *Linguistic Inquiry* 23, 1–28.

References

Contreras, H. (1984). "A Note on Parasitic Gaps." *Linguistic Inquiry* 15, 698–701.

Epstein, S. D. (1986). "The Local Binding Condition and LF Chains." *Linguistic Inquiry* 17, 187–205.

Ernst, T. (1991). "On the Scope Principle." *Linguistic Inquiry* 22, 750–56.

Fiengo, R., C.-T. J. Huang, H. Lasnik, and T. Reinhart (1988). "The Syntax of *Wh*-in-situ." In *Proceedings of the West Coast Conference on Formal Linguistics*, vol. 7, 81–98. Stanford Linguistics Association, Stanford University, Stanford, California.

Haïk, I. (1984). "Indirect Binding." *Linguistic Inquiry* 15, 185–223.

Heim, I. (1982). "The Semantics of Definite and Indefinite Noun Phrases." Doctoral dissertation, University of Massachusetts, Amherst.

Heim, I., H. Lasnik, and R. May (1991). "Reciprocity and Plurality." *Linguistic Inquiry* 22, 63–101.

Higginbotham, J. (1980). "Pronouns and Bound Variables." *Linguistic Inquiry* 11, 679–708.

Higginbotham, J. (1983). "Logical Form, Binding, and Nominals." *Linguistic Inquiry* 14, 395–420.

Higginbotham, J. (1985). "On Semantics." *Linguistic Inquiry* 16, 547–93.

Higginbotham, J., and R. May (1981). "Questions, Quantifiers, and Crossing." *Linguistic Analysis* 1, 41–79.

Hoji, H. (1985). "Logical Form Constraints and Configurational Structures in Japanese." Doctoral dissertation, University of Massachusetts, Amherst.

Hoji, H. (1986). "Scope Interpretation in Japanese and Its Theoretical Implications." In *Proceedings of the West Coast Conference on Formal Linguistics*, vol. 5, 87–101. Stanford Linguistics Association, Stanford University, Stanford, California.

Hornstein, N. (1984). *Logic as Grammar*. MIT Press, Cambridge, Massachusetts.

Hou, J. (1979). "Grammatical Relations in Chinese." Doctoral dissertation, University of Southern California, Los Angeles.

Huang, C.-T. J. (1982). "Logical Relations in Chinese and the Theory of Grammar." Doctoral dissertation, MIT, Cambridge, Massachusetts.

Huang, C.-T. J. (1988a). "Comments on Hasegawa's Paper." In W. Tawa and M. Nakayama, eds., *Proceedings of Japanese Syntax Workshop*, 77–93. Connecticut College, New London, Connecticut.

Huang, C.-T. J. (1988b). "*Wo pao de kuai* and Chinese Phrase Structure." *Language* 64, 274–311.

Huang, C.-T. J. (1990). "Reconstruction, the A/A' Distinction, and the Structure of VP." Paper presented at the Second Northeast East Conference on Chinese Linguistics, University of Pennsylvania, Philadelphia.

Huang, C.-T. J., and C.-Z. Tang (1989). "On the Local Nature of the Long-Distance Reflexives in Chinese." In *Proceedings of NELS 19*, 191–206. GLSA, University of Massachusetts, Amherst.

Huang, S. F. (1981). "On the Scope Phenomena of Chinese Quantifiers." *Journal of Chinese Linguistics* 9, 226–43.

Hudson, W. (1986). "Predication Operators and Licensing of Indefiniteness." Ms., University of Southern California, Los Angeles.

Hudson, W. (1989). "Functional Categories and the Saturation of Noun Phrases." In *Proceedings of NELS 19*, 207–22. GLSA, University of Massachusetts, Amherst.

Jaeggli, O. (1982). *Issues in Romance Syntax*. Foris, Dordrecht.

Jaeggli, O. (1985). "On the ECP." Ms., University of Southern California, Los Angeles.

Jackendoff, R. (1972). *Semantic Interpretation in Generative Grammar*. MIT Press, Cambridge, Massachusetts.

Katada, F. (1991). "The LF Representation of Anaphors." *Linguistic Inquiry* 22, 287–313.

Kayne, R. S. (1981). "Two Notes on the NIC." In A. Belletti, L. Brandi, and L. Rizzi, eds., *Theory of Markedness in Generative Grammar*, 317–46. Scuola Normale Superiore, Pisa. [Reprinted in Kayne 1984.]

Kayne, R. S. (1984). *Connectedness and Binary Branching*. Foris, Dordrecht.

Kayne, R. S. (1986). "Connexité et inversion du sujet." In M. Ronat and D. Couquaux, eds., *La Grammaire modulaire*, 127–47. Editions de Minuit, Paris.

Kim, S. W. (1991). "Chain Scope and Quantification Structure." Doctoral dissertation, Brandeis University, Waltham, Massachusetts.

Kitagawa, Y. (1986). "Subjects in Japanese and English." Doctoral dissertation, University of Massachusetts, Amherst.

Koopman, H. (1984). *The Syntax of Verbs: From Verb Movement Rules in the Kru Languages to Universal Grammar*. Foris, Dordrecht.

Koopman, H., and D. Sportiche (1982). "Variables and the Bijection Principle." *The Linguistic Review* 2, 139–60.

Koopman, H., and D. Sportiche (1985). "Extraction and Theta-Theory." *GLOW Newsletter*, 14, 57–58.

Koopman, H., and D. Sportiche (1991). "The Position of Subjects." *Lingua* 85, 211–59.

Kuroda, S.-Y. (1988). "Whether We Agree or Not: A Comparative Syntax of English and Japanese." *Lingvisticae Investigationes* 21, 1–46.

Larson, R. (1985). "Bare-NP Adverbs." *Linguistic Inquiry* 16, 595–621.

References

Larson, R. (1987). "'Missing Prepositions' and the Analysis of English Free Relative Clauses." *Linguistic Inquiry* 18, 239–66.

Larson, R. (1988). "On the Double Object Construction." *Linguistic Inquiry* 19, 335–391.

Larson, R. (1990). "Double Objects Revisited: Reply to Jackendoff." *Linguistic Inquiry* 21, 589–632.

Lasnik, H., and M. Saito (1984). "On the Nature of Proper Government." *Linguistic Inquiry* 15, 235–89.

Lasnik, H., and M. Saito (1992). *Move α*. MIT Press, Cambridge, Massachusetts.

Lebeaux, D. (1983). "A Distributional Difference between Reciprocals and Reflexives." *Linguistic Inquiry*, 14, 723–30.

Lebeaux, D. (1984). "Nominalizations, Argument Structure and the Organization of the Grammar." Ms., University of Massachusetts, Amherst.

Lee, T. (1986). "Studies on Quantification in Chinese." Doctoral dissertation, UCLA, Los Angeles, California.

Li, Y.-H. A. (1990). *Order and Constituency in Mandarin Chinese*. Kluwer, Dordrecht.

Li, Y.-H. A. (1992a). "Indefinite *wh* in Mandarin Chinese." *Journal of East Asian Linguistics* 1, 125–56.

Li, Y.-H. A. (1992b). "DOU: Syntax or LF." Paper presented at the Fourth North American Conference on Chinese Linguistics, University of Michigan, Ann Arbor.

Lin, J.-W. (1991). "The Syntax of *Weishenme* and *Zenme(yang)* in Mandarin Chinese." Ms., National Tsing Hua University, Taiwan. [To appear in *Journal of East Asian Linguistics*.]

Liu, C.-S. (1992). "The Syntax of DOU: A Case of Unselective Binding." Ms., National Tsing Hua University, Taiwan.

May, R. (1977). "The Grammar of Quantification." Doctoral dissertation, MIT, Cambridge, Massachusetts.

May, R. (1985). *Logical Form: Its Structure and Derivation*. MIT Press, Cambridge, Massachusetts.

May, R. (1988). "Ambiguities of Quantification and *Wh*: A Reply to Williams." *Linguistic Inquiry* 19, 118–34.

Nishigauchi, T. (1990). *Quantification in the Theory of Grammar*. Kluwer, Dordrecht.

Ouhalla, J. (1990). "Sentential Negation, Relativized Minimality and the Aspectual Status of Auxiliaries." *The Linguistic Review* 7, 183–231.

Pesetsky, D. (1982). "Paths and Categories." Doctoral dissertation, MIT.

Pesetsky, D. (1985). "Morphology and Logical Form." *Linguistic Inquiry* 16, 193–246.

Pesetsky, D. (1987). "*Wh*-in-Situ: Movement and Unselective Binding." In E. J. Reuland and A. ter Meulen, eds., *The Representation of (In)definiteness*, 98–129. MIT Press, Cambridge, Massachusetts.

Pollock, J.-Y. (1989). "Verb Movement, Universal Grammar, and the Structure of IP. *Linguistic Inquiry* 20, 365–424.

Reinhart, T. (1983). *Anaphora and Semantic Interpretation*. Croom Helm, London.

Riemsdijk, H. van, and E. Williams (1981). "NP-Structure." *The Linguistic Review* 1, 171–217.

Rizzi, L. (1982). "Negation, *Wh*-Movement and the Null Subject Parameter." In *Issues in Italian Syntax*, 117–84. Foris, Dordrecht.

Rizzi, L. (1990). *Relativized Minimality*. MIT Press, Cambridge, Massachusetts.

Ross, J. R. (1983). "Inner Islands." Ms., MIT, Cambridge, Massachusetts.

Safir, K. (1983). "On Small Clauses as Constituents." *Linguistic Inquiry* 14, 730–35.

Safir, K. (1984). "Multiple Variable Binding." *Linguistic Inquiry* 15, 603–38.

Safir, K. (1986). "Relative Clauses in a Theory of Binding and Levels." *Linguistic Inquiry* 17, 663–89.

Sag, I. (1976). "Deletion and Logical Form." Doctoral dissertation, MIT, Cambridge, Massachusetts.

Saito, M. (1985). "Some Asymmetries in Japanese and Their Theoretical Implications." Doctoral dissertation, MIT, Cambridge, Massachusetts.

Saito, M., and H. Hoji (1983). "Weak Crossover and Move-alpha in Japanese." *Natural Language and Linguistic Theory* 1, 245–59.

Schneider-Zioga, P. (1988). "Are Double Object Constructions Small Clauses?" Ms., University of Southern California, Los Angeles.

Shi, T. (1987). "On Chinese Passives." Ms., University of Southern California, Los Angeles.

Shi, T. (1992). "The Nature of Topic Comment Constructions and Topic Chains." Doctoral dissertation. University of Southern California, Los Angeles.

Speas, M. J. (1986). "Adjunctions and Projections in Syntax." Doctoral dissertation, MIT, Cambridge, Massachusetts.

Sportiche, D. (1988). "A Theory of Floating Quantifiers and Its Corollaries for Constituent Structure." *Linguistic Inquiry* 19, 425–49.

Stowell, T. (1981). "Origins of Phrase Structure." Doctoral dissertation, MIT, Cambridge, Massachusetts.

Stowell, T. (1986). "Null Antecedents and Proper Government." In *Proceedings of NELS 16*, 476–92. GLSA, University of Massachusetts, Amherst.

Stowell, T. (1989). "Subjects, Specifiers and X'-Theory." In M. Baltin and A. Kroch, eds., *Alternative Conceptions of Phrase Structure*, 232–62. University of Chicago Press, Chicago, Illinois.

Stowell, T. (1991). "Determiners in NP and DP." In K. Leffel and D. Bouchard, eds., *Views on Phrase Structure*, 37–56. Kluwer, Dordrecht.

Stowell, T., and H. Lasnik (1991). "Weakest Crossover." *Linguistic Inquiry* 22, 687–720.

Suh, J. (1990). "Quantifier Scope in Korean." Doctoral dissertation, University of Southern California, Los Angeles.

Tang, C.-C. (1990). "Chinese Phrase Structures and the Extended X'-Theory." Doctoral dissertation, Cornell University. Ithaca, New York.

Tang, T. C. (1979). *Studies in Chinese Syntax*. Student Books Co., Taipei.

Teng, S. H. (1977). *A Semantic Study of Transitivity Relations in Chinese*. Student Books Co., Taipei.

Thompson, S. (1973). "Transitivity and the *ba* Construction in Mandarin Chinese." *Journal of Chinese Linguistics* 1, 208–21.

Torrego, E. (1984). "On Inversion in Spanish and Some of Its Effects." *Linguistic Inquiry* 15, 103–29.

Travis, L. (1984). "Parameters and Effects of Word Order Variation." Doctoral dissertation, MIT, Cambridge, Massachusetts.

Tsai, W.-T. (1991). "On Nominal Islands and LF Extraction in Chinese." In *MIT Working Papers in Linguistics* 15, 239–74. Department of Linguistics and Philosophy, MIT, Cambridge, Massachusetts.

Wang, P. C.-T. (1970). "A Transformational Approach to Chinese *ba* and *bei*." Doctoral dissertation, University of Texas, Austin.

Wible, D. (1990). "Subjects and the Clausal Structure of Chinese and English." Doctoral dissertation, University of Illinois, Urbana-Champaign.

Williams, E. (1977). "Discourse and Logical Form." *Linguistic Inquiry* 8, 101–39.

Williams, E. (1980). "Predication." *Linguistic Inquiry* 11, 203–38.

Williams, E. (1987). "Implicit Arguments, the Binding Theory, and Control." *Natural Language and Linguistic Theory* 5, 151–80.

Williams, E. (1988). "Is LF Distinct from S-Structure? A Reply to May." *Linguistic Inquiry* 19, 135–46.

Williams, E. (1989). "The Anaphoric Nature of θ-Roles." *Linguistic Inquiry* 20, 425–56.

Xu, L.-J. (1986). "Free Empty Category." *Linguistic Inquiry* 17, 75–93.

Yoshimura, N. (1989). "Parasitic Pronouns." Ms., University of Southern California, Los Angeles.

Zagona, K. T. (1988). *Verb Phrase Syntax*. Kluwer, Dordrecht.

Zubizarreta, M. L. (1987). *Levels of Representation in the Lexicon and in the Syntax*. Foris, Dordrecht.

Index

A-bound, 22, 24, 58
A-position, 26, 57, 88
A-relation, 88–89
$\bar{\text{A}}$-binder, 3–5, 8, 11, 19, 56, 57, 86 (*see also* Potential antecedent)
$\bar{\text{A}}$-bound, 5, 24
$\bar{\text{A}}$-disjointness, 4–6, 24
$\bar{\text{A}}$-element, 88–89
$\bar{\text{A}}$-free, 3–4, 24
$\bar{\text{A}}$-indexing, 88, 124
$\bar{\text{A}}$-position, 2–6, 8, 19, 26, 73, 79–80, 85–86, 88, 103, 138
$\bar{\text{A}}$-relation, 88–89
Abney, S., 101, 106
Absorption. *See* Scope
Active sentence, 12–13, 20–21, 38, 55, 74–76
  Chinese, 7, 12, 26
  English, 7, 12, 26
Adjunct, 151–152. *See also Wh*-adjunct; *Wh*-operators;
  nonreferential, 154–155, 157–160, 208n4
  position, 32
  referential, 154–156, 208n4
Adjunction, 79. *See also* Move α, NP-adjunction; Move α, Q-adjunction)
  to (non)argument position 20, 74
  to X^0, 35
Adverb, 181–184. *See also* Scope
Agreement, 23–24, 133–134, 148. *See also* Specifier; Spec/head agreement
Anaphor, 5–6, 9, 170–172. *See also* Reciprocals; Reflexives
  binding, 30
  long-distance, 5–6
  nonraising, 6

raising, 6
short-distance, 6, 132
Antecedent contained deletion, 77–78
Antecedent Requirement. *See* Minimal Binding Requirement
Aoun, J., 3–4, 19, 21, 24, 56, 68, 87–88, 105, 134, 138, 153–155, 169–171, 173
Argument
  internal, 33
  structure, 152
  variable
    external, 161
    internal, 161

Barss, A., 18–19, 30, 126
Bijection Principle, 20
Binding theory, 56, 87, 171–172. *See also* Minimal Binding Requirement
  Generalized, 173
  Principle A, 109, 131
  Principle C, 56–57, 68, 153–154
  Proper binding, 23
Bowers, J., 102–103, 162

C-command, 8, 11–12, 15–18, 31, 45, 68–69, 71, 201n8
Case, 31–33, 36
  assignment, 30
  filter, 29, 33, 36
  inherent, 31–32
  structural, 32
Chain, 8, 11–12, 21, 26, 59, 71, 73, 83, 123
Chinese. *See* Mandarin Chinese
Chiu, B., 137

Index

Chomsky, N., 1–6, 15, 19–20, 23, 29, 56, 68, 74, 88, 103, 124–126, 155, 169–172, 175, 187
Cinque, G., 153–155, 169
Clark, R., 77
Condition on Analyzability. *See* Move α
Construal mechanism. *See* Interpretive rules
Constituent structures, 22, 25, 38
  Chinese, 22, 24, 38
  English, 22, 24, 38
Contain, 172, 187
Contreras, H., 126

D-Structure, 1, 22
Dative constructions, 29–31, 34, 36, 38
Determiner (phrase), 101–106. *See also* Specifier
Disjointness (requirement), 3–5
  A-disjointness, 3
  $\bar{\text{A}}$-disjointness, 3–4, 24 (*see also* Minimality)
Dou, 136–140, 148, 166, 181–183, 211n23
Double complement. *See* Double object construction
Double object construction, 12–13, 20, 29–34, 36, 38, 55, 70

Each ... the other. See Reciprocals
Empty category, 23
Empty Category Principle (ECP) 2, 19, 21, 28, 87, 151
English, 5, 7–9, 12, 15, 17–20, 69, 111, 113, 157
Ernst, T., 181
Extended Standard Theory, 1
Extraposition, 16

Generalized binding. *See* Binding theory
Governing category, 109, 132, 134, 148, 171
Government, 45, 53, 80, 138, 203n2
  definition, 45
  lexical, 23
  between operators, 45, 51, 54

Head, 16
Head-final, 16
Head-initial, 15
Heim, I., 73, 79, 137, 170–171
Higginbotham, J., 3, 15, 18, 117, 161, 170
Hoji, H., 40, 49, 189–190, 192, 194, 197–198

Hornstein, N., 3–4, 19, 23–24, 56, 68, 87, 131, 134, 138, 153–155, 169, 173
Hou, J., 27
Huang, C.-T. J., 4, 7, 11, 13, 15–16, 27, 46, 100, 101, 106–107, 110–111, 132, 137–138, 151, 153–155, 169, 181–182
Huang, S.-F., 11, 13
Hudson, W., 101, 103

Incorporation, 30
Indexicals, 153
Indexing, 124
Inflection (Infl), 23, 105
Intermediate trace. *See* Trace
Interpretive invariance, 11, 91
Interpretive rules, 8, 13, 22, 123–125, 127, 148
Inversely linked quantification, 100, 110–111
Isomorphic Principle, 11–12, 15–19

Jackendoff, R., 160
Japanese, 7, 9, 189–198
Jaeggli, O., 23, 51

Katada, F., 138
Kayne, R. S., 2, 19–20, 29–30, 167
Kim, S. W., 196–198
Kitagawa, Y., 13, 190
Koopman, H., 13, 20, 33, 162, 170
Kuroda, S.-Y., 13, 101, 190–194, 198

Language variation. *See* Variation
Larson, R., 12–13, 18, 29–34, 36, 70, 77
Lasnik, H., 1, 18, 30, 49, 84, 87, 126, 137, 155, 169–171
Lebeaux, D., 5, 12, 18, 170
Lee, T., 13, 15, 131–132, 137–139
Lexico-semantic structure, 161
Li, Y.-H. A., 4, 23, 27, 105, 137, 138
Lightfoot, D., 23, 87, 153–155, 169, 173
Lin, J.-W., 162, 181
Liu, C.-S., 138
Load/spray constructions, 36, 38
Locality, 9, 19, 109, 134–136, 201n12
Locality Requirement, 172, 187, 210n15, n21. *See also* Minimality
Logical Form, 1–3, 5–6, 8, 12–15, 19, 88–89, 138, 199n2
  component, 1, 4, 99
  derivation, 78

Index 223

parametric variation, 8, 13, 27
representation, 1–2, 5
Logical interpretation, 91

Mandarin Chinese, 3–9, 11–12, 15–20, 39, 46, 50, 55, 69, 111
May, R., 1, 7, 13–15, 19, 21, 39–40, 44–46, 53–55, 77, 85, 100, 110, 117, 137, 170–172, 187
Minimal Binding Requirement (MBR), 8, 11–13, 19–22, 38–40, 56, 60–61, 66, 71, 79, 82–83, 157, 163, 165–167, 172, 186
  context sensitivity, 167
  relativized, 166, 173
  rigid, 79
Minimality, 4, 210n15
Modal, 4
Modification, 160–164, 179. *See also* Scope
Modify, 160, 184
Move α, 1–2, 5, 8, 13, 23, 196
  Condition on Analyzability, 205n3
  lowering, 21
  NP-adjunction, 73, 79–83, 88, 94–95, 99, 109, 121, 134 (*see also* Locality)
  NP-raising, 101, 104–106, 111, 113 (*see also Seem*-type construction)
  pied-piping, 74
  Q-adjunction, 73, 79–80, 82–83, 88
  Q-raising, 74–75, 77–79
  QP-raising, 75, 77–79
  restriction, 80–81
  subject raising, 13, 23, 27, 101, 105–106, 190
  V-raising, 23, 28
  wh-raising, 4–5

Negation, 79, 87–88, 167
  interaction with adverbials, 167
  interaction with QPs, 168, 175–177
  interaction with *wh*-adjuncts, 169, 177
  interaction with *wh*-arguments, 167–169, 177–178
  phrase, 175
Negative element. *See* Negation
Negative polarity items, 2, 30–31
Nishigauchi, T., 196, 198
Nonargument position. *See* Ā-position
Nonthematic position, 8, 74–75, 80
Noun phrase, 8. *See also* Determiner (phrase); Specifier

complex
  Chinese, 128–131
  English, 127–128
simplex
  Chinese, 92–101, 106–107, 111–114, 118–120
  English, 92–101, 106–110, 114–118
structure, 101–106
  Chinese, 104–106
  English, 104–106
NP-adjunction. *See* Move α
NP-model, 89
NP-structure, 89

Object, 11, 15, 70
Opacity, 8
Operator, 8, 85–87
  endocentric behavior, 91, 100–120
  exocentric behavior, 91–100
  interaction, 121, 181
  nonovert, 125–127, 138
  types of, 153–154
Ouhalla, J., 175

Parametric variation. *See* Variation
Parasitic gap construction, 123–126
Passive sentence, 12, 17, 21, 38, 55, 74–76, 199n5
passivization, 32, 63
Path, 40–44, 51
  embedded, 52
  intersecting (*see* Path, overlapping)
  overlapping, 40–44, 49, 52
  segment, 40
Path Containment Condition (PCC), 7, 39–40, 45–46, 49, 50–53
Pesetsky, D., 7, 39–40
Phrase structure constraint. *See* Phrase structure rule
Phrase structure rule, 12, 15, 16
Pied-piping, 77–78, 147. *See also* Move α
Pollock, J.-Y., 175
Possible antecedent. *See* Potential antecedent
Potential Ā-binder. *See* Potential antecedent
Potential antecedent, 19–20, 26, 39, 57, 58, 68, 71, 166–167
Predicate phrase, 162
Predication, 123–124, 127
Pronominals. *See* Pronouns

Pronouns, 2–3, 5–6, 24
  bound, 3–5, 24–25
  referential, 3, 24
Proper binding. *See* Binding theory

Quantificational element. *See*
  Quantificational phrases
Quantificational phrases (QP), 6–8, 11, 15,
    17–19, 79, 83, 155–156. *See also* Scope;
    Trace
  interaction with negation, 175–177
  interaction with QPs, 7–8, 11, 38–39, 53,
    55, 86, 92–96, 100–102, 106–113, 114,
    189–194
  interaction with *wh*-adjuncts, 9, 155–157,
    159–161, 163–164, 168–169, 173–175,
    178–179
  interaction with *wh*-arguments, 8, 38–39,
    53, 56–71, 77, 86, 97–100, 114–120,
    161, 168–169, 173, 194–198
Quantifier 4, 11, 71. *See also* Move α
  binding, 30
  in nonthematic position, 8
Question marker, 195, 198

Raising. *See* Move α
Raising structure, 28, 74–77. *See also*
  Seem-type construction
Reanalysis, 28
Rebracketing, 16
Reciprocals, 170
Reconstruction, 77–78, 126, 138
Reflexives, 125, 132–133, 170
Relativized construction, 123–124. *See also*
  Noun phrase, complex
Restriction. *See also* Move α
Restructuring, 11–12, 15–17, 19
Riemsdijk, H. van, 89
Rizzi, L., 79, 153–155, 162, 166–167, 169,
    173, 181
Ross, J. R., 167

S-Structure, 1, 2, 4, 12, 14, 15, 23, 89
Sag, I., 77
Saito, M., 49, 84, 155, 169, 190, 192
Scheneider-Zioga, P., 18
Scope, 1–2, 8, 11, 13, 16–18, 21, 61–63,
    71–72, 79–80, 84–85, 125–126, 148,
    161–162, 205n8
  absorption, 117–118, 121
  of adverbs, 183–184, 210n22
  and configuration, 68
  role of chain, 83

role of intermediate traces, 85–88
role of modification, 161–164, 178–182
role of NP-traces, 74–83, 88
role of operators, 73, 77, 85–87
role of variables, 77, 84–85, 87–88, 148
Scope Principle, 8, 11–13, 21–22, 27,
    38–40, 56, 59–61, 66, 71, 73, 88,
    124–125, 202n16, 205n9
  May's, 45, 52–55,
Scrambling, 190, 192–193, 198
Seem-type construction, 27, 38, 74. *See*
  also Move α
Shi, T., 49
Σ-sequence, 45, 51
Small clause, 20, 29
Spanish, 39, 46, 59
Speas, M., 13
Spec/head agreement, 161–162
Specifier, 103–106, 121
  of Comp, 4, 52, 58, 60, 86
  of DP, 102–106
  of IP, 13, 23, 58
  of NP, 102–106
  of VP, 13, 23, 33, 58
Sportiche, D., 4, 13, 20, 153, 162, 170
Stowell, T., 23, 29–30, 101, 126, 161
Subjacency, 56, 84
Subject, 4–5, 11, 15, 22, 23, 70, 162
Subject raising. *See* Move α
Suh, J., 193
Superiority, 30–31
Syntax, 2, 6, 88

Tang, J., 138, 162
Teng, S. H., 27
θ-Criterion, 74, 79
θ-position, 74, 75, 79
θ-role, 30, 153–154
  directionality requirement, 33
  possessor, 29
θ-theory, 79
Topicalization, 46, 48, 49
Torrego, E., 51
Tough construction, 123–125
Trace
  intermediate, 73, 85–88, 125–127, 180
  of NP, 21, 22, 26, 40, 61–63, 66, 72, 74,
    77, 83, 88
  of QP, 12, 109 (*see also* Variables)
  of *wh*-element (*see* Variables)
Travis, L., 33, 167
Tsai, W.-T., 162

Index

V-raising. *See* Move α
V′-reanalysis, 32
Vacuous quantification, 19
Variables, 2–3, 8, 11, 19, 56, 71–72,
    83–85, 87–88, 153–154, 180
  antecedent requirement on (*see* Minimal
    Binding Requirement; Minimality)
  in argument position, 86, 151
  bound by QP, 56–57, 68, 125, 131–132,
    134–136, 138–139, 148
  bound by *wh*-element, 56–57, 60, 68, 125
  locality requirement on (*see* Locality
    Requirement)
  in nonargument position, 151
  type
    nonreferential, 153–155
    referential, 153–155
Variation, 7–8, 15, 27, 91
VP-copying, 77
VP-deletion, 77

Weak crossover, 2, 30–31, 126, 192
Weinberg, A., 23, 87, 153–155, 169, 173
wh-adjuncts, 9, 151, 167, 169. *See also*
    Quantificational phrases, interaction
    with *wh*-adjuncts
wh-arguments, 86, 154–155, 167, 169. *See
    also* Quantificational phrases,
    interaction with *wh*-arguments
wh-island, 46, 52
wh-operators, 2, 4–7, 52, 56, 87, 151. *See
    also* Quantificational phrases,
    interaction with *wh*-adjuncts;
    Quantificational phrases, with
    wh-arguments
  wh-in-situ, 4–5
wh-raising. *See* Move α
wh-structure, 89
Wible, D., 23
Williams, E., 19, 40, 77–78, 89, 124, 161

Yoshimura, N., 193

Zagona, K. T., 13
Zubizarreta, M. L., 160–161